REFLECTIONS
ON SACRED TEACHINGS

Volume Four: Sri Isopanisad

B.T. SWAMI

Copyright © 2004 by John E. Favors

All rights reserved. No part of this book may be reproduced, stored in a retrieval system, or transmitted in any form, by any means, including mechanical, electronic, photocopying, recording, or otherwise, without prior written consent of the publisher.

Hari-Nama Press gratefully acknowledges the BBT for the use of verses and purports from Srila Prabhupada's books. All such verses and purports are © Bhaktivedanta Book Trust International, Inc.

First printing 2005
Second edition printing: Amazon KDP 2020

Interior layout by Sthayi Bhava dasi and Subala dasa
Cover design by Brahma Muhurta dasa and Subala dasa
Cover photo by Stephen Knapp (Sri Nandanandana dasa)

The cover: Statue of Lord Vishnu at the Sri Rangam temple in India.

ISBN 9798642248812

Reflections
ON SACRED TEACHINGS

Volume Four: Sri Isopanisad

INTRODUCTIONS

Dedication

Sri Isopanisad, with a translation and commentary by His Divine Grace A.C. Bhaktivedanta Swami Prabhupada, was the first book I read by my future spiritual master. Reading *Sri Isopanisad* helped to situate me nicely on the path of *bhakti*. In turn, I dedicate this commentary as an offering both to newcomers to Krishna consciousness, as well as to older devotees. My wish is that this book will serve as a reminder for all of us about the need to reflect constantly on the sacred teachings made available to us by Srila Prabhupada.

Contents

Acknowledgements .... **i**
Foreword .... **iii**
Introduction **1**
    Ordinary versus Extraordinary Knowledge •
    Situational Ethics versus Eternal Truth • Lack of
    Knowledge Brings Misery • A Low-Trust Culture
    Sabotages Devotion • A Universal Religion? • Is
    the Spiritual Master All-Knowing? • Why Choose
    Bhakti-Yoga? • Ten Pramanas, or Evidences
    of Truth • Understanding What Is Favorable •
    Connecting Internally • The Importance of Sadhu-
    Sanga • Preach by Example • Applying Intelligence
    Properly • Questions and Answers
Invocation **23**
    Searching for Wholeness • Nama, Rupa,
    Guna, and Lila • The Body Is a Prison Suit •
    Partial Understandings of God • The Mystery
    of Acintya-bhedabheda-tattva • Principles of
    Spiritual Giving • The Craziness of Separation •
    Completeness in the Lord's Creation • Questions
    and Answers
Mantra One **37**
    The Problem of False Ownership • Connecting
    with Various 'Isms' • Spiritual Communism •
    Beyond Mundane Piety • The Value of the God
    Factor • Questions and Answers
Mantra Two **45**
    The Universal Law • Free Will versus Destiny •
    Three Divisions of Activity • Group Karma • Mixed
    Karma • Doctoring the Soul • Creating Our Own
    Happiness and Distress • Compassion for the
    Suffering of Others • The Four Stages of Karma •
    No Happiness in the Material World? • Questions
    and Answers
Mantra Three **57**
    Vedic Divisions of Human Society • Those Who
    Do Not Surrender • Mudhas—Beasts of Burden •
    Naradhamas—Uncivilized Human Beings •
    Mayayapahrta-Jnana, or Those Whose Knowledge

Is Stolen by Illusion • Asuram Bhavam Asritah—
Those of Demoniac Nature • Killers of the Soul •
Religious Pretenders • The Price of Knowledge •
Questions and Answers

Mantra Four **65**
Krishna Possess All Opulences • We Choose Our
Relationship with Krishna • Why Preach Krishna
Consciousness? • We can Only Know Krishna by
Devotion • Endeavor or Mercy? • Making Excuses
and Blaming the Environment • Why do Some
Advance Faster than Others? • Krishna Responds
to Quality of Devotion • Questions and Answers

Mantra Five **77**
Can We See God? • Devotional Service Gives
Us the Eyes to See • Prisoners cannot Make
Demands • The Limits of Mundane Scholarship •
Understanding Spiritual Realities • Questions and
Answers

Mantra Six **85**
The Nature of a Sadhu • The Importance of
Environment • Three Types of Devotees •
Characteristics of the Kanistha-Adhikari •
Characteristics of the Madhyama-Adhikari •
Characteristics of the Uttama-Adhikari • Healthy
versus Unhealthy Discrimination • Genuine
Respect • Devotional Fraudsters • Questions and
Answers

Mantra Seven **95**
A Higher State of Consciousness • Love: The Most
Powerful Weapon • A Story of Hope • Leaving the
World of Duality Behind • Questions and Answers

Mantra Eight **103**
Gratitude and Reciprocation • Material Senses
and Spiritual Senses • How to Strengthen
Memory • The Greatest Sense Gratification •
The Importance of Arca-Vigraha • Questions and
Answers

Mantra Nine **113**
Does Knowledge Mean Sorrow? • Breaking
Spiritual Laws • The Higher the Knowledge, the

Greater the Consequences • Insider Deviation • A Cobra Decorated with a Valuable Jewel • Sri Isopanisad Is a Powerful Weapon • Questions and Answers

Mantra Ten 123
Light Always Dispels Darkness • Building Community • Diversity and Dedication Result in Victory • Recovering from Amnesia • Eighteen Methods for Developing Real Knowledge • Questions and Answers

Mantra Eleven 149
Making Healthy Distinctions • Liberation via Material Indulgence? • Discernment Strengthens Determination • Should Indulgence Precede Renunciation? • Developing a Higher Taste • Dodging Death Is Futile • Advice from the Expert Preacher • Avoiding Extremes • Institutional Knowledge or Misinformation? • The Illusion of Wedded Bliss • Studying the Experiences of Others • Gratitude Is Essential • Questions and Answers

Mantra Twelve 171
The Destination of the Worshiper • Is Sastra Subject to Interpretation? • The Exploitation of Religion • How to Research the Goal • Scripture: Literal or Allegorical? • Various Types of Study Lead to Different Goals • The Dangers of Fundamentalism • Madhurya-Rasa in Diverse Spiritual Traditions • The Experience of Krishna Consciousness • Fanaticism Leads to Destruction • Desiring Heaven • Running Away from God • Practice and Perseverance Makes Perfect • Sincere Desire Produces Miracles • More Humble than a Blade of Grass • Questions and Answers

Mantra Thirteen 193
Purchasing a Ticket to Goloka Vrndavana • Obtaining a Specialization in Devotion • The Ultimate Beneficiary of All Sacrifices • Qualifications for Hearing Confidentially • Questions and Answers

Mantra Fourteen **203**
True Knowledge • Philanthropy: A Distraction? • Prasadam Alters Karma • Time Consciousness • The Importance of Setting Personal Goals • Honest with Ourselves • The Value of Enthusiasm • Stepping Stones to Surrender • Questions and Answers

Mantra Fifteen **215**
Desiring for Krishna • Why Krishna Takes Away • Do We Want Krishna or Maya? • Maya's Attacks Are Unavoidable • Arrive at Gratitude • Going for the Gold • Be Prepared to Pay the Price • Lord Buddha Attains Realization after Many Tests • The Trials of Queen Kunti • Is Krishna Consciousness Too Difficult? • Maharaja Pariksit Welcomes Death • The Austerities of Dhruva Maharaja • How We Sabotage Ourselves • Maya: Krishna's Secret Agent • The Sorrows of Devaki and Vasudeva • Haridasa Thakura's Beatings • Srila Prabhupada's Sacrifice • Jayananda Thakura's Battle with Leukemia • Eliminating Distractions • Questions and Answers

Mantra Sixteen **239**
Approach Krishna through Humility • The Dangers of Distractions • Dealing with Tricks of the Mind • Developing Intense Spiritual Greed • Begging for Captivity • "Take Away My Will, Krishna!" • Faith and Trust in God • Hoping against Hope • Diunital Realities • Why Think Small? • An Honest Broker • Conclusion • Questions and Answers

Mantra Seventeen **261**
A Temporary Dwelling Place • Evaluation After Death • The Story of King Citraketu • The Story of Ajamila • Near-Death Experiences • Death Indicates a Change of Body • Understand the Science of the Soul • God's Many Representatives • Antimaterial Desires • Questions and Answers

Mantra Eighteen **277**
The Principle of Saranagati • A Dangerous Prayer • Asking for Pure Love • Taking the Proper

Prescription • Claiming Our Rightful Inheritance • Rights versus Responsibility • Krishna's Greatest Opulence • Intense Concentrated Desire • The Selfless Devotion of Advanced Devotees • The Power of Forgiveness • Who Returns to the Spiritual World? • The Svarupa-Laksana • Petition the Lord for Mercy • Asking for More than We Deserve • Questions and Answers

Glossary **301**
Bibliography **309**
Index **311**
About the Author **319**

Acknowledgements

I would sincerely like to thank Deborah Rochelle Klein for her work as the chief editor, and Parijata dasi, Dhruva Maharaja dasa, Diana Caulton, Matthew Gerhold, Lila Katha dasi, Murti dasi, and Acyuta dasi for further assistance with editing and proofreading. I also want to thank Karttika dasa along with the many others who assisted with the transcription of the numerous audiotapes.

I would further like to thank Syamananda Krsna dasa and Purusa-sukta dasa for scriptural editing; Jambavan dasa for Sanskrit editing; and Karen van Wvk for assistance with the Biblical references. I also thank Subala dasa and Stayi Bhava dasi for the layout and cover design of the book; Sri Nandanandana dasa for the cover picture; and Kripa dasi and Aja dasa for all the final details involved in bringing this book to press.

I am so appreciative of how the devotees in South Africa worked together as such an efficient team to assist me in the preparation of this book and to even pay for its printing. I am most grateful and look forward to other projects in the future in which we can work together.

Reflections on Sacred Teachings, Volume Four

Foreword

Sri Isopanisad is an ancient work. It is counted as the first of the 108 *Upanisads*, and is part of the *Yajur Veda*—among those literatures which are accepted by followers of the Vedic tradition to have come from God Himself at the time of creation. As such it is, one could say, about as foundational a text as one could hope to find, anywhere, dealing with the most primeval and fundamental concepts of reality as we know it, presented in a context that is both timeless, in that it comes from the person who put time into motion, and simultaneously eternal.

It deals with issues that are as broad and universal as its origins. Essential issues such as our responsibilities as integral parts of the universe, in one sense uniquely individual but simultaneously interrelated with everything else in an arrangement so delicate that one wrong move may adversely affect the existences of so many others. Some may be surprised that a book, which might be considered ostensibly "religious" in the more limited sense of the term, could be so practical and real. This is not the stuff that legends are made of, but rather a pragmatism that is as down to earth as Newton and his apple, while at the same time giving a tangible link to subjects transcendent to the current scope of our experience.

Not surprisingly, *Sri Isopanisad* deals with themes that are familiar to the reader of Vedic literature. The living entity is presented as *atma*—spirit soul—by nature not a part of this material world, but still deeply implicated and entangled in its permutations and fluctuations. Not at home here, but not easily able to extricate himself from its clutches. The Absolute Truth is presented at His inscrutable best—He is fixed in His abode, but is swifter than the mind. He is far away, but very near as well; He is within everything but also outside of everything. Many would say that such qualities demand that He not be defined as "He", but rather in impersonal terms.

But wait! As we approach the final pages of the book we find the speaker appealing to the Absolute in deeply heartfelt, emotional terms. It appears he is coming to the final moments in his life, and is experiencing a type of communion with God that is driving him into areas of realization that seem clearly to defy impersonalism. Beyond that blinding spiritual light, that apparently all-consuming oneness, he sees a face! With excitement rising to a transcendental crescendo as everything material is torn away from him, he senses the presence of an extraordinary Supreme Person, full of mercy, who he has access to, and who will surely reciprocate with him as he opens his heart and fully takes shelter.

This is no stoic, emotionless non-entity that we are talking of. Rather this is that personal Absolute Truth accepted in the Bhakti school of the Vedic tradition as the Supreme Personality of Godhead, who reciprocates with those pure devotees who surrender wholeheartedly to Him. Thus *Sri Isopanisad* seems to ultimately direct us to the personal conception of the Supreme Truth, in this way resolving a dispute that is almost as old as the book itself is. At the same time it acknowledges an impersonal element, with characteristics distinct from personality as we know it, but behind that impersonal manifestation lies the personal feature, inasmuch as behind displays of energy we always find energetic sources.

Into this complex ocean of truth dives our commentator, His Holiness Bhakti Tirtha Swami. His background is eminently suitable for dealing with the subject matter of *Sri Isopanisad*. As a leading practitioner of *bhakti-yoga* for nearly 35 years, he has been living a Vedic lifestyle for the greater part of his life, and has immersed himself in the philosophy of the Vedic tradition. But then as a graduate and lecturer in political science and psychology he has a perspective on the application of the philosophy in the current age that is quite unique. In his own life the synthesis of ancient wisdom and modern day relevance has become complete, and this is reflected in his capacity to communicate with today's audiences, even including business and political leaders, in dynamic ways that empower them to successfully take on the problems of life in the 21st century from a higher platform of spiritual awareness and truth.

Bhakti Tirtha Swami is no esoteric armchair philosopher. Nor is he a purveyor of watered down clichés, designed to win the attention and financial support of dabblers in the so-called New Age. With exacting integrity he takes us through some of the most essential basic elements of transcendence and gives us the keys to unlock their secrets and put them to work for us.

Please read on. I am sure that when you finish this significant book you will feel the same as I do—grateful for having received a gift of such value that you will keep realizing it every day for the rest of your life, and perhaps beyond.

—His Holiness Bhakti Caitanya Swami
International GBC Chairman of ISKCON

Introduction

Ordinary versus Extraordinary Knowledge
When we approach the *Vedas*, or the Vedic literatures, it is imperative to remember that we are not entering the realms of mundane religion or history. Hearing from the *Vedas* means immersing ourselves in a deep spiritual culture that is saturated with the highest knowledge. *Sri Isopanisad* is an ancient Vedic text written in Sanskrit, one of the earliest languages known to humankind. It is also the language spoken by many *devas*, or demigods, to communicate with one another. In his introduction to *Sri Isopanisad*, Srila Prabhupada explains that *Veda* means 'knowledge'. *Vedanta*, or Vedic philosophy as elucidated by bona fide scriptures, means 'ultimate knowledge'. *Sri Isopanisad*, the foremost of the one hundred and eight *Upanisads*, or the section of the *Vedas* that contains philosophical treatises, offers us a dense summary of essential Vedic teachings. Comprised of nineteen *mantras, Sri Isopanisad* presents unique insight into the structure of the universe and our place within it.

The Sanskrit word *'mantra'* is derived from two roots: *'man,'* or mind and *'tra,'* which means to deliver. Thus, the very composition of the word indicates that *mantra* meditation is a technique for the deliverance of the mind. In this day and age, most of us desperately yearn to break free from unhealthy connections, impositions, and mindsets. *Sri Isopanisad* conveys a very powerful understanding about the nature of the soul, of the cosmos, and of humanity's relationship with the Supreme Personality of Godhead. These *mantras* were compiled by the direction of Srila Vyasadeva approximately five thousand years ago at the dawn of Kali-yuga, or the current age of quarrel and hypocrisy, in order to reawaken our dormant consciousness and to deliver us from ignorance.

As Vaisnavas or aspiring devotees of the Lord, we may have read *Sri Isopanisad* many times already. It is important for us to continually revisit our sacred scriptures, especially *Bhagavad-gita As It Is, The Nectar of Instruction, The Nectar of Devotion, Srimad-Bhagavatam*, and *Caitanya-caritamrta*. Each time we reflect on the same scripture, we should try to understand it from a deeper perspective. If our understanding does not deepen, something is wrong. Acquiring spiritual knowledge does not necessarily mean acquiring new information. In fact, within the first couple of days of coming to devotional service, we are given everything we will ever need: the process as well as the goal. Advancement is merely a matter of deepening our understanding. As our desire to know Krishna intensifies; as we engage in *bhajana*, or the practice of devotional service; and as we read spiritual books, realizations should blossom unbidden in our hearts. One of the beauties of *bhakti*, or love and devotion for Krishna, is that if we hear the realizations of a dozen devotees on the same *sloka*, or verse, we will receive just as many shades of meaning. Our tradition of honoring variegated ways of reading sacred texts resonates, too, throughout the writings of our *acaryas*, or spiritual teachers who lead by example. In fact, many of the texts composed by our *acaryas* are commentaries on pre-existing scriptures.

In various cultures over time, different philosophical methods have been developed by thinkers to assist in the understanding of the interrelation between truth and knowledge. For example, ontology is concerned with theories about the nature of being, or existence; epistemology involves an analysis of the methods of acquiring knowledge; and cosmology pertains to metaphysical speculation regarding the nature of the universe as an ordered whole. Theology is the systematic study of and inquiry into the attributes of God, while axiology is concerned with how we ascribe values to experience. Aesthetics involves an assessment of the nature of beauty. All these systems of codifying knowledge suggest ways of defining reality. However, intelligent people want to define the world not according to their own flawed perceptions, but through the lens of a higher viewpoint. While Krishna is *sarva-jna*, or all-knowing, human beings possess only partial knowledge at best. Therefore, to attain perfect knowledge, we must see through the eyes of the *sastra*, or revealed scripture. More specifically, we seek a healthy interdependence between *sastra*, *sadhu* or saintly persons, and *guru* or the spiritual master. It is healthy to avoid both an attitude of extreme dependence on any of these three as well as one of extreme independence.

Situational Ethics versus Eternal Truth

Sri Isopanisad is a very powerful book. It was one of the first books written by Srila Prabhupada that I read. At the time, I was attending Princeton University in America. I was delving into many sorts of illusory systems of knowledge, including metaphysics and *astanga-yoga*, an eightfold system of mysticism. After reading *Sri Isopanisad*, I remember thinking that out of the numerous volumes

Introduction

of other literatures I had read, this small book crystallized for me so many phenomena that were unclear in other studies. It contained a set of simple meditations with explanations, yet at the same time, it was so inclusive. I was encouraged to explore further.

We bring our consciousness to bear on anything we hear or read. In mundane scholarship, truth is based on what is functional in the present. Situational ethics, which is the standard in most academic communities, implies that no ultimate truth exists. Interest lies merely in what is true for the moment and, more specifically, in what will assist in the attainment of sense gratification. In general, intellectuals are suspicious of those who claim to have found 'The Truth.' In the academic world, if one joins a spiritual institution, one is often considered to have lost one's rational intelligence. As a member of a group, a devotee is seen to have 'sold-out' his or her intelligence, which is now supposedly contaminated by 'subjectivity.' Intellectuals prefer to reflect, to observe, or to study at a distance rather than to participate actively in the experience of new realities. Unfortunately, the philosophy of 'objectivity' suggests that life is not about commitment or accountability, and that nothing deeper exists than the mind or the intellect. Frequently, scholars feel it honorable to be mere spectators, going through life without giving their hearts to anything. Sadly, millions of people live out their time on earth without any real passion.

Lack of Knowledge Brings Misery

In America, the average person will change his or her profession three or four times, and his or her job ten times during the natural life span. Individuals commonly replace their cars three times within ten years, and change houses every seven years. Alterations constantly take place in most people's lives. In middle age, many people undergo crises, feeling cheated because life did not give them what they really expected. If their children leave to attend college, they lament, "They don't think about us any more. We are left at home by ourselves now." If their children decide not to go to college, they also feel depressed, thinking, "What kind of imbecile child do we have? We thought he was going to be a doctor, a judge, or an engineer, but then he got a low-paying job straight after high school." Often, when daughters get married, the parents are happy, but cry at the same time.

Generally, people experience many complexities because they do not have a clear idea about the meaning of life. Therefore, they keep trying new things. "Maybe I didn't get the right husband or wife," they reflect, "or maybe I need to travel. Or perhaps I just need to lose weight." If we define truth as what feels comfortable to the mind and the senses, then we contribute towards an animal-like civilization, in which people come together merely to exploit one another. Thinking about taking and not giving, everyone suffers. The *Vedas*, however, offer universal knowledge that gives us the *siddhanta*, or ultimate conclusion of the revealed scriptures and the goal of existence. The *Vedas* give us access not merely to one aspect of reality, which may be full of speculations, but to a multi-dimensional vision of crystal-clear truth.

Srila Jiva Gosvami, in his work *Tattva Sandarbha*, or *The Essence of Truth*, notes that all conditioned souls or living entities deluded by the material energy, possess four major flaws, which interfere with their attempts to acquire sublime knowledge:

- *Bhrama*, or our tendency to make mistakes
- *Pramada*, or our tendency to fall prey to *maya*, or illusion
- *Karanapatava*, or our imperfect senses
- *Vipralipsa*, or our cheating propensity

Usually, people get angry when they are deceived, often because they want to be the ones to deceive others first. The best lawyers on the planet are those who assist their clients in cheating, and getting away with it. Currently, it is so difficult to know whether or not someone or something is genuine. With the proliferation of virtual reality, many ways to project illusion exist. Posturing occurs everywhere, including within governmental and spiritual institutions.

A Low-Trust Culture Sabotages Devotion

After recently completing a thirty-five-country tour, I was shocked to see that a low-trust culture has permeated ISKCON, or the International Society for Krishna Consciousness, too. When I studied the situation more closely, however, I realized that we cannot have anything *but* a low-trust culture in many places. Devotees are disappointing one another terribly. Leaders are failing their followers, husbands are abandoning their wives, parents are disillusioning their children, and vice versa. When vows are broken, and when we are wounded, we begin to trust less and less. When information is not sufficiently provided, it promotes suspicion. When expectations are not clearly communicated, confidence is depleted. Lack of trust sabotages *bhakti*. Strong *bhakti* cannot exist without strong *sraddha*, or faith. When faith is weak, *bhakti* cannot grow.

Introduction

Cultivating love and devotion for Krishna is much like tending a garden. If the soil in the garden is depleted, then no matter what else we do, our plants will not grow luxuriantly. Similarly, if we sow our *bhakti-lata-bija*, the seed of our devotional creeper, in the soil of weak faith, then how can it possibly flourish? However, if the soil is rich with assurance and conviction, then our creeper will develop healthily and ultimately produce good fruit.

One way to strengthen our faith is to search for deeper truths. Everything is contained within the scriptures. In fact, not taking advantage of our scriptures indicates laziness. We accept Krishna because of the Vedic authority. Therefore, we explore the *Vedas* for guidance, for clarity, and for solace. Unfortunately, our tendency to cheat is so pervasive that even when we come to Krishna consciousness, we still want to put in as little as possible while getting out as much as possible. We approach the Lord externally, but very few of us really give our hearts. In general, our tendency is to engage in deviations, without realizing that Krishna is monitoring everything. We can find so many ways to justify our digressions, but who are we really hurting? Only ourselves. The Lord in the heart is monitoring us. He is not just in some people's hearts, but in everyone's hearts. As Krishna tells Arjuna in *Bhagavad-gita* 15.15:

> *sarvasya caham hrdi sannivistho*
> *mattah smrtir jnanam apohanam ca*
> *vedais ca sarvair aham eva vedyo*
> *vedanta-krd veda-vid eva caham*

> *I am seated in everyone's heart, and from Me come remembrance, knowledge and forgetfulness. By all the Vedas, I am to be known. Indeed, I am the compiler of Vedanta, and I am the knower of the Vedas.*

Krishna is all-cognizant, but we are not. With all of the cheating taking place both around us and inside of us, it is difficult to know what is best. Therefore, we must take shelter of higher authority. It takes intelligence to dedicate oneself genuinely. We can give the body to the Lord without the mind and intelligence, but this is not complete giving.

A Universal Religion?

In his introduction to *Sri Isopanisad*, Srila Prabhupada mentions that although some may see the *Vedas* as Hindu, the word 'Hindu' itself is a misnomer. "Our real identification," he writes, "is *varnasrama*" (*Sri Isopanisad*, 3). Referring to the division of society into four *varnas*, or societal orders, and four *asramas*, or stages of spiritual life, as ordained by Krishna, Srila Prabhupada notes that these divisions are to be "found everywhere." Ultimately, however, we are adherents of *sanatana-dharma*, which means that the occupation of each one of us is to serve Krishna eternally and blissfully. Divisions that we make based on the body are temporary and can be confusing at times. For example, if someone says, "I am Jewish," what does that mean? He or she could be referring to his or her identification with a religion, a culture, a language, an ethnicity, or a political persuasion. As devotees of Lord Krishna, we are connected with the Hindu family. Hinduism, for some, means being born in Bharata-varsa, which today is generally defined as the country of India. For others, Hinduism denotes a political calling, perhaps a posturing against Muslims or other nationalities. For some, Hinduism indicates worshiping the demigods. For others, Hinduism is synonymous with impersonalism.

Ultimately, however, there is only one religion, *saranagati*, or surrender to Krishna, and one culture, the culture of *bhakti*. In fact, although all the different cultures of the world are transitory, they include various aspects of *bhakti*. If we explore the roots of history on this planet with great scrutiny, we will discover that ancient civilizations were in tune with natural rhythms and higher truths. Western culture is quite modern, and acculturation to urban norms has distanced us from our true nature. However, as we identify with the soul, we will again be able to honor *sanatana-dharma*.

Sometimes people look at us and think, "There goes a cult member, brainwashed by obscure mythology," when, in fact, average people are fervent adherents of the dangerous ideology of materialism. We are knowledge-seekers. We seek knowledge for the sake of knowing how to act in the world. Instead of trying to impose our subjective conceptions of truth on the planet, we want to let divinity descend upon us. Srila Prabhupada points out that another word for the *Vedas* is *sruti*, or "knowledge which is acquired by hearing" (*Sri Isopanisad*, 4). We need to hear the *Vedas* from the mouth of a bona fide spiritual master.

Is the Spiritual Master All-Knowing?

Sometimes devotees ponder upon the question: "Did Srila Prabhupada know and see everything?" Some will say, "Yes, he must. Of course he is all-knowing and all-seeing, because he is a pure devotee of Lord Krishna." Others will emphasize that Srila Prabhupada was not Krishna, but a pure servant of the Lord. As a servant of God, he was aware of anything that Krishna wanted him to know. Srila Prabhupada was neither an auto-mechanic nor an engineer. Knowledge of these things was not required. Since he understood the essence, Krishna revealed to him whatever was required according to time, place, and circumstance. When Srila Prabhupada was confronted with this question, he explained that the *guru* is not God. Sometimes, people carry unusual conceptions in their minds about what constitutes purity, not realizing that purity means becoming a puppet for Krishna. Often, when people find out that we have a *guru*, they ask, "What magic can he do?" Similarly, they would demand of Srila Prabhupada, "Swamiji, what miracles can you do?" Sometimes, reporters would inquire, "Why did you come here on a 747 jet? Why are you wearing a gold ring on your hand? Why are your disciples driving you around in a Rolls Royce?"

The general understanding of spiritual life is that it is the opposite of material life; that matter is sinful; and therefore, that spirit means automatic disassociation from matter. Pure devotees, however, always see everything in relation to Krishna's service. Krishna describes that different energies emanate from Him: namely, *antaranga-sakti*, or His internal potency; *tatastha-sakti*, or His marginal potency; and *bahiranga-sakti*, or His external potency. These energies have intrinsic value relative to their source, Lord Krishna. However, when they are perceived by us to have value separate from the Lord, these energies appear to us in a perverted or incomplete form. Fully aware of a higher nature, pure devotees engage everything in Krishna's service in order to please the Lord, as opposed to conditioned living entities who try to exploit the material energy for their own pleasure.

Why Choose Bhakti-Yoga?

Krishna consciousness is an extraordinary philosophy because it allows us to honor all the bona fide prophets, their teachings, as well as the scriptures connected with those traditions. However, just as the *Oxford English Dictionary* is available in both the abridged and unabridged editions, so too do different teachings supply us with varying levels of wisdom. When we open the unabridged edition of the dictionary, for instance, we will discover many more words and detailed explanations than can be found in the abridged edition. Basic religiosity is like the abridged edition—it will provide us with elementary information about serving God, such as 'Do not kill,' 'Follow your heart,' and 'Honor thy neighbor as thyself.'

These basic teachings are also present in Krishna consciousness as *dharma*, or the observance of occupational roles according to religious principles. However, the *Vedas* supply knowledge about our eternal *dharma* called *sanatana-dharma*, which is higher than mundane religiosity. *Dharma* is automatically included in *sanatana-dharma*. Similarly, the culture of *bhakti-yoga*, which emphasizes connection with the Lord through love and devotion, encompasses all other systems of *yoga*, or the linking of the self with the Supreme, including *jnana-yoga*, the study of the impersonal aspect of the Lord; *hatha-yoga*, the execution of bodily postures to control the five kinds of air in the body; *karma-yoga*, the discharge of one's prescribed duty to satisfy the Lord; and *astanga-yoga*. All forms of *yoga* are paths which ultimately lead to *bhakti*. Srila Prabhupada compares the path of *bhakti* to an elevator which can take us to the topmost floor whereas other *yoga* systems take us step by step up the staircase. However, before we can even attempt to rise to the topmost floor, at the very least we must be inside the building; that is, we have to be on a bona fide spiritual path. As we reach the topmost level, many wonderful opportunities unfurl.

Ten Pramanas, or Evidences of Truth

According to Srila Jiva Gosvami and the great Vaisnava scholar and devotee Srila Madhvacarya, ten different *pramanas* are customarily accepted as philosophically sound in Eastern thought. *Pramanas* mean evidences of truth, or ways of acquiring knowledge. They are as follows:

1. *Arsa*, or the statements of authoritative sages or demigods. For example, the *Brahma-samhita* contains prayers spoken by Lord Brahma in glorification of the Supreme Personality of Godhead. Lord Brahma is also a *mahajana*, or one of the twelve designated authorities on religious principles in the material world.

2. *Upamana*, or the explanation of a particular phenomenon by comparison with another. For instance, the *Vedas* often compare the material world to a prison house, or to a shadow of the spiritual world.

3. *Arthapatti*, or assumption due to the presence of known facts.

A perception that is clear functions as an indicator of another that is unclear. One piece of information acts as a catalyst for another. For example, if we see a peacock feather, we may think of Krishna. If we observe that animals eat, sleep, reproduce, and defend, just like humans, then we can assume that, just like us, they also have souls.

4. *Abhava*, or understanding gained through an absence of indicators. For instance, when we see a corpse, we know that the soul has left the body because it is not breathing or responding to stimuli.

5. *Sambhava*, or inclusion. A smaller concept is validated by its inclusion within a larger one. For example, ten dollars is automatically incorporated within a hundred-dollar bill, just as a single soldier is integrated within an army of a thousand soldiers.

6. *Aithya*, or tradition. Practices which have been passed down from generation to generation. For instance, in North America, it is a tradition to celebrate Independence Day every July 4th with fireworks.

7. *Cestha*, or gesture. Another way of knowing truth is through *mudra*, or bodily gesticulations and mannerisms. Those who are learned in the science of *mudras* can understand a great deal about others by studying their posture, their body language, and their physiognomy, or general outward appearance. In Vedic cultural dance, for instance, the movements of the dancer's eyes and hands tell an intricate story. In more mundane environments, people make the victory sign or sometimes offensive gestures, communicating either that we are wanted, or that we should go away.

8. *Pratyaksa*, or direct perception by the senses. For example, we can understand that something is sweet or bitter by tasting it, or that something is hot or cold by touching it.

9. *Anumana*, or induction. A method of reasoning from particular cases to general conclusions. A classic example is the story of Isaac Newton observing an apple dropping from a tree, then formulating his general theory of gravity.

10. *Sabda*, or verbally revealed testimony. This includes the testimony of both mundane experts like doctors and teachers, and statements transmitted by divine authoritative sources, such as the *Vedas*. The first type of testimony is not exempt from contamination by the four human defects, whereas the second type of testimony, termed *sabda-pramana* or *apauruseya-sabda*, is faultless.

In his *Tattva Sandarbha*, Srila Jiva Gosvami accepts only the last three *pramanas*. Ultimately, however, he notes that the only evidence of truth that Vaisnavas embrace fully is *sabda-pramana*. *Sabda-pramana* is transcendental, whereas the other nine *pramanas* are material. *Sabda-pramana* is the source of our real solace because the transcendental vibrations of the *Vedas*, which include the words of the *acaryas*, are not ordinary sources of knowledge. They are divine sources. When we hear from them, we connect with Krishna Himself. At the same time, we honor *pratyaksa* and *anumana* to the degree that they complement the primary goal of life. When these secondary methods do not support our principal focus, we should discard them. As Vaisnavas, we rely on *pratyaksa* and *anumana* only to the extent that they reinforce *sabda-pramana*.

Sometimes, as devotees, we may mistakenly think that we are to use only *sabda-pramana*. However, if secondary techniques like *pratyaksa* or *anumana* support *sabda-pramana*, to that degree we should make use of them. As a general principle, if we can apply a secondary facility for the purpose of enhancing or amplifying the primary, then there is no reason we should not utilize it. We accept what is favorable for Krishna's service. As Srila Rupa Gosvami writes in his *Bhakti-rasamrta-sindhu* 2.255-256:

> *anasaktasya visayan*
> *yatharham upayunjatah*
> *nirbandhah krsna-sambandhe*
> *yuktam vairagyam ucyate*
>
> *prapancikataya buddhya*
> *hari-sambandhi-vastunah*
> *mumuksubhih parityago*
> *vairagyam phalgu kathyate*

When one is not attached to anything, but

at the same time accepts everything in relation to Krishna, one is rightly situated above possessiveness. On the other hand, one who rejects everything without knowledge of its relationship to Krishna is not as complete in his renunciation.

Understanding What Is Favorable

We must learn to discriminate between what is constructive for our spiritual lives, and what is not. We can understand that a facility, a relationship, or a service is genuinely favorable if it allows us to concentrate our attention on our primary objectives. For instance, while a central point of concern for most devotees is upholding the four rules and regulations, how each one of us manages our lives in order to keep these guiding principles in focus remains an individual matter. A devotee may ask himself or herself, "Should I remain single or should I get married? Should I marry this person or that person? Should I stay in my current service? What is good for me?" To answer these questions, analyze the situation. Note to what degree the secondary arrangement complements the goal. Meditate on the following questions: To what extent will this involvement harmonize with those activities that are an essential part of our identity as Vaisnavas? To what degree is it encouraging me in my chanting or in reading Prabhupada's books mindfully? To what degree is it inspiring me to want to go back to Godhead faster? Whatever is secondary that genuinely facilitates the primary should not be rejected. It should be honored and even celebrated!

Honestly appraising our lives is not always an easy process. Sometimes, a secondary arrangement that is beneficial for one devotee may be detrimental to another. For example, taking up a particular type of profession may be extremely positive for one individual, as it helps him or her to keep body and soul together while focusing on Krishna. For another, engaging in the very same profession will simply take him or her further from his or her identity as a Vaisnava. For some, obtaining opulence can turn into their biggest *maya* because it distracts them from devotional service. For others, having nothing becomes their biggest *maya*. When they have to worry about getting the basic necessities, they are prone to neglect their *sadhana*, or regulated practice of *bhakti-yoga*. Anyone who has been in the community of Vaisnavas for some time will observe that occasionally once-serious devotees will drift away from Krishna when they suddenly acquire wealth (through an inheritance or other means). "Sorry, no time for Krishna now," they wave, as they drive off into the sunset in a luxury car. Before, when the same devotees did not have much, they were humble and dedicated, always begging for Krishna's mercy. However, once Krishna gave them some mercy, they say, "Thank you, Krishna. You must realize how busy we are now that we have all these assets to manage. Please understand that we just do not have much time to come to the temple, or to read and chant anymore."

Conversely, others, who have always had a nice financial situation, may be quite Krishna conscious. When their situation reverses one day, however, they may begin to curse Krishna. As long as they had a good position and support coming to them from many different sectors, they liked to come to the temple and to chant. But when Krishna Himself arranges to take away, they do not want to accept His mercy. The same Krishna who gives so generously also removes in the blink of an eye. He gives and He takes, He takes and He gives, noticing all the while how we react to His various modes of reciprocation. "Now that I have given you so much," He evaluates, "how are you going to serve Me? Now I have taken away, how are you going to behave?" Krishna will test us. "Are you trying to connect more with My *sakti*, or energy, than with Me as a *saktiman*, or the source of those potencies? Are you accepting My love only when it comes in the package you want, or are you accepting My love however I choose to give it, knowing that I am making it available for you unconditionally?" Surrendering to Krishna, no matter how He chooses to reciprocate with us, can be a difficult challenge in devotional life. At the end of the day, however, transcendence really means that despite any obstacles we may experience, we find a way to glorify Krishna even more. Whatever occurs externally can never impede our internal focus unless we allow it to.

Connecting Internally

When I was in Croatia some years ago, I visited an elderly devotee in the hospital. She had served the Deities faithfully as a *pujari*, or priest, for nearly two decades, but currently she was afflicted with a serious disease, which was almost certainly terminal. I was amazed to note that although she was bedridden, she was incredibly vibrant. Although now she was physically restricted from doing her *pujari* service, day after day she engages in even more elaborate *puja* in her mind. Humbly accepting whatever Krishna arranged in her life, she still found powerful ways in which to give love and receive love from the Deities. During periods when our bodies are practically dysfunctional, we can nevertheless think of Krishna and serve Him intensely in our minds. There is never a time in which we cannot serve the Lord if we really want to.

Experiencing a crisis is really a chance for us to reflect with greater sincerity, and to truly understand the higher truth. It is a chance for us to take close inventory of what is going on in our lives. It is a chance for us to develop even more gratitude for the wonderful things that have taken place within and around us. In the depth of the pain of these critical moments lie great opportunities for us to make serious advancement.

We grow more at times when we are confronted with some difficulty rather than at times when everything is going well in our lives. How can we grow within a comfortable situation if our basic position in this material world is as prisoners? As prisoners trying to escape, we will inevitably face turmoil and incoherence. As we work towards making a difference in the world, natural calamities, conflict, bewilderment, frustration, anxiety, and gloom will be part of our experience. However, if we choose to simply accept that we are incarcerated by the environment, then we may feel an illusory sense of peacefulness, stemming from ignorance. If a prisoner accepts his or her situation, he or she may feel content in captivation. But when we finally make a bid to escape our conditioning, then without doubt we will undergo a struggle. Unquestionably, it is very difficult to get free from the prison house of the material world without sufficient support, encouragement, and good examples.

The Importance of Sadhu-Sanga

Sadhu-sanga, or the association of devotees, can stimulate and encourage us, thus enabling us to become very animated in our devotional service. However, it can also become discouraging if we allow it to deteriorate into a low-trust culture. Quality association is indispensable. If we do not have sufficient support, then inevitably we will get weaker and weaker. We are all locked into one another's consciousness much more than we normally consider. If we experience very exhilarated Krishna consciousness, our mood automatically spills over and touches someone else's psyche. It encourages others, assisting them in watering their own devotional creepers. Our firm Krishna consciousness will give others shelter and protection. But if our minds are captured with overwhelming doubts, fears, anxieties, and the enemies of the mind—namely *kama* (lust), *krodha* (anger), *lobha* (greed), *moha* (illusion), *mada* (madness), and *matsarya* (envy)—then that consciousness will seep through and contaminate others. We should be honest: genuine work on our own issues is required, not blind following. Let us dive deep into the culture of *bhakti* in order to acquire greater potency to act upon higher truths. Let us truly cultivate the ability to share positively with others.

In *Bhagavad-gita* 7.16, Krishna tells Arjuna:

> *catur-vidha bhajante mam*
> *janah sukrtino 'rjuna*
> *arto jijnasur artharthi*
> *jnani ca bharatarsabha*

> *O best among the Bharatas, four kinds of pious men begin to render devotional service unto Me—the distressed, the desirer of wealth, the inquisitive, and he who is searching for knowledge of the Absolute.*

Of the four types of people who are attracted to Krishna consciousness, only one is primarily after knowledge. We must be aware that the majority of those who take shelter of Krishna are chiefly motivated by distress, curiosity, or financial difficulties. Either due to *sukrti*, or credits accrued from previous pious activities, or *ajnata-sukrti*, devotional service unknowingly performed, a particular person says 'yes' to Krishna. If people who are grappling with anxieties or problems arrive for the Sunday feast only to hear a *sannyasi*, or a leader-renunciate, tell them that Krishna will take everything away, down to their last twenty dollars, they will not be encouraged to remain. After taking *prasadam*, the remnants of vegetarian food offered to the Lord, our guests will sneak out the back door. We might never see them again if we do not preach to them in the proper way.

When a person approaches us out of knowledge, however, his or her experience will be different, because he or she is more qualified to continue to say 'yes' to Krishna, regardless of whatever is happening in the immediate environment. Even if these kinds of people hear information that is materially discouraging, the knowledge factor will keep propelling them forward. Ultimately, however, everyone is influenced by the quality of *sadhu-sanga* in his or her environment. Therefore, we should be extremely careful not to cause pain to anyone, especially those closest to us. It is important that we function in such a way as to act upon our Krishna conscious

Introduction

principles while not imposing them on others. We have a duty to try to find techniques to help people appreciate Krishna. Most importantly, we must behave in such a way that will lessen the possibility of causing others to make offenses. If our colleagues at work or our relatives feel Krishna consciousness is not relevant, then they will minimize what the great *acaryas* have given us.

Devotees should cultivate concern, mercy, selflessness, and compassion. We should never have an arrogant mood or force our philosophy on people; rather, we should convey our sincere desire to share it. By living it, we show that it is vibrant and potent. The best way of sharing Krishna consciousness is to align our speech with our actions. It is so vital that we 'walk our talk,' because in this way people will naturally think, "Without a doubt, there is something special about this Hare Krishna devotee. I don't really understand why, but I want to be close to this person. Although she is a little unusual, I want to learn more about her lifestyle, because she projects such a loving energy."

The pain we experience in intimate relationships is the deepest we will ever endure. While no one can give us love like those who are closest to us, nobody can hurt us like those we love the most. Sometimes, it is awkward to break family or cultural traditions, because doing so may cause those who are very dear to us to feel disturbed. They may interpret our abandonment of their tradition as a message that we do not honor them. They may feel that we are rejecting their love and that they may even lose us. It can be very difficult. On the basis of *aithya*, many people accept family customs as ultimate realities. After all, these are the ways in which their parents, their grandparents, and their great-grandparents have always done things in terms of theology and culture. Often, rituals that have been in the family for years are very hard to break. Following mundane traditions too rigorously generally distracts us from the transcendental. Observing them encourages us to focus upon the immediate experiences that bombard us rather than allowing us to move beyond the bodily conception of life.

Preach by Example

One way to facilitate Krishna consciousness is to become expert in whatever we do. People admire expertise in any area, whether it is in sportsmanship, music, art, engineering, finance, or medicine. Competency naturally draws people's attention. They will become curious as they try to understand what assists us in achieving our levels of excellence. "What is your secret?" they wonder. "What is your solace, your support? What is your stimulation?" As they uncover our connection with Krishna consciousness, they will be more likely to embrace the philosophy when they see that it is followed by such high achievers.

Let us consider the converse situation: when we behave in a way that sends out a message of failure, people will associate the theology we follow with our inability to succeed. Recently, after speaking with some devotees from Australia, I was shocked by what I could see was a negative indicator for the future. While preaching against the government, many devotees simultaneously rely on the welfare system for their maintenance. Devotees disparage governmental policies on war, taxation, slaughterhouses, and meat-eating in schools. At the same time, they take the government's money and do not work. At some point, those in charge of the country will realize that while 'Hare Krishna people' criticize their drinking and their lotteries, they themselves have failed to become productive citizens and are living off the profits of the very systems they deride. Leaders will conclude that our philosophy does not lead to the creation of mature citizens, and moreover, that it is hypocritical.

It is an unfortunate fact that in some areas over eighty percent of marriages in ISKCON end in divorce. When intelligent people perceive these kinds of indicators, they will not feel encouraged to take shelter of our philosophy, because they will think, "If I join, before I know it, my marriage will be on the rocks. I do not want to be the next statistic." A few years ago, someone confided in me that some young women do not want to become very involved in Krishna consciousness because they think it will prevent them from finding husbands. Recently, in Durban, South Africa, a father revealed to me that he did not want his daughter to join ISKCON. "Do not get too close to the Hare Krishna movement," he advised her, "because then you will end up alone." However, when people see that Krishna consciousness is inclusive, that they can join the movement and associate with people who are ethical and supportive, they will feel more inclined to surrender. We should be in a strong position to demonstrate that while we recommend a simple life, we also offer an opportunity to attain solace and security in conjunction with spiritual advancement. Alternatively, if people observe that by joining the Hare Krishna movement, they stand a good chance of being on welfare, divorcing three or four times, or having no opportunity at all to find a husband or a wife, then they may very well think, "I do not know about this 'Hare Krishna' stuff. Perhaps it is safer to visit the church down the road, or to worship Lord Siva instead."

Introduction

Applying Intelligence Properly

Our movement often attracts people with strong brahminical inclinations, for whom acquiring knowledge has a strong appeal. Very intellectual devotees can become the best devotees—or the worst. They become the worst devotees when they research quotes from the most obscure scriptures to justify nonsense, or when they use their intelligence to rationalize deviations. At the same time, if we do not use our intelligence, then our senses will simply dominate the mind, capture it, and lead us to hell. The senses, confronted with the environment, are constantly assaulting the mind. If our minds are not strengthened by good intelligence, then we will be at the mercy of the environment. If the intelligence is not constantly reflecting on transcendental knowledge, then when the senses send a demand to the mind, the mind will not have the power to resist it. A devotee who has an intellectual propensity, yet is unable to engage it properly, will find spiritual life very cumbersome. Intellectually inclined devotees who do not immerse themselves in *sabda-pramana* will be afflicted by restlessness. They will engage their intelligence in contemplating sense gratification. Thinking leads to feeling, feeling to willing, and willing to acting. Absorbing the mind in mundane knowledge leads to material entanglement. Conversely, absorbing the mind in transcendental knowledge leads to spiritual freedom.

As discussed, the *Vedas* reveal that the conditioned living entity has four defects. These patterns are so dominant in most of our minds that they can be rooted out only by the potency of devotion. In his introduction, Srila Prabhupada contrasts inductive and deductive methods of reasoning: induction leads us to limited conclusions derived from personal analysis, while deduction enables us to obtain understanding from universal principles. Both processes are useful to the extent that they assist us in attaining greater love and devotion for Krishna. However, as Vaisnavas, our goal is not to analyze and prove everything ourselves. We cannot possibly capture reality based on our limited perception and insignificant intellectual power. Therefore, we want to use our intelligence to sustain the mind properly, in order to prevent it from being dragged under by the senses. We want to use our intelligence to open ourselves up to receiving divine intervention. We want to use our intelligence to inquire beyond the orthodox scheme of things. We want to use our intelligence to truly understand how to become a genuine lover of the Lord.

Questions and Answers

Question: Do Western religious and philosophical traditions contain transcendental knowledge, or are they merely material systems?

Answer: All bona fide philosophical traditions contain some degree of transcendental knowledge. Certain philosophies are part of the Vedic family, while others exist outside of it. Krishna has expressed Himself more directly through the Vedic connection. Therefore, the more a philosophy is aligned with the Vedic conclusion, the more mature and evolved it is. Every bona fide theology can also be verified based on how closely it is aligned with its own authorized scriptures, holy men and women, and spiritual masters. To the degree that the actions of the followers of a particular school or tradition faithfully reflect their own bona fide *sadhu*, *sastra*, and *guru*, to that degree they will also be able to connect meaningfully with other bona fide religions.

Question: Are the words of demigods and sages to be read as *sabda-pramana*?

Answer: As discussed, we accept authoritative statements by sages and demigods, but they are secondary. We do not base our whole lives on them. Numerous types of demigods and sages exist whose statements fall into different categories. We accept them to the degree that their words are in alignment with our authorized scriptures and *sadhana*. When they are not in harmony with our scriptures, we need to look closer to find the essence. For instance, Lord Siva makes hundreds of statements that are not all directly supportive of *bhakti-yoga*, and at times he behaves in ways that we should not emulate. While we recognize that Lord Siva is a pure devotee of Krishna, and we accord him all honor, we only follow the conduct or embrace the statements of demigods that fall in line with Vaisnava *sastra*. Words of sages and demigods are to be considered directional indicators only. We cannot accept them wholeheartedly or categorically.

For instance, each of the eighteen *Puranas*, or the division of Vedic literature known as histories, asserts its particular deity as superlative and absolute. In his *Tattva Sandarbha*, Srila Jiva Gosvami explains that Srila Vyasadeva wrote the different *Puranas* for different reasons. Six sattvic *Puranas* exist for persons in the mode of goodness, six rajasic *Puranas* exist for those in the mode of passion, and six tamasic *Puranas* exist for those in the mode of ignorance. All are bona fide, but serve variegated purposes. Simply put, what we worship is what we get. Various bona fide ways to worship are available, many of which are based on goals that lie outside of unalloyed devotional service. Therefore, when evaluating the statements of sages and demigods, we need to adhere faithfully to the standards set by the previous *acaryas*.

Question: How can we strengthen our faith in Krishna?

Answer: Nothing strengthens faith like positive experience. Our faith deepens when we receive affirmation that what we are doing is right, and when we see others around us accorded similar encouragement. Our faith grows stronger when we gain a better understanding of the philosophy through reading or discussion. Strengthening our *sadhana* has a great impact on faith. When we find our association inspiring, our faith increases automatically. If we feel enthused by the devotees around us, then naturally our conviction in the science of Krishna consciousness intensifies. Emulating a role model whose qualities we would like to acquire is also encouraging. It follows that engaging in the opposite of these activities will debilitate our faith. Strong faith is not something we can fake. Our level of conviction is directly connected to how we choose to apply our bodies and our minds.

What we think is often more important than what we do. Although we may complete many services expertly, if our internal dialogue is rebellious, then gradually our thoughts will manifest in the world around us. We must reflect externally what we feel internally. For instance, when a *brahmacari*, or celibate male student, wears white, we realize that he is thinking of marriage, but has just not found his sweetheart yet. However, at other times, the external does not always match the internal. When we see a *brahmacari* wearing saffron, for example, we may wonder initially if he is genuinely renounced. There is a chance that he might be keeping a white set of cloth in his drawer with the intention to change his *asrama* the next Janmastami, or when he discovers that the girl with whom he is captivated is also interested in him.

Thinking leads to speaking and speech leads to action. The mind is very, very powerful. More intimately than our external behavior, our thoughts reflect who we really are. From time to time, I hold workshops for devotees at which I assist them in monitoring their own thoughts. Often, devotees who previously considered themselves to be happy were shocked to notice how many of their thoughts are actually negative meditations. If we constantly tell ourselves that we are useless and low achievers, then those meditations will determine our actions, and ultimately our reality. We must be very careful to pull our minds back from unhealthy reflections based on lust, greed, and fear. If we are able to become more and more devotional in our thinking, however, then even while we remain in physical bodies, our mindsets can gradually become connected with our spiritual forms in the spiritual world. As Krishna advises Arjuna in *Bhagavad-gita* 6.5:

> *uddhared atmanatmanam*
> *natmanam avasadayet*
> *atmaiva hy atmano bandhur*
> *atmaiva ripur atmanah*

> *One must deliver himself with the help of his mind, and not degrade himself. The mind is the friend of the conditioned soul, and his enemy as well.*

Our minds can be either vicious adversaries or supportive companions. Introspect and examine your own thoughts closely. If your thinking is unhealthy, then it is advisable to adjust it immediately, as our thoughts produce so much of what happens in our lives.

The mind is more powerful than the body and the senses. The body will follow the mind to any reality that the mind absorbs. The *Vedas* describe that the mind is *cancala*, or constantly flickering between *sankalpa*, or acceptance and *vikalpa*, or rejection of the same idea. Therefore, we have to harness the mind, to tame it as we would a wild animal. We have to trick it sometimes in an auspicious manner. If the intelligence is properly nourished and stimulated, then it will be able to control the mind. If the intelligence is neglected, however, then the senses will dictate the environment.

The eyes will see something appealing, the nose will smell something tantalizing, the genitals will become aroused, and they will send a message to the mind. "We are needy," they will tell the mind. "What are you going to do? There are more of us than you. If you do not do something, we will beat you." And the mind says, "Okay. I remember last time how you jumped on me when I denied you. So, yes, let me arrange to give you what you want this time."

However, when the intelligence is strong, it can say to the mind, "Do not be a coward! You do not have to give in. We will deal with these senses together. I am standing next to you." When the intelligence is strong, we will be less affected by the four defects, and we will be in a better position to accept *sabda-pramana*.

Reflections on Sacred Teachings, Volume Four

Invocation

*om purnam adah purnam idam
purnat purnam udacyate
purnasya purnam adaya
purnam evavasisyate*

The Personality of Godhead is perfect and complete, and because He is completely perfect, all emanations from Him, such as this phenomenal world, are perfectly equipped as complete wholes. Whatever is produced of the Complete Whole is also complete in itself. Because He is the Complete Whole, even though so many complete units emanate from Him, He remains the complete balance.

Searching for Wholeness

Most people find it difficult to imagine that anything on this planet can be perfect or complete. Although we may search constantly for external objects to enhance our lives, a sense of wholeness continues to elude us. When we attempt to make all kinds of alterations to the twenty-four elements of the *mahat-tattva*, the total material energy, we often experience disappointment and bewilderment. In one sense, material life consists simply of different combinations and permutations of the same ingredients, Krishna's separated energies. Imagine, for a moment, being confined to an area where there are only twenty-four things to do. After a while, we would exhaust our options and become bored. For example, when children obtain new toys, or even when adults acquire something unusual, they are initially fascinated with their latest object of interest. After a short period, however, the novelty wears off. They no longer get the same satisfaction from it.

This is a central feature of material nature: the same object or experience that can make us happy one moment can bore us to death in the next. It is amazing how the mind can experience satisfaction for a brief period of time, and then minutes later shift into disillusion in the blink of an eye. This is the nature of the duality of the material world. People are constantly trying to become more fulfilled by manipulating the material energy. Some seek this fulfillment through travel, while others take up extra curricular activities such as sports. Often, people address the opulences of Krishna indirectly by seeing them in relation to themselves. They might focus on developing beauty, strength, fame, knowledge, or wealth, and, in some rare cases, they pursue renunciation. Most people hope to become happy by becoming expert in one of these areas.

We all feel a deep internal desire to experience these opulences because ultimately they are all qualities of Krishna. Lord Sri Krishna is the original Supreme Personality of Godhead: *krsnas tu bhagavan svayam* (*Srimad-Bhagavatam*, 1.3.28). One of the most profound understandings of God is that He is the ultimate possessor of all opulences to their greatest extent. The Godhead is *purnam*, or perfectly complete, the *summum bonum*, or the highest end of all ethical systems. He is the Supreme Good who naturally possesses all the qualities the *jiva-atma*, or the individual soul, pursues, but is unable to achieve completely. We cannot obtain wholeness without Krishna because we are parts and parcels of the Lord. We suffer because we do not honor our completeness. We suffer because the senses and the mind prevent the soul from recognizing its original nature. We suffer because we are not in harmony with the source of our existence. As Krishna says in *Bhagavad-gita* 15.7:

> *mamaivamso jiva-loke*
> *jiva-bhutah sanatanah*
> *manah-sasthanindriyani*
> *prakrti-sthani karsati*

> *The living entities in this conditioned world are My eternal fragmental parts. Due to conditioned life, they are struggling very hard with the six senses, which include the mind.*

Nama, Rupa, Guna, and Lila

Understanding Godhead means realizing that He is the reservoir of all pleasure and of all life. We evaluate everything of importance in the world based on four attributes, namely *nama, rupa, guna,* and *lila*. We even assess ourselves based on these attributes:

- *Nama* means name. In the material world, there are many names: everything is called something. Nomenclature refers to systems of naming and categorization. We usually categorize an object or an experience by the words that label it. We refer

Invocation

to it by a particular appellation. "What is it called?" we ask. "Is its title really dealing with its essence?" Two entities can have similar appellations, but may be of a totally different orientation. For example, a human being and a pet animal, although completely different, may be called the same name. Hearing a name is merely the first step in understanding the true nature of a phenomenon.

- *Rupa* is form. A comprehension of form naturally follows from an understanding of name. After obtaining information about the outward appearance of an object, we search for how it interacts in the world, and for the activities in which it participates.

- *Guna* refers to qualities. Usually, after we have named a phenomenon, we begin to describe its form and then proceed to talk about its character and its individual traits. All the 8,400,000 different species in the universe have specific names and qualities. By understanding the quality of something, we can discern whether it is in the mode of ignorance, passion, or goodness. By assessing its qualities, we can comprehend to what degree illusion is active in the life of a *jiva* or a particular living entity.

- *Lila* signifies pastimes. A significant way to appraise those *jivas*, or the living entities under the spell of the material energy, is to observe their activities. Although we are distinguished from one another by many different types of bodies, our activities indicate to what extent we are running towards or away from Krishna. What we call ourselves, what people call us, what kind of form we have acquired by the three modes of material nature, and how we identify with the qualities that permeate our day-to-day experiences are also keys to understanding our affinity for or separation from Krishna.

When we think about anything, we immediately think about it in relationship to something else. Without name, form, quality, or relationship, a phenomenon is meaningless. It simply does not exist. If something exists, then if we study it closely, these four attributes must be present. If they are not present, then this means that we do not possess total knowledge of that object. Therefore, as we study the world around us closely, we will naturally see that we exist as part and parcel of Krishna. While all these attributes must be present in everything, they exist in full only for Krishna.

The Body Is a Prison Suit

The soul can suffer in many different kinds of prison suits. In most countries, convicted prisoners are kept in jails. When it comes time for parole, the judge may ask: "Is this prisoner rehabilitated? Did the prison environment and the prison suit remind him or her that he or she needs to undergo transformation and reformation? Or, have the inmates settled into their jail, identifying with and continuing to create an environment based on a life of incarceration?" Sometimes, prisoners worsen their own situation by identifying with the penitentiary.

In everyday life, people copy their fellow inmates by calling themselves by the names of their idols and by trying to acquire some of their qualities. Often, they attempt to imitate their idol's activities, and may even try to copy his or her form, or actual prison suit. All species follow the *nama, rupa, guna,* and *lila* of their leader. Therefore, these attributes will naturally be much more prominent in Krishna who is *sac-cid-ananda-vigraha* or eternal, full of knowledge, and full of bliss. The soul, our real identity, is also full of eternity, full of knowledge, and full of bliss. In addition, over and beyond those attributes, it has *vigraha,* or form. Spirit soul is real form and everything else is a temporary, perverted reflection.

Partial Understandings of God

Some individuals attempt to make understanding God a complex matter. Such people have to work hard just to accept the idea of God. Often they will recognize only a particular aspect of the Godhead. Those who have some understanding of the Lord as the impersonal Brahman will refer to Him as 'cosmic consciousness,' 'eternal energy,' or 'all-encompassing light.' These terms refer to the *sakti* that is connected with the *summum bonum,* but encompass only an appraisal of the *sat* feature of the Lord, or His potency of eternality.

God is present in everyone as the Supersoul, or the Paramatma. The Paramatma represents the *cit* feature of the Lord, or His potency of knowledge. As Krishna instructs Arjuna in *Bhagavad-gita* 13.23:

> *upadrastanumanta ca*
> *bharta bhokta mahesvarah*
> *paramatmeti capy ukto*
> *dehe 'smin purusah parah*

> *Yet in this body there is another, a transcendental enjoyer, who is the Lord, the supreme proprietor, who exists as the overseer and permitter, and who is known as the Supersoul.*

According to the living entity's desires, he or she has been afforded a certain level of realization, both materially and spiritually. However, a possibility for complete understanding always exists, as the Supersoul is ever-ready to accommodate the desire of the *jiva*. Unfortunately, many seekers of transcendence are only interested in the Brahman conception. This type of spiritual searcher may be compared to a hungry man, who finds the aroma of foodstuff enticing. However, we all know that the aroma alone is not really fulfilling.

As devotees, not only do we desire to smell *prasadam*, but we also desire to taste it. Just as the aroma is an indicator of the *prasadam* itself, so the Brahman aspect is a symptom of the presence of God. We do not want to merely think about love of Godhead, but we want to experience it. This is the *ananda*, or the bliss aspect, of our conception of Godhead. As stated previously, we are all *sac-cid-ananda-vigraha*. We understand Krishna as the Supreme Personality and the *adi-purusa*, or the original person. Not only is He the youngest, but simultaneously He is the oldest. He is *purnam*, the complete balance who encompasses all these attributes. We recognize that His Brahman and His Paramatma aspects, taken alone, cannot be *purnam*, or completely perfect.

The Mystery of Acintya-bhedabheda-tattva

We are simultaneously one with the Lord and different from Him. This understanding of Godhead is explained by Lord Caitanya as the philosophy of *acintya-bhedabheda-tattva*, or simultaneous and inconceivable oneness and difference. Krishna is the greatest and at the same time He is the most personal and the most aware. He is outside of everything and inside of everything simultaneously. While He possesses an energetic aspect, He is also the Supreme Energetic.

Ordinary religionists cannot appreciate that while God can be everything, He also has intimate names and participates in specific activities. At the same time, He can create everything, maintain the entire creation, and even enter into it. When they hear these transcendental truths, they think, "Oh, this is mythology. How can God do that?" They might hear our understanding of different *avataras*, or incarnations of God such as *guna-avataras*, or incarnations who rule the modes of material nature, such as Lord Brahma or Lord Siva. They also hear us refer to *lila-avataras*, or incarnations who come specifically to enact amazing pastimes, such as Lord Krishna and Lord Nrsimhadeva; and *saktyavesa-avataras*, or empowered representatives of the Lord, such as King Prthu and his wife Arci. They might listen to wonderful pastimes about the Lord's various activities on the earth planet as Lord Ramacandra; as Matsya, the fish *avatara*; and as Kurma, the tortoise *avatara*.

After being exposed to such transcendental narrations, they sometimes say, "It is completely implausible that the Lord incarnates in so many diverse forms." But we reply, "Why not?" In fact, not only do we say, "Why not?" but we declare that it must be the case. How is it possible that we, as humans, can have so many pastimes, so many qualities and forms, and even so many names, without God possessing those same attributes? People can know us by so many names. There are so many diverse qualities associated with various experiences and environments in our lives. To get an idea of our many *rupas*, we simply need to glance at our photographs from when we were babies, schoolchildren, teenagers, and young adults. As we enter into progressive stages in life, certain *lilas* accompany us. So, why do we think that God would not have them? Logically, it follows that not only must God have these attributes, but He must possess them in even greater abundance than we do.

Our theology is complete because of our understanding of the inconceivable simultaneous oneness and difference of the Godhead. We do not say that Krishna has no energy. As mentioned in the discussion of the ten *pramanas* in the Introduction, a philosophy can be understood to be inclusive when it encompasses smaller conceptions (*sambhava*). Therefore, when we have greater knowledge about the Supreme, the lesser knowledge is already included within it. Integrated within Krishna consciousness is the knowledge of the *yogi*, that of Paramatma; and also the knowledge of the impersonalist, that of Krishna's *sakti* or the effulgence of Brahman. However, we realize that the Paramatma and the Brahman effulgence exist because they are emanating from the spiritual *rupa* of Krishna Himself.

Through the following practical example, let me illustrate the relationship of partial conceptions of God to a fuller understanding of the Absolute Truth. Who would be satisfied if the cook announces at *prasadam* time, "Everyone, I made all of these wonderful dishes for the Lord. He has seen, He has eaten, and He has taken. Now you can smell them, but nothing more"? Will it satisfy us to interact only with the aroma? The cook might even say generously, "Devotees, circle around—today is a festival and we will have a great feast. Therefore, not only can you smell, but you can also look." Everyone might then come with big eyes and stare at the delicious preparations, but still we would not feel complete. We would not feel satisfied and we would certainly not feel nourished. We can compare having a theoretical knowledge of God to merely relishing the scent of *prasadam*, but not the taste of it. Knowledge on its own is not enough. Completeness comes from experiencing, from involving oneself with the Godhead. Some people work hard at various kinds of *yoga*, and also at other types of spiritual processes, but the end result is devoid of relationship. The final outcome does not lead to any appreciation of *sac-cid-ananda-vigraha* and does not sound very exciting to Vaisnavas. We know that love involves *sambandha*, or relationship. We cannot have real love without *sambandha*. Knowledge must be present, but more important than knowledge is association. Some people may say, "I love everybody." That is a nice general sentiment, but it is not deep, because it does not involve knowledge or association. However, when association, knowledge, and involvement are present, then it is possible to say, "I have great affection." We love someone because we find particular characteristics exciting about our beloved. Again, we return to *nama, rupa, guna,* and *lila*. If all of these are pleasing, then we will truly be able to say, "Yes, I feel intense appreciation."

Principles of Spiritual Giving

Although complete worlds continuously emanate from Him, Krishna's completeness remains undisturbed. How He can exist in full is a great mystery to us. We usually cannot experience such wholeness in this world of matter. For instance, if we have certain commodities but then share them with others, we will usually end up with less and they will possess more. This is not true of the spiritual paradigm, however. In the spiritual model, we do not have less after we give. This point is illustrated nicely by Srila Prabhupada. He told a story of a contemporary *yogi* named Ramakrishna. Ramakrishna supposedly gave some of his mystic power to a disciple, and then cried, "Now you have taken all my *sakti*, and I have nothing." This kind of giving is not spiritual. When a person gives something and ends up with less, then he or she is operating on the material plane, whether gross or subtle. It is imperative to keep in mind that as spiritualists, when we give, we do not end up with less, but we actually receive more. The more we genuinely activate our spiritual facilities, knowledge, and realizations in our dedication to Krishna, the more Krishna will give us in return. As the Supreme Lord promises Arjuna in *Bhagavad-gita* 4.11:

> *ye yatha mam prapadyante*
> *tams tathaiva bhajamy aham*
> *mama vartmanuvartante*
> *manusyah partha sarvasah*

> As all surrender unto Me, I reward them accordingly. Everyone follows My path in all respects, O son of Prtha.

Krishna explains that every living being must abide by His rules. This statement applies not just to some people, or to certain species, but to everyone. The difference between living entities lies simply between those who are cognizant of Krishna's rules, and those who are not. In contrast to the laws of the material world, in which giving usually means loss, as we give ourselves to Krishna, so we reap rewards. We actually enter into a competition with Krishna to see who can give the most. Of course, Krishna always wins. Krishna always accommodates us to a greater extent than our actual level of qualification. Therefore, if we give, we are going to get more and more. A simple way of understanding whether a devotee is advanced, intermediate, or neophyte is to assess his or her quality of giving. The more a devotee is authentically determined to give, the more advanced that devotee is. As an individual intensifies his or her desire to dedicate themselves and their assets, the more Krishna will work through that particular being. There are two categories of *saktyavesa-avataras*. The first category concerns beings who are totally liberated, who come into this world simply to act as puppets for Krishna. The second category concerns beings who possess an intense desire to serve, to be an instrument for grace and mercy beyond their own capacity in the conditioned state. In such a case, a ray of Krishna will enter the *rupa* of that entity, and it will move that entity in various ways. That individual's accomplishments and abilities will far exceed his or her ordinary capability.

We should always have a big desire, even if our capacity is not very large. I underwent a health challenge recently, which involved

Invocation

a surgical procedure and a period of prescribed recuperation. This experience made me very aware of my limitations. At the start of my world tour in 2002, I was thinking how difficult it would be for me. I am used to being very active, participating often in *kirtana*, or public chanting and dancing, with the devotees, but the doctor said I could not dance for another two months. The body has limitations, but, at the same time, our desire can still be very strong in spite of some physical restrictions. As our desire gets stronger and stronger, Krishna will find ways for us to go beyond our normal capacities. We do not want to preach based purely on our own resources. We want to use our resources in such a way that Krishna will be willing to give more. We are not *karma-kandis*, or fruitive workers, yet at the same time, we definitely want to surpass what we have in order to engage it all in Krishna's service.

The Craziness of Separation

Sometimes, we are forced to interact with someone we struggle to appreciate. Perhaps that individual's qualities are not pleasing to us, or perhaps his or her *rupa* annoys us. This antipathy may be related to a previous pastime between us. If we hold onto fears and doubts, and maybe even nurture a grudge, then these negative emotions will certainly interfere with our relationships. We are in material bodies as a result of holding a grudge against Krishna. We thought, "Hey, Krishna! Why do you have to be the all-in-all? I refuse to play into it. I am not going to accept it!" Then Krishna said, "No problem, you can be the all-in-all. Get into a material body, and experience what that is like." In one sense, material life consists solely of people trying to be the all-in-all. Ironically, we are already complete, because the soul is complete when it is in harmony with its true identity. Srila Prabhupada gives the example of the hand and the body. The hand cannot enjoy on its own. When the hand picks up some type of food, it must put it into the mouth. After the food enters the mouth, so many different processes need to occur in order for the whole body to be nourished. When we serve Krishna, we are really serving ourselves, just as when the hand serves the mouth, it benefits along with all the parts of the body. Our position as servitors is not unusual or outside of the parameters of what is healthy. It is simply a matter of being in unison with our complete existence. But our crazy mind tells us, "Why should I have to be the servant?" This is similar to the hand saying, "Why can I not experience the foodstuff directly and benefit without the body?" This is material life: an insane attempt to enjoy separately, disconnected from a genuine relationship with Krishna, in which everything is flowing and in harmony.

As we give, we receive more. However, as we misuse, Krishna will take away. Occasionally, we may notice that devotees have become very nonchalant in taking care of what Krishna has given them. If this occurs, then Krishna will reciprocate accordingly. If devotees waste supplies and *prasadam*, then after a while it is likely that the temple will start to have trouble just feeding its residents. If devotees do not take good care of their vehicles, then after some time, they will fall apart or accidents will occur. Occasionally, devotees even become sinful. When they make offenses by deviating, then the temple may get robbed or catch on fire. In the past, some of these inauspicious incidents occurred in different projects because we abused what Krishna gave us. We want to see the opposite amongst devotees: whatever we have, we should use to the best of our ability. The wages for devotional service is more service. As devotees execute their service nicely, according to the transcendental arrangements of payment, Krishna will give them more opportunities to serve.

A sign that a temple is doing nicely is that it is expanding. At times, it can be overwhelming since devotees have to be very active in their services, which may involve making numerous preparations of *prasadam* or serving many guests in order to facilitate preaching opportunities. Almost everyday there is a project to execute. Projects are blessings, even though at the time, they may feel quite taxing. However, as each person tries to do his or her part, a task that is quite demanding becomes less difficult. If we serve with a sense of honor and commitment, then difficulty will gradually turn into realization and bliss.

Completeness in the Lord's Creation

Everything is complete, even in the material world. *Kama* is actually *prema*, or pure love of God, which is covered over. The anxiety we normally experience is really a symptom of the true anxiety that is present in our pure state, an indication of the excitement and the sense of adventure inherent in serving Krishna. The anxiety of working within the limits of time, the anxiety of trying to be present, and the anxiety of coordination are all perverted reflections of a great spiritual anticipation to do something very wonderful for Krishna, and the pleasure associated with that experience. Usually, we will feel anticipation before any fulfilling event. For example, if we plan to undertake a four-day fast, we will undergo some anxiety about not eating. However, as the end of four days approaches, we feel increased excitement in knowing that the fast will soon be over. Similarly, in the spiritual world, there is constant anxiety in the pure sense. This is because the unconditioned souls realize how pleasurable the actual experience of associating with Krishna can be. Reflecting back on the magnificence of their previous experiences, they naturally become filled with great expectations. As they prepare for the opportunity to dance for Krishna, or to make all kinds of astonishing arrangements, they feel ever-increasing eagerness and anticipation.

Not only is the spiritual world complete, but even the material world is completely arranged—to harass us! The material environment is expertly designed to help us maintain the illusion that we are controllers. However, Krishna does not condemn us forever: the material world is also completely arranged to allow us to escape. We are not perpetually trapped in the material energy. Krishna gives us all facilities to rise above the world of limitations, but most people refuse to accept them. The moment we want to say 'yes' to Krishna, and we really mean it, all facilities become available to us. While the material world is completely arranged for the illusory, perverted reflections of *nama, rupa, guna,* and *lila,* the spiritual world is completely situated for the eternal, faultless performance of *nama, rupa, guna,* and *lila.* At any second, we can gain higher and higher levels of realization to reach total understanding and completion. If we are not attaining these kinds of realizations, and if we are not arriving daily at a sense of greater and greater completion, then we need to look introspectively at the nature of our desires. We should remind ourselves that completeness means understanding that whatever happens to us has a higher purpose.

Sometimes people who endeavor to understand the Lord conjure up unusual *namas* and *rupas*. They say, "God is She," and we say, "Yes, that is true, but there is more." Some say God can only be He. We say, "Yes, that is true, but there is more." We have Father God, and we have Mother God. God in the form of Lord Caitanya is the perfect teacher, also. If everything comes from the Lord, then He must encompass all those features and more. He must possess all attributes fully, and therefore He does not assume only one attribute of Himself. He must be the best dresser, the best fighter, and the best lover. If not, then something greater than God exists. He must also possess a feminine aspect, which is the *hladini-sakti,* personified in the form of Srimati Radharani. When Radha is present, Krishna is also there. While They appear to be separate,

They are one. We can view them as one Supreme Soul, manifested in two different *rupas* at different times.

It is exciting to realize that no theology as complete as ours exists. Krishna consciousness encompasses all other theologies, while still remaining balanced in its completeness. If people want to think of God as She, we say, "Sure, no problem. Come and join us." If people want to approach the Supreme Lord as a friend, then we receive them with open arms. If they conceive of God in a more formal way, then that is acceptable, too. Those who have strong maternal or paternal instincts may think of the Lord as their son. Those who have a great desire for intimacy may approach the Lord as their lover. It is so rare to find such a pervading understanding of the Supreme. However, when we preach to people, we should remember not to be condescending. Rather, we should realize that they may have special affection for a particular aspect of God, or they know the Lord as God, but have not yet accepted His intimate names.

Questions and Answers

Question: Is it possible to confuse the desire to give with the desire to take?

Answer: Yes. Everything depends on our consciousness. Sometimes, we can give in order to make a connection that will allow us to take. On occasion, we posture as givers, while our real motive is to get. Therefore, we must examine our own motives on a regular basis. Desire is a natural part of the living entity. Even in Krishna consciousness, we have desires. We want to go back to Godhead. Actually, Srila Prabhupada said that, in our present state, we should want to return to the spiritual world and that we should not desire to remain here in the material world. The *nitya-siddhas*, or those who are perpetually liberated, can go any place and serve anywhere, because they are always in connection with Krishna. Even when they go to the lower realms, they are not really separate. But, of course, *our* desire is to be able to return home. At the same time, we must be careful not to be fruitive. This is called *karma-mimamsa* or performing spiritual austerities while in the back of our minds, we think, "Krishna, I did this for you. Now what are you going to do for me? You owe me." Krishna will not respond to or be fooled by that kind of mentality.

We have a complete understanding of Godhead that is *purnam*. Krishna has even arranged a complete illusory environment to

Invocation

frustrate us, in order to help us analyze the situation quickly, so that we will desire to return to Him without delay. As we continue to study the *mantras*, we will gain clearer insight into what Krishna has given us, and how we can reclaim what we have temporarily forgotten.

Reflections on Sacred Teachings, Volume Four

Mantra One

*isavasyam idam sarvam
yat kinca jagatyam jagat
tena tyaktena bhunjitha
ma grdhah kasya svid dhanam*

Everything animate or inanimate that is within the universe is controlled and owned by the Lord. One should therefore accept only those things necessary for himself, which are set aside as his quota, and one should not accept other things, knowing well to whom they belong.

The Problem of False Ownership

Mantra One directly addresses the problem of false ownership on the planet. In general, when people make a discovery, they claim it as their own. In such a way, continents and natural resources are appropriated. Just because we discovered a territory, a phenomenon, or a so-called new species does not mean that we created it. To discover simply means to be a little more observant of what is already in existence. The main question we should ask when analyzing historical, geographical, and scientific data is not who discovered them, but who was responsible for their creation. Merely noticing something that was already present is not a great achievement. In fact, discovering something new simply indicates the degree to which we were in illusion previously.

Formerly, we were in deep delusion. Now, after making a discovery, perhaps we are a little less deluded. We realize that previously we were blind to part of the Lord's existence. The philosophy of Krishna consciousness helps to dispel our illusions once and for all. As we realize the extent to which we are lacking knowledge, any discovery should assist in humbling us. When scientists, researchers, and philanthropists discover new facts, or devise innovative ideas, they should feel in awe of God's creative power as they sense the weight of all the other possibilities that, though available, are unfathomable to them at present. This is the point at which spirituality enters the material scheme.

In *Bhagavad-gita* 7.4, Lord Krishna informs Arjuna about some of the elements that constitute the material universes:

> *bhumir apo 'nalo vayuh*
> *kham mano buddhir eva ca*
> *ahankara itiyam me*
> *bhinna prakrtir astadha*

> *Earth, water, fire, air, ether, mind, intelligence and false ego—all together these eight constitute My separated material energies.*

Together with these eight, another sixteen elements exist which comprise the twenty-four elements of the *mahat-tattva*, or the entire material energy. While people generally focus on manipulating different material energies in order to gain varieties of experience, it is important to remember that a higher nature concurrently exists:

> *apareyam itas tv anyam*
> *prakrtim viddhi me param*
> *jiva-bhutam maha-baho*
> *yayedam dharyate jagat*

> *Besides these, O mighty-armed Arjuna, there is another, superior energy of Mine, which comprises the living entities who are exploiting the resources of this material, inferior nature.*
> *Bhagavad-gita 7.5*

In this verse, the Lord mentions that while this world is composed of *apareyam*, or His inferior energy, *prakrtim param*, or a higher nature, is available. We should feel intimidated by the Lord's words. Everyone is always searching for the best, the highest. When we continue to search, but we find nothing higher, we will realize that we have gone back home, back to Godhead.

Connecting with Various 'Isms'

Customarily, governmental and managerial leaders approach an understanding of life by connecting with different man-made philosophies, or 'isms,' within the inferior nature of the Lord. One such 'ism' is capitalism, the goal of which is to profit from the misfortune of others. Capitalism is a philosophy of getting and taking. Greed becomes manifest wherever there is a mentality of ownership and proprietorship. And wherever greed exists, perpetual struggle arises from the domination of one class over another for the purposes of enjoyment.

Other 'isms' include socialism and communism. Under communism, all the citizens are meant to own all the country's facilities. However, this verse tells us that Krishna owns and controls everything within the universe. According to the *Manifesto of the Communist Party* (1848) by Karl Marx and Friedrich Engels, the perfection of communism means a classless society in which everyone is guided by the dictum "from each according to his ability, to each according to his needs." However, when this philosophy is implemented, what usually happens is that a certain elite group controls the key resources. While its members pay lip-service to caring for everyone, government by this group results in an oligarchic arrangement, whereby the elite elects a leader from amongst itself: one group of little monarchs chooses another little monarch to oversee everything for their own profit.

Spiritual Communism

In his books, Srila Prabhupada refers to the idea of spiritual communism. He emphasizes that under such a system, the needs of individuals would be addressed as most important, while at the same time, those needs would be dealt with from a Krishna-centered perspective. Initially, the concepts of communism and spirituality seem to contradict each other. Once, when I shared Srila Prabhupada's idea of spiritual communism with the president of Ghana in relation to the governance of his country, he practically jumped out of his chair. He could not believe that communism and spirituality could work together, until I explained what was meant by spiritual communism. Usually communism means the annihilation of God. However, the basic idea of communism is good when one addresses the God factor. Concern about the welfare of various kinds of people is present within the philosophy of communism. It also advocates a system that guarantees that the needs of all citizens are addressed. In capitalism, concern for the welfare of others is almost completely absent. Therefore, in capitalistic societies, we find many people without homes, food, and jobs. Ultimately, communism, in a genuine sense, cannot exist without spirituality. Communism without spirituality means lack of consistency. People cheat, pretending to share, but in actuality they still endorse an elitist arrangement. Some people still suffer, while others enjoy. Once we bring Krishna into the picture, however, then communism can become very powerful.

Once, I discussed the concept of spiritual communism with President Kaunda of Zambia. We were sitting with his Central Committee, who were mostly communist-aligned. I challenged them, asking them how it was possible that they supposedly supported a family model of government, while they did not acknowledge a mother or a father. Without parents, how can there be a real sense of benefit for the people? Misalignment will naturally occur. In a healthy family, all the family members attempt to please the mother and the father. Therefore, if we discard the mother and the father, then how can we possibly have a real family? Ultimately, Radha and Krishna are the Divine Mother and Father of all of creation. In certain circumstances, when our father or mother dies, we have no choice but to accept the situation. However, we structure our lives around an understanding and appreciation of their presence, of their past *nama, rupa, guna,* and *lila.* Spiritual masters also leave their bodies. Srila Prabhupada has left the planet, but still his *nama, rupa, guna,* and *lila* from the past dominate our minds. We continually try to focus on his desires when we think about what to do, how to act, and how to serve. Thus, the influence of the father is perpetual. Therefore, we should manifest a culture of spiritual communism, where we can be fixed on God as the *summum bonum,* but at the same time we remain concerned about His parts and parcels. We should ask ourselves, "How do we serve the well-being of other living entities?"

In general, the concepts underlying spiritual communism are difficult for ordinary people to understand. A few years ago, I spoke to the Board of the Centre for Conflict Resolution in South Africa, which is composed of pious individuals who exert some influence on the military and political structure in that country. Fortunately, they inquired about a model for bringing spirituality to governmental leaders. This is usually an awkward subject, because politicians frequently care about spirituality only as far as they can exploit it for other means. At the same time, it is our duty as *sadhus,* as carriers of brahminical culture, to live our theology and make it relevant to our communities. As Krishna consciousness is a spiritual culture and not just a religion, it can make a profound difference. If we are not making a difference in the world through Krishna consciousness, then we should ask ourselves, "Why are we even following this process? Do we perceive Krishna consciousness as merely a religion, or as simply an activity we perform at festivals, on weekends, or only in our temples?" Our temples are actually universities, environments for study and processing transcendental information, which empower us to own this philosophy. If we consider this philosophy to be part of us, then we can live it and share it effectively.

Before trying to spiritualize others, however, we need to undergo transformation ourselves. This is such an exciting process! We must embody the change we expect to see in others. I explain this principle regularly to leaders around the world, to those who propose to help people, but at the same time participate in smoking, drinking, fornicating, and eating food acquired through violence. I instruct them to raise their own consciousness first. Then, naturally they will be able to influence others. We bring who we are to any situation, especially one that involves negotiation, facilitation, and guidance. The more we are endowed spiritually, the more we can share our gifts in any type of environment.

Beyond Mundane Piety

In his purport to *Mantra One*, Srila Prabhupada describes that calamity occurs when we do not honor *isavasyam idam sarvam*, the fact that everything within the universe is controlled by the Lord. Much of the world is in a state of fragmentation because people cultivate unhealthy greed. Therefore, the scenario of the cheater and the cheated is perpetuated: one living entity is food for another. People position themselves based on gender, ethnicity, and religion. These are all sectarian identifications stemming from external material designations, which result in on-going conflict. All conflict stems from false proprietorship. However, once we recognize our true identity and original nature, we will be able to foster genuine unity based on sincere service to Krishna.

Srila Prabhupada evokes the example of mundane vegetarianism in order to help us understand that just doing the right thing is not enough; it must be done in the right consciousness. Firstly, we do the right thing because we are vegetarian. However, we need to step beyond nutritious eating, beyond just taking care of the body nicely, and beyond being sensitive to nature, and kind to animals. We need to act in the right consciousness, also. Therefore, we offer our food to Krishna first, and eat it in the spirit that it is mercy from Krishna, to be received in a worshipful way.

While our philosophy includes vegetarianism, it contains much more than *ahimsa*, or nonviolence. Yes, we acknowledge the impersonal aspect of the Lord, the *sat* factor. But there is more. Yes, we have access to the knowledge, the *cit* factor. But, there is more still! When we connect the *sat* and *cit* factors together with the *ananda* factor and with an understanding of God's form, then we have completeness: *sac-cid-ananda-vigraha*. This is the *purnam*, the Complete Whole. Even if the Complete Whole shares itself, it still remains complete. Even though Krishna enters into His own creation, He still remains complete. Not only is He complete, but He makes Himself available according to the desires of living entities. In this way, He stands as the complete Personality of Godhead. He lets Himself connect with so many desires for service. This is called *rasa*, or mellow of completely satisfying spiritual exchanges, enacted through the myriad ways in which Krishna gives Himself personally to each living entity. Because Krishna's level of reciprocation is so complete, each entity in the spiritual world thinks, in a pure sense, that Krishna is exclusively engaging with him or her.

The Value of the God Factor

The concept of spiritual variegatedness is so refreshing, because it encompasses all the heterogeneity in creation. It also helps us to realize that the cause of creation, the Lord, must be greater than His creation. Unfortunately, many people have a tendency to want to describe the universe and its mysteries while leaving out the God factor. Eradicating God from philosophical depictions and scientific discoveries is often considered to be a sign of excellence. When academics put spirituality into their dissertations, they are often met with disapproval. "Religion?" their colleagues exclaim, "We want scientific fact! Try to examine, understand, and describe the universe in as many ways as possible. But do not bring in this 'God stuff.' You will mess it all up." It is very powerful when we are able to show them that we cannot discover anything or describe anything without Krishna. Once we bring Krishna into the discussion, then everything makes sense.

Questions and Answers
Question: I notice that the male devotees shave their heads, leaving a little ponytail. What does this hairstyle signify?

Answer: Not only in the Vedic system, but throughout the world's various cultures, people shave their heads as an expression of renunciation and simplicity. This custom is especially prominent in the monastic orders of Buddhism, Christianity, and Hinduism. A shaven head in a religious context signifies the avoidance of worldliness and disassociation from secular culture. Most of us associate a shaven head with vows of simplicity, humility, and a commitment to a life of religiosity.

This is not always the case, however. Some years ago, when I returned to the United States after a stint in the Communist Block and West Africa, I spotted a group of people at a gas station with shaven heads and what seemed to be *sikhas*, or tufts of hair at the back of their heads. Thinking they were devotees, I called out to them, but when they turned around with puzzled looks on their faces, I realized that they were merely wearing their hair in a new fashion style. Fifteen years ago in Lagos, I was involved in a comparable incident. I was on my way to the library, where I was to meet up with a friend. A fancy limousine drew up next to me. As the window of bulletproof glass slowly slid down, the passenger sitting in the backseat asked me who my tailor was, because he liked my style. Mistaking my devotional appearance to be a new fashion, this wealthy man wanted to acquire it.

Generally, however, a shaven head is associated with vows and commitment. In some African countries, when the title of chieftainship is bestowed upon a leader, he must shave his head in order to show that he is dedicated to serving the people. Changes in the appearance of the leader are meant to encourage him or her to make concurrent shifts in consciousness, and also to influence positively the tribe's perception of his or her role in a positive way. Male devotees shave their heads in recognition of the fact that we are not the physical body, and that we want to be picked up out of the material world and to be brought back into the spiritual existence without delay.

Reflections on Sacred Teachings, Volume Four

Mantra Two

*kurvann eveha karmani
jijivisec chatam samah
evam tvayi nanyatheto 'sti
na karma lipyate nare*

One may aspire to live for hundreds of years if he continuously goes on working in that way, for that sort of work will not bind him to the law of karma. There is no alternative to this way for man.

The Universal Law

During a world tour a few years ago, I encountered an interesting discussion in the English media on *karma*, a concept that is often misunderstood. A famous sports coach had made a statement implying that people win or lose on the basis of their *karma*, or reactions accrued as the result of their previous activities. The statement, which ultimately led to the coach's dismissal, disturbed many authorities as well as the general public. Some physically challenged people, as well as survivors of rape and torture, were indignant at the idea that their own misfortune along with the misfortune of others was the result of their own *karma*, rather than of a series of unjust coincidences. However, if we consider the coach's statement in the cool light of logic, then we may conclude that it is not so far removed from the truth.

In various religious traditions and belief systems, the concept of action and reaction exists. For example, in the New Testament, St. Paul advises the people, "Do not deceive yourselves; no one makes a fool of God. A person will reap exactly what he sows" (Galatians 6: 7). We find that a similar understanding is implicit within most scientific systems. In physics, for instance, Newton's third law of motion states that every action has an equal and opposite reaction. The main focus of *Mantra Two* is the law of *karma*, by which all living beings are bound to suffer and enjoy the results of their own work. The law of *karma* is merely one of a set of universal laws arranged by the Supreme Personality of Godhead to act upon humankind.

Mature people who have a sense of accountability intuitively comprehend that what they think and what they do ultimately produces some kind of reaction in their lives, while those who are immature simply want to enjoy a life without responsibility. It is this immature approach to life that is now becoming more prevalent in the world today, manifesting in the international arena as individuals, institutions, corporations, and nation-states plunder one another without considering the effects of their actions. In the Vedic scriptures, this selfish mentality is called *aham mameti*, or 'I and mine.' As Srila Prabhupada writes in his purport to *Srimad-Bhagavatam* 5.18.4, "As soon as someone thinks, 'I am this material body (*aham mameti*) and everything in relationship with this material body is mine,' he is in illusion (*moha*)." This false identification with the body and the mind results in the delusion that one's individuality is a temporary manifestation stemming from a chance combination of material elements. In actuality, we are eternal: our personalities are products of numerous experiences, not just from this life, but also from previous lives.

Thirty years ago, when I conducted research into hypnotherapy as part of an undergraduate program at Princeton University, I discovered that phobias peculiar to individuals in this lifetime often stem from underlying impressions carried through from the past. The bulk of my study involved analyzing the effects of hypnosis on people suffering from traumas, neuroses, and psychoses. Through hypnosis, I learned that it was possible to take patients back to earlier events in their lives using a technique called regression. It was also possible to use the same technique to regress a patient back to events from previous lives. In one instance, a patient I regressed was able to speak German with a perfect accent, even though she had never been to Germany, never learned German, nor lived with German people. Her case served to strengthen my conviction that reincarnation was an irrefutable fact.

Karma is intimately connected with our innermost personal wishes. While numerous thoughts assail our minds at every moment, those we dwell upon develop into our desires, and these thoughts create our reality. *Karma* does not necessarily dictate what happens to us specifically, but it does determine our general pattern of experience. For example, a student may fail an exam, and shrug it off, believing that it was simply due to *karma*. This may very well be the case, but, at the same time, many other factors are involved, such as free will and time utilization. All these factors, together with *karma*, count towards the final result. The student who failed the exam needs to be accountable for his or her actions and to ask honestly, "Did I use my time positively? Did I study? And if I did study, did I do so properly?" *Karma* works with the way we think and act to create effects in our environment.

Some people take issue with Eastern thought, feeling that it is fatalistic. When we examine this philosophical system closely, however, we find that the study of *karma* is simply a scientific analysis of the effects that certain actions will produce. Fatalism means that we have no free will, while *karma* is integrally interwoven with free will and its specific ramifications across time.

Free Will versus Destiny

Since time immemorial, questions regarding the relationship between free will and destiny have plagued the minds of great philosophers. How do we reconcile these two apparently contradictory concepts: free will and destiny? In the higher realms of understanding, any deep philosophical or spiritual subject matter will present seemingly paradoxical perspectives at first. However, the more we genuinely explore and analyze these questions, we see that their resolutions lie less in the realm of 'either/or,' and more in an interplay between both concepts. Some contemporary philosophers call such an idea 'diunital,' as it encapsulates seemingly opposing terms. Often, when we study different polarities, we notice that taken together, they give us a greater understanding of the whole. This is particularly applicable to the nature of the soul and of God. For example, sometimes it may seem that God's laws for governing the universe are at odds with those prescribed by humankind, but if we explore the situation in a prayerful mood, we will often be able to appreciate the congruency that emerges between them.

Frequently, spiritual seekers ask, "How can the Lord be all-merciful if at times we experience chastisement and seemingly unhealthy reciprocation?" The *acaryas* reply that we have all been given the facility of free expression. To understand the interplay between free will and *karma*, the following image may be helpful. Imagine that choices available to us in any given situation are buttons on an elevator command panel. Whichever button we choose to push represents the expression of our free will. After we touch a certain button, we will be carried to a specific destination. Similarly, when we make life decisions, we receive distinct reactions that we ourselves have initiated. Therefore, we must be very careful about the choices we make in our lives, because such choices produce varying responses.

Often, we do not want to accept that so much power is invested within each one of us. It is very easy to use others as scapegoats, or to rationalize some weakness within us by pinning it on someone else or by blaming the environment. Ultimately, however, we are responsible for how we behave, and for how we respond to what we perceive to be happening around us. In a situation of conflict, for example, one person may respond with anger, a second with fear, while a third may react with empathy. One person may choose to feel degraded after hearing a critical remark, while another will use the same remark as a catalyst for change. Some people will adopt combative, violent moods based on their unhealthy past experiences, while others will use a similar circumstance to gain a more profound understanding of themselves and others. If we truly recognize that whatever reactions we receive in the present are the result of karmic factors, then we will be able to accept them with more humility and tolerance.

Three Divisions of Activity

In his purport to this verse, Srila Prabhupada describes three divisions of activity:

- *Karma*, or actions performed according to one's prescribed duties, as laid down by the revealed scriptures. These actions are also termed *punya-karma*, or pious work. Although these activities are neither completely spiritual in nature nor completely liberating, they bring about a positive material result, such as a long life and elevation to the heavenly planets

- *Akarma*, or actions that free one from the cycle of birth and death

- *Vikarma*, or actions that are performed through the misuse of one's free will, which direct one to the lower species of life

As living entities are always active, their actions will be aligned with one of these three categories. If a person's lifestyle is based on degradation or on transgressing spiritual laws, then his or her resultant actions will fall into the category of *vikarma*. Such people may prosper in this lifetime, but undoubtedly they will receive reactions for their sinful activities in future births. For example, a person who is extremely wealthy, yet at the same time incredibly obnoxious and arrogant, may have to take birth as a beggar in the next life. Nowadays, many women who would love to have children are barren. Often, these women had the chance to bring forth children in the past, but because they aborted their fetuses, they are unable to carry a child to term in the present.

If we had the ability to see a person's previous lives, we would be amazed by the spectacle that would unfold before our eyes, as we view the soul's transmigration from one body to another. In previous lives, the soul might have been in a male body, then in a female body. In this life, the soul may be incarcerated within a European body, while in a past life, it might have been in either an Asian or an African body. Our souls continually move from body to body to facilitate our desires as well as our personal growth; therefore, we should not become overly absorbed in any of the various bodies we happen to inhabit at any specific point in time.

In *sastra*, the symptoms of *punya-karma* are specifically described as follows:

- *Janma*, or a good birth
- *Aisvarya*, or riches
- *Sri*, or beautiful features
- *Sruta*, or a good education
- *Yasah*, or fame

Symptoms associated with *vikarma* are also detailed. They include:

- Poverty
- Unattractive or deformed bodily features
- Legal problems
- Lack of education
- Chronic illness

In general, our current life situations reflect the nature of our activities in previous lives. However, it is important to bear in mind that exceptions exist in specific situations.

Group Karma

Karma works not only individually, but also collectively. Group *karma* can be divided into family *karma*, tribal *karma*, race *karma*, national *karma*, and planetary *karma*. It is not an accident that at different times in history, one civilization rises while another falls. These kinds of alterations in group *karma* occur continuously. When one cultural group uses what Krishna gives them wisely, then they are the recipients of both great auspiciousness and an elevated culture. For example, Satya-yuga was an age of great piety, in which most individuals were God conscious. As a result, people in this age possessed almost unimaginable levels of wealth, health, and longevity. During the following ages, from Treta-yuga to Dvapara-yuga and finally to Kali-yuga, people become progressively less God conscious. Consequently, the level of suffering they experienced increased in proportion to their sinful activities. Therefore, our group *karma* in this current age is quite debased.

Most bona fide scriptures of the world, such as the *Bible*, the *Koran*, and the *Torah*, mention periods in which people will struggle. During these times, inhumane behavior will be on the rise and spirituality will be placed in the background, to be called upon only when convenient. For instance, in the Book of Revelations in the New Testament, St. John describes visions of an age of degradation comparable to the advanced stages of Kali-yuga. In this age, people in general do not desire to be servants of the Lord or even servants of their fellow human beings. Their lack of desire produces effects in society that are progressively more negative. At present, everyone on this planet is experiencing the effects of a massive release of negative *karma*, and therefore we find ourselves embroiled in a constant struggle for survival.

Mixed Karma

Misra-karma, or mixed action, is a slightly more complex concept than *karma*, *akarma*, or *vikarma* in the sense that it involves mixed reactions for deeds that cause both positive and negative effects in the lives of others. As the result of performing an action that leads to an assortment of consequences, the doer will experience both auspicious and inauspicious results. For example, if we offer assistance to a blind man, we undertake an auspicious action, but if we assist him by leading him to a liquor store, then we simultaneously reinforce his deviation. By our 'kind deed,' some inauspiciousness is also invoked. By helping the blind man, we will receive certain positive rewards in this life or the next, but concurrently in having misled him, we will accrue negative reactions, too. Hence, the process of karmic reaction is extremely scientific and specific.

Doctoring the Soul

People who are aware of the scientific nature of *karma* often attempt to undertake pious work for material benefit, such as donating funds toward the opening of a hospital. However, assisting in the patching up of the body is ultimately not the most noble or spiritual action a person can perform. It is no doubt virtuous to assist others in this way, but we must go beyond just caring for the body. As opposed to the pious materialist, the spiritualist or transcendentalist goes directly to the root of all suffering by undertaking actions that are far more beneficial to everyone than merely dealing with the immediate situation. The transcendentalist aims to check those metaphysical patterns that have produced inauspiciousness in the first place. For example, a person may be sickly due to *karma* that has already manifested in this life. Therefore, even if a doctor succeeds in curing the disease, the patient may simply develop another ailment. Doctors may heal the immediate illness, but in the long run, their efforts may be ineffectual if the patient has a basic karmic pattern for disease.

Instead of merely addressing the symptoms, the transcendentalist seeks to address the patterns that cause disease to manifest in the first place. The transcendentalist will look at the thoughts, the deeds, and the emotional issues in the patient's life that have produced the effects of illness. We can compare *punya-karma* to the efforts of the doctor, who addresses the immediate effects of the illness, while *naiskarmya*, or freedom from the results of fruitive activities, is connected with the work of the transcendentalist, who analyzes the causes of the illness deeply. The job of the transcendentalist is to uncover the root of the problem and to eradicate it, transforming negative patterns into an outcome that is not only positive but also sublime.

Creating Our Own Happiness and Distress

Ultimately, *karma* means reciprocity. We undergo experiences in the present based on what we planted at an earlier time. Although we sometimes feel miserable when events or relationships do not turn out as planned, we are responsible for what occurs in our lives based on our previous activities. For instance, when we order a particular meal from the menu at a restaurant, we make a choice based on our free will. When the meal arrives, we reap the results of our action. However, if, after taking a few bites, we decide that this type of food is not really what we want, we will find ourselves in a difficult situation. We may call the waitress back and tell her that we are unhappy with the meal. She may ask, "Is this the item you ordered? If it is, unfortunately you will have to pay for it." Although we made the request, now that the result has arrived, we find ourselves dissatisfied by the taste.

This example clearly illustrates that while our mindsets invite certain experiences into our lives, once they become a part of our environment, sometimes we become unhappy. Often, the reason many people have trouble accepting the idea of *karma* is their refusal to recognize that what happens to them is the perfect result of their own actions. Since we are all parts and parcels of the Supreme Lord, we have similar qualities to Him, but are different in quantity. Therefore, we are also creators since we possess the ability to attract various experiences into our lives, although frequently we end up feeling discontented with what we have created. The lesson here is to be more mindful about our own thoughts and actions, so what we ultimately produce is beneficial not only for ourselves, but for others.

Compassion for the Suffering of Others

According to Vedic philosophy, three *gunas*, or modes of material nature, control us in various ways, namely *sattva-guna*, or the mode of goodness; *rajo-guna*, or the mode of passion; and *tamo-guna*, or the mode of ignorance. A person influenced primarily by *sattva-guna* is very clean, thoughtful, and righteous. Someone who is dominated by *rajo-guna* is often self-centered, erratic, and arrogant, while a person predisposed to *tamo-guna* is often rather obnoxious. Sometimes, those predominated by ignorance are even empowered for destruction. These sorts of people constantly look for opportunities to bring about chaos in society. As opposed to those who relish the suffering of others, a real *sadhu* is pleased when someone else experiences happiness and feels pain when observing the distress of another. In *Vilapa-kusumanjali* 6, Srila Raghunatha dasa Gosvami prays to Srila Sanatana Gosvami in this mood: *para-duhkha-duhkhi krpambudhir.* A Vaisnava is an ocean of mercy who is always unhappy to see others suffer. If we love someone, then naturally we will be sensitive towards the feelings of our beloved. If we are able to extend that loving mentality towards all of humanity, we will be concerned about the welfare of every living entity, and not only with our personal happiness. Great *acaryas* possess this loving mentality to an unlimited extent. Out of their causeless mercy, they perpetually try to guide us towards a higher level of understanding in order to bring about a genuine sense of well-being and peace for every living being without exception.

The Four Stages of Karma

In his book, *Madhurya-Kadambini: Cloud Bank of Nectar*, the great Vaisnava saint Srila Visvanatha Cakravarti Thakura delineates the nine stages of *bhakti* from *sraddha* to *prema*. In his discussion of the five types of *klesas*, or miseries, which are gradually eradicated by the process of devotional service, Srila Visvanatha Cakravarti Thakura includes the four effects of sin: *prarabdha*, or sin that has already matured; *aprarabdha*, or sin which is not yet fructified; *bija*, or the germinated seed of sin; and *rudha* or *kuta*, or the fertile environment in which the seed of sin can take root and grow. Thus, he describes the different phases in which *karma* manifests in an exacting, systematic way.

In order to understand how the different stages of *karma* follow one on another, it may be useful for us to apply the analogy of the various periods in the farming cycle. For example, before a farmer plants his seeds, he normally scouts the land, checks the soil, and ploughs it. This stage can be compared to *kuta*, the creation of a fertile environment for sin. At a particular time of the year, the farmer plants the seeds and nourishes them. This stage can be compared to *bija*, the germinated seed of sin. Daily, the farmer waters his germinated seeds, watching over them as their leaves push through the earth. The point before harvest, when the plants are flourishing, but not yet fully mature can be compared to *aprarabdha*, while the stage of harvesting the crop is similar to *prarabdha*. Thinking of the stages of *karma* in terms of growing crops enables us to understand easily that when we decide to engage in sense gratification, we merely cheat ourselves. Although we may get some immediate pleasure from our actions, we will have to suffer consequences later.

The final stage of reaction, *prarabdha*, is the manifest result of past activity. If the past activity was sinful, then the reaction will be characterized by the full-blown expression of chastisement or inauspiciousness in the life of the living entity. When *karma* begins to unfold, one may undergo a series of positive experiences, or alternatively, negative experiences, depending on the nature of one's past deeds. Sometimes, these phases can even continue into future lives. During a phase when negative *karma* is unfolding in a particular person's life, he or she may find the experience very difficult.

It is possible to see the results of *karma* from observing the world around us. We may notice that, for some people, no matter what kind of financial investment they make, inevitably it will fail to bear fruit. While some obviously do not have the *karma* to make money, others seem to be able to turn sand into gold with very little effort. Similarly, students will often notice that while some of their peers barely need to study in order to attain very good results, others need to invest a huge amount of energy just to scrape through to the next grade. Many of us know of someone who spent his or her entire life making all kinds of endeavors to stay healthy, such as exercising regularly and following a balanced diet, but who died early from a common cold or a heart attack. Those who are expert in the field of martial arts, who are able to defend themselves from any outside attack, may nevertheless slip on a banana peel one day and end up paralyzed for life. In all of these cases, endeavor is present, but the results of endeavor are quite different due to the varying natures of individuals, and the karmic influences to which they are subjected.

No Happiness in the Material World?

Often amongst devotees, we hear the familiar maxim that 'there is no happiness in the material world.' Critics may question the truth of these words, as most of us have experienced that some temporary pleasure may be gained through the senses. However, because this pleasure is fleeting and is often followed by unpleasant consequences, the senses cannot bring lasting happiness. As sometimes we do not receive immediate chastisement, the tendency of those in the material world is to think that they can get away with all types of nonsense. Generally, people with an atheistic mentality believe that they can do what they want, when they want. Because they assume that no ultimate agent is present, they suppose that existence is merely the random struggle of individuals for survival in a hostile environment, and that whoever manages to be the best exploiter attains the greatest level of success. This may be the case in the short term, but the karmic factor will undoubtedly ensure that justice is served in the future.

How should we approach the influence of *karma* in our lives? On the one hand, we can choose to become insensitive to results and fail to endeavor by thinking, "Whatever happens, happens."

On the other hand, we can always try to do our best in whatever we undertake, with the understanding that certain influences may facilitate us, while others will make it more difficult to achieve the desired results. Some karmic patterns have the potential to block our spiritual advancement if we are not aware of the power they exert in our lives. Fortunately, however, the more we connect with transcendence through God conscious activities, the more the ties of inauspicious *karma* become loosened and ultimately disappear. By surrendering to Krishna, we immediately transcend the influence of *karma*.

Questions and Answers
Question: Is it possible to become free from all *karma* eventually?

Answer: Yes, chanting the *maha-mantra*, Hare Krishna, Hare Krishna, Krishna Krishna, Hare Hare/ Hare Rama, Hare Rama, Rama Rama, Hare Hare, is an integral part of becoming *karma*-free. Keep in mind, though, that chanting is not a mere articulation. Chanting means calling on the names of the Lord in a genuine consciousness of wanting to experience God and of inviting His presence into your life. Insincere chanting may be compared to the calls of a crazy man who stands at his front door, beckoning his friends to enter. However, once his friends begin to approach, he starts laughing at them, cursing them, and throwing objects at them. Obviously, if we invite our friends in such a mood, they will not want to come and visit us. In the same way, offenses, doubts, fears, lust, anger, and envy within our consciousness act as static, interfering with the reception of mercy. If I call you over in order to speak with you, while in my heart I am harboring harshness and violence, then how can healthy communication occur? Just like the crazy householder, I will receive your attention, but you will not want to talk with me. If we want to receive the Lord's mercy, we must invite Him into our lives in a prayerful mood. A sincere meditation on attracting the Lord's attention must be present as we engage in the chanting of *mantras*. Always bear in mind that when we chant the *maha-mantra*, or engage in prayers or worship, everything must be done with genuine quality as far as possible.

Question: Is it someone's *karma* to commit sinful activities?

Answer: While the temptation factor for sense gratification is present in everyone, we all possess the ability to say "yes" or "no." Previously, we explained how free will and predestination interact. If we compare a person's vulnerability to illness with the propensity to commit sinful activities, then the interaction between choice and destiny becomes clearer. Germs are always present in the atmosphere around us. When our immune systems are weak, we become more susceptible to the their influence, but when our bodies and minds are healthy, our immune systems naturally repel them. Whether or not we become sick depends, to some extent, on how we interact with our environment. Temptations, like germs, are always present. The onus is on us to strengthen our spiritual immunity. We can never blame a decision to sin simply on the presence of temptation. We have a responsibility to keep our immune systems healthy through hearing and chanting. In this way, we will find it easier to resist infection.

Mantra Three

*asurya nama te loka
andhena tamasavrtah
tams te pretyabhigacchanti
ye ke catma-hano janah*

The killer of the soul, whoever he may be, must enter into the planets known as the worlds of the faithless, full of darkness and ignorance.

Vedic Divisions of Human Society

According to the Vedic literatures, human society is divided into four main categories of spiritual seekers, namely *karmis, jnanis, yogis,* and *bhaktas.* The main focus of *karmis* is worship of the demigods through fruitive work, as opposed to *jnanis,* who immerse themselves in intellectual pursuits. By attempting to understand the material world through empiric methods, *jnanis* hope to become detached from sense objects and thus merge into the Supreme. *Yogis,* occupied with developing psychic talents, immerse themselves in metaphysical phenomena, while *bhaktas* absorb themselves in a culture of love and devotion with God at the center. These four divisions of spiritualists are distinct from the four social and economic classes that constitute the Vedic *varnasrama* system, ordained by Krishna to facilitate the proper function of community. Unlike the class structure of materialistic societies in which the upper classes usually exploit the lower classes, Vedic class structure ensures a harmonious integration and interchange between various sections of society, according to their different desires and vocational propensities. Regardless of social position, however, it is always possible to connect intimately with the Godhead.

Those Who Do Not Surrender

Human society may also be divided more generally into two categories. In his purport to this verse, Srila Prabhupada describes the *suras*, who are godly by nature and the *asuras*, who are opposed to the service of God, and therefore considered to be miscreants (*Sri Isopanisad*, 29-30). In *Bhagavad-gita* 7.15, Krishna describes the four types of people who never surrender unto Him:

> *na mam duskrtino mudhah*
> *prapadyante naradhamah*
> *mayayapahrta-jnana*
> *asuram bhavam asritah*

> *Those miscreants who are grossly foolish, who are lowest among mankind, whose knowledge is stolen by illusion, and who partake of the atheistic nature of demons do not surrender unto Me.*

Four classes of humans, namely the *mudhas*, the *naradhamas*, the *mayayapahrta-jnana*, and the *asuram bhavam asritah*, experience great difficulty in living genuine theistic lives. They struggle to recognize that higher laws govern the universe, that we are more than the material body, and that other worlds and entities exist beyond the physical realm. Such people cannot maintain any kind of ethical integrity. In the following paragraphs, we will examine their mindsets more closely.

Mudhas—Beasts of Burden

The first category of those who have misdirected their intelligence is the *mudhas*, or those whose lifestyle might compare to that of a donkey. A donkey is neither a thoughtful nor an innovative animal. It merely tries to enjoy the immediate environment. People within this category desire instant gratification from the world around them. Often, due to circumstantial conditions, their distress is so intense they can think only about survival. For some, distress can serve as a catalyst for spiritual growth, but in the case of those with a donkey-like mentality, distress serves as yet another distraction from realizing their true spiritual identity.

Naradhamas—Uncivilized Human Beings

The second category is the *naradhamas*, who are considered

to be the lowest of humankind because they neglect to utilize their human form of life properly. Failing to regulate their lives according to religious principles, such living entities choose not to apply their intellectual capacity, an integral part of the human condition, in the understanding of spiritual subject matters. Although such living entities may have the facility of human bodies, they choose not to apply their intellectual capacity, which is an integral part of the human condition in the understanding of spiritual subject matter. While the animal body is meant for eating, sleeping, mating, and defending, the human form of life is meant to enable us to transcend these behavioral patterns through the following of regulative principles.

As opposed to the *naradhamas*, the *jnanis* attempt to transcend their immediate physical environments by utilizing their intelligence to approach realities beyond the scope of the material senses. Nevertheless, in an indirect way, they also want to enjoy interacting with their material surroundings without recognizing the source of their enjoyment. They want to experience the Lord's energies, but do not give credit to the energetic—the true possessor of innumerable potencies.

Mayayapahrta-Jnana, or Those Whose Knowledge Is Stolen by Illusion

The third category of miscreants is called the *mayayapahrta-jnana*, or those persons whose intelligence has been misdirected due to the influence of the illusory energy. This class consists of the so-called cream of society, including well-known intellectuals, writers, filmmakers, technical inventors, and financial innovators, who use their intelligence to disobey the Supreme Lord. Scholars who misinterpret the *Bhagavad-gita* fall under the category of *mayayapahrta-jnana*. All unauthorized interpretations of the *Bhagavad-gita*; those written outside of the guidance of a bona fide *parampara*, are merely obstacles to spiritual advancement. These misguided analyses of Krishna's transcendental advice to Arjuna on the battlefield of Kuruksetra fail to convey the principle of surrender, one of the Supreme Lord's most basic instructions.

Asuram Bhavam Asritah—Those of Demoniac Nature

The forth and final category of spiritual deviants is *asuram bhavam asritah*, or professed atheists. People who are intensely influenced by the mode of ignorance fall within this category. These are the kind of people who enjoy hurting others and who are often aggressive towards those who are pious and spiritual. Due to envy, they will attempt to create situations in order to tempt ordinary people into forgetting their own humanity and spirituality. Atheists are usually forced to undergo very difficult experiences due to previous *karma*. Some of them are possessed, which means that they experience psychic intrusions that cause them to act negatively. They have great difficulty in accepting the simple reality that life is more than just a type of animalistic survival.

Killers of the Soul

As the soul cannot be burned or killed, the concept of a 'soul-killer' may sound strange. Nevertheless, this concept aids us in the realization that the soul experiences a death-like state in the material body as it waits for that wonderful chance to break out of its incarcerated situation. The Vedic literatures often describe the material world as a large ocean and the human body as a boat, with the capacity to carry the individual soul across the vast, treacherous waters. The spiritual master and religious scriptures are like skilled boatmen, while auspicious situations associated with the body and the mind act as favorable breezes, blowing the boat onwards. The various categories of *asuras* correspond to different types of people who have been shipwrecked, but do not wish to be saved. Adrift on an open sea, they are given an opportunity to reach the safety of the shore, but they do not take advantage of it. Rather, they choose to be stranded on the dangerous ocean of death, and therefore they are called *atma-hanah*, or killers of the soul. After millions of births, they have finally risen to the human platform. They have been given the intelligence to inquire, "Why am I suffering? Why is there death? Why is there old age, and why is there disease? If I am only a material entity, then why do I have all these anti-material desires? Where did I get them? If this is not my real home, then where is my real home?" The human form is meant for us to ask such questions. The spiritual master is present in order to help us to solve them.

Religious Pretenders

Another type of *atma-hanah*, especially prevalent in this day and age, refers to those hypocrites and pretenders who hide out in spiritual or moral institutions, using religion to attain their own selfish goals. Such people seek refuge in theology while they corrupt the innocent. These degraded people are manipulative, exploitative, and sometimes out-right evil. Perceiving the power of religion, they take shelter of sacred organizations while desiring to use them for destruction. What we experience as religious fanaticism in the world today has very little to do with true religion, but it has a lot to do with corrupt people who misuse religion to further their own ulterior motives. These people desire the money, the power, and the influence that religion can generate, and therefore they take full advantage of it. *Sri Isopanisad* explains that the karmic reactions for such people are very inauspicious, as they are not merely ordinary miscreants. If someone is sinful due to a poor fund of knowledge, they will suffer some reaction. If someone is sinful while possessing a full understanding of what is proper and while employing theologies to create negativity in the world, their penalty will be far greater. Their reaction will fit the crime of sabotaging authentic religious systems, a transgression which brings about great confusion, and often causes people to become atheistic.

The Price of Knowledge
To the degree that knowledge and grace have been bestowed upon us to represent the Krishna conscious philosophy, to that degree we suffer the consequences of violating it. Therefore, it should be very clear to us that knowledge has a price. Through spiritual knowledge we are given an opportunity to elevate ourselves, but if we do not take advantage of that opportunity, we will be held accountable. We should use this life for spiritual elevation to obtain the Lord's mercy. If we do not, then our lives will become miserable. We will have to experience the consequences for misusing this human form. In order to experience auspicious results, we must be alert to employing our gifts in the proper way and to hearing attentively from *sadhu, sastra,* and *guru*.

Questions and Answers
Question: Even though I have full faith that Krishna is the Supreme Personality of Godhead, I still pray to angels and archangels. Is it wrong to take shelter of angels as well as the Lord?

Answer: As discussed previously, the scriptures identify different agents of Krishna. We are not to be offensive towards any of them, because they are highly elevated beings. We can even take advantage of their presence by praying to them to assist us in becoming genuine servants of the Supreme Lord. However, taking shelter of angels and archangels may become a distraction if we place them before service to Krishna. Engaging in this kind of distraction is called idol worship. Idol worship means anything that we substitute for service to God. Directing too much attention towards a car, a job, or acquiring money is also considered to be idol worship. Essentially, idol worship indicates an infatuation with anything that does not bring us closer to the Godhead. Therefore, we should think of angels, archangels, the *devas, apsaras, vidyadharas,* and *gandharvas* in the spirit of servitorship. They can be elevated servants of the Lord; therefore, we can pray to them to help us improve our quality of service to Krishna. However, if we try to bribe them subtly for some material benefit, or if we attempt to give them the love that should be given to the Lord, then we have a problem. Those who minimize the Supreme Lord cannot cross the devastating ocean of *samsara* or repeated birth and death—they sink, or at best, merely stay afloat. Those who take shelter of anything other than Krishna are killers of the soul. Unfortunately, they will fail to make the transition.

Question: We are told that we should return to the Kingdom of God we originally came from. Supposedly, we left the Kingdom of God because we had a desire to enjoy separately from Him. If this were true, would that very desire not indicate that it is in our nature to explore life without God?

Answer: It is definitely in our nature to express our free will. From one perspective, we have left the Kingdom of God, but, in an esoteric sense, no one has ever left God or the spiritual world. For instance, imagine that I cover the ring on my hand with a handkerchief. The ring will still be on my hand, although it is concealed by the handkerchief. While it is under the handkerchief it has its own existence; nevertheless, it is still in the room. Like the handkerchief, the *mahat-tattva* acts as a covering within an eternal arena compared here to the room. We are always in the spiritual world. However, some of us are under the illusion that the world beneath the handkerchief is all that exists, and therefore our activities are focused on the environment of the covering. Spiritual realization is really just a matter of uncovering the soul, which is always pure and has simply acquired a form of amnesia. Tricked by the material energy, the living entity identifies with many false designations. Simultaneously, we frequently feel bereft, because we are separated from the source of our natural bliss.

All the teachings of the great prophets, of the *nitya-siddhas,* and of the *saktyavesa-avataras* communicate the same basic message—we are not these bodies and the earth is not our eternal home. The rituals, prayers, scriptures, and traditions of any bona fide religion are merely tools for awakening our spirituality, enabling us to regain what we have forgotten. As Prahlada Maharaja instructs Hiranyakasipu in *Srimad-Bhagavatam* 7.5.23-24:

> *sravanam kirtanam visnoh*
> *smaranam pada-sevanam*
> *arcanam vandanam dasyam*
> *sakhyam atma-nivedanam*
>
> *iti pumsarpita visnau*
> *bhaktis cen nava-laksana*
> *kriyeta bhagavaty addha*
> *tan manye 'dhitam uttamam*

> Hearing and chanting about the transcendental holy name, form, qualities, paraphernalia and pastimes of the Supreme Lord (Krishna), remembering them, serving the lotus feet of the Lord, offering the Lord respectful worship with sixteen types of paraphernalia, offering prayers to the Lord, becoming His servant, considering the Lord one's best friend, and surrendering everything unto Him (in other words, serving Him with the body, mind and words) – these nine processes are accepted as pure devotional service. One who has dedicated his life to the service of Krishna through these nine methods should be understood to be the most learned person, for he has acquired complete knowledge.

All of the devotional activities described by Prahlada Maharaja can be used to help us revitalize our dormant consciousness. When we approach spiritual life from this perspective, we realize that it is not very difficult. We are our own greatest enemies, because so often we impose and identify with difficulties. Our interference with God's plan for us can be compared to the chaotic situation that results when the passenger in a speeding car suddenly grabs the steering wheel away from the expert driver. The Paramatma in the heart, or what is referred to in the Judeo-Christian tradition as the

Holy Ghost, is an indwelling presence of the Supreme, who is able to guide us at any time. Having little or no faith, however, we try to take over. We grab the wheel, crash the car into different objects, and then, for a while, let the trained driver regain command of the vehicle. The process of healthy *sadhu-sanga*, of taking shelter of *sastra*, and of seeking out mentors helps us to redirect our consciousness. The practice of Krishna consciousness is simple and straightforward. Unfortunately, we often minimize the sweetness of what the Lord arranges for us by creating complexities. Therefore, again and again we are obliged to enter into additional material bodies on different material planets and to take birth in places full of ignorance and darkness, especially designed for the deviant and faithless.

Question: The *Bible* speaks about an Apocalypse. Is there a similar prediction in the Vedas?

Answer: Yes, we find the concept of a colossal universal destruction in all the major scriptures of the world. Great teachings emphasize that events occur in cycles, that humanity will be confronted with different challenges during various periods. In all bona fide scriptures, we can locate discussions about creation and maintenance, as well as about devastation and annihilation. The Vedic scriptures are encyclopedic, providing much more detail about universal cycles and catastrophes than most other scriptures. The Vedas can assist us in understanding that various sorts of annihilations and manifestations occur continuously in the material worlds. In the West, people normally think that the world is created and then destroyed. However, if we read the *Bible* carefully, we will see that during different periods, cycles of creation and destruction are initiated, as during the time of Adam and Eve, Noah, as well as during the time of Lot. The Vedic scriptures provide specific calculations regarding how long each cycle will prevail, as well as an analysis of the conditions that lead to the destruction of each particular age.

Mantra Four

*anejad ekam manaso javiyo
nainad deva apnuvan purvam arsat
tad dhavato 'nyan atyeti tisthat
tasminn apo matarisva dadhati*

Although fixed in His abode, the Personality of Godhead is swifter than the mind and can overcome all others running. The powerful demigods cannot approach Him. Although in one place, He controls those who supply the air and the rain. He surpasses all in excellence.

Krishna Possess All Opulences

One understanding of Krishna's supremacy is that He is topmost in all areas. Within the Lord's supreme dominion, we will always find somebody who is more powerful, more beautiful, more renounced, more knowledgeable, more famous, or wealthier than the next person. Upon studying all living entities, however, we find one who is the greatest of all, the *summum bonum*. In this verse, Krishna is compared to the fastest runner in the universe. No one can overtake Him, not even the most powerful of the demigods. Although His influence is felt everywhere, the Vedas narrate that Krishna never leaves His original home. How can beautiful Syamasundara (Krishna), who is continually playing His captivating flute, enchanting all of creation by engaging in His amorous pastimes, bear to depart from Vrndavana, the land of the Lord's most intimate and complete relations? How can He possibly abandon the company of His most lovable associates? At first, our understanding of Krishna in Vrndavana may appear contradictory to the conception of an all-pervasive Godhead described in this *mantra*, and elsewhere in *Sri Isopanisad*. How can Krishna be so involved with His eternal servants that He is never able to leave them, while at the same time making Himself available to the conditioned souls who are perpetually engaged in running away from Him? The truth is that He is simultaneously connected with His intimate friends and relatives, as well as with those who have left the spiritual kingdom.

When someone very powerful and loving is faced with hostility or indifference, he or she does not adopt the same type of mentality. Powerful, loving people will try to do the best even for those who do not care for them, in the hope that in time those individuals will ultimately accept them. In the same way, when we turn our backs on Krishna, He does not turn His back on us. The Supersoul is within all things, observing everything we do. If we are behaving improperly, we will not want to accept this idea! It can be frightening to think that everything is being monitored in such a sophisticated way. If we are trying to do the right thing, however, then it is a great solace to realize that we are never alone. Krishna is always trying to arrange for our rescue. When we are struggling, lonely, or confused, it is very comforting to know that Krishna is always present and ready to assist us. In the absence of devotees, we should never feel forsaken or totally alone. Help is on the way. In fact, help is already there!

Krishna has many different expansions. He also manifests through His different energies. Ultimately, all expansions are coming from the original *summum bonum*, Krishna as Lord Syamasundara. In one sense, only the *antaranga-sakti* exists, or the original potency of the Lord, which is directly connected with the spiritual world. However, when the living entities come in contact with the three modes of material nature, they become bewildered by the *bahiranga-sakti* of the Lord. Because the living entity is composed of *tatastha-sakti*, its nature is to either connect with the Lord's external energy, *bahiranga-sakti*, or to be in harmony with His superior energy, *antaranga-sakti*. *Ahankara*, or false ego which is an element of the external energy, is responsible for creating separated conceptions of the self. *Ahankara* causes the conditioned souls to engage in activities apart from those that aim to please Krishna directly. When the living entity turns from the original nature, he then enters into a perverted reflection of that nature, called the *bahiranga-sakti*. This is a shadow of the internal energy, and therefore stands as one with, but also distinct from the internal potency.

Krishna's internal energy consists of three potencies:

1. His *samvit* potency of knowledge, awareness, and cognizance

2. His *sandhini* potency of eternal existence
3. His *hladini* potency of internal pleasure

The *samvit* potency in its true form provides us with awareness of our true existence as eternal servants of Krishna and of Krishna's different *nama, rupa, guna,* and *lila*. When we turn away from God, *samvit* in its perverted form provides for us an awareness of a temporary and illusory material identity. As devotees, we should ask ourselves scrutinizingly from time to time, "Am I taking full shelter of this knowledge?" As conditioned living entities, often we see but do not see, or hear but do not hear: *pasyann api na pasyati* (*Srimad-Bhagavatam*, 2.1.4). *Maya* interferes with our ability to receive transcendental knowledge properly. Real seeing and real hearing are not just a matter of distinguishing the sense objects as they inundate the eyes, or of discriminating between various sound vibrations as they bombard the ears; it is a matter of *realized experience*.

We Choose Our Relationship with Krishna

Krishna is so merciful that He allows us to choose how we wish to live with Him. We can live either in the most divine and sublime arrangement within our eternal abode, or we can live by associating with some of Krishna's manifestations in the material world. God is known in many ways. For example, He may be known as the supreme *isvara*, or autocrat. He may also be recognized in His Vaikuntha form, in which He oversees everything with great pomp and opulence. As opposed to these more formal expansions, Krishna may also be worshiped in His most intimate and revealing form as Govinda in Goloka Vrndavana, the highest planet in the spiritual sky that is the Lord's personal abode. Even in His form of Govinda, we can relate to Him in many different types of *rasas*: as a senior, as a peer, or as a subordinate. Occasionally, Krishna may see that His associates desire to connect with Him in a different mellow from their usual one, and in some cases, He allows it. The variety and the spice are unlimited when serving the Lord.

Occasionally, religionists adopt a dull consciousness, assuming that the soul is inactive while it waits to return to God. Another misconception about the Supreme Personality is that He desires to punish us. If another human being in our environment behaves as a disciplinarian, we do not feel very comfortable, protected, or loved. Therefore, if we conceive of the Supreme Lord as a supreme watchman who is simply waiting to reprimand us, then it is natural for us to become fearful of Him, and want to deny Him. If we are afraid of Krishna, imagining that He marks all our foolish attempts to become God with a punishing eye, then how can we ever love Him? If we visualize Krishna as thinking, "I can easily destroy these miscreants and make them suffer! Yes, I know, I will make them burn in hell for all eternity!" then we lack a healthy conception of the Godhead.

The *samvit* potency of the Lord acts upon us according to our own *karma* and desire. Some people want to know God only fifty percent, some ten percent, while the desire of others to invite Him into their lives is less than a fraction of a percentage. There are also those, such as atheists, who might not want to know Him at all. Depending on the degree to which we wish to relate to the Supreme Personality of Godhead, we will be attracted to a specific religion or scripture that will impart to us our desired level of knowledge. In one sense, this is the reason why various religions and philosophies exist. If someone wants to know Krishna fifty percent, he or she will be drawn to a religion that will give him or her that kind of knowledge. If a person wishes to know the Lord only as the great creator and annihilator, he or she will be given facility to approach Him in that way. However, those so-called religions that sanction actions against *dharma*, or religious principles, are not authentic and are considered to be in a separate category. Genuine religions may be defined as such by a close examination of the correlation between their own *sadhu*, *sastra*, and *guru*.

Why Preach Krishna Consciousness?

If we acknowledge that the Lord arranges for us to experience and associate with Him in whichever way we desire, then some devotees may inquire whether it is really necessary to preach Krishna consciousness. If Krishna orchestrates a separate arrangement for people who do not want to know Him, as well as for those who want to know Him only piecemeal, then why should we expend our energy trying to encourage others to experience Him in full? It is true that the *maha-bhagavata*, or the topmost devotee who has reached the highest stage of God realization, does not perceive any need to preach because he or she appreciates that everyone is already following the Supreme Personality of Godhead in one way or another. We cannot avoid Krishna because His energies are everywhere. However, in this age of Kali, the Lord has descended as His most merciful incarnation, Sri Caitanya Mahaprabhu, who is freely distributing love of Krishna to everyone, whether they desire it or not.

As part of his service to Lord Caitanya, the *maha-bhagavata* or *uttama-adhikari* sometimes descends to the second-class platform, acting as a *madhyama-adhikari* in order to be effective in urging different types of conditioned living entities to turn to the Lord. The *madhyama-adhikari* relates to the situation of the conditioned souls personally by discerning the specific type of coverings that separate them from their truly divine nature. In this way, the *madhyama-adhikari* can best assist them in their journey back to the spiritual world.

We can Only Know Krishna by Devotion

How may we know Krishna? Is it possible to know Him by *jnana* (intelligence), by *yoga* (the practice of mysticism), by *tapasya* (austerity), by *yajna* (the performance of sacrifice), by *vrata* (the taking of a vow for religious rituals), or by *dana* (giving of charity)? No. We cannot know Him by any of these methods, although they may assist us. Intelligence is a prerequisite for us to appreciate how much we do not know. An awareness of the amazing manifestations that can result from the practice of *yoga* can aid us in appreciating how intricately Krishna's potencies permeate the entire universe. Austerities, sacrifices, rituals, and giving in charity may make it easier for us to disassociate from the material energy, but even these activities cannot help us to know Krishna in full. As the Lord says in *Bhagavad-gita* 18.55:

> *bhaktya mam abijanati*
> *yavan yas casmi tattvatah*
> *tato mam tattvato jnatva*
> *visate tad-anantaram*

> *One can understand Me as I am, as the Supreme Personality of Godhead, only by devotional service. And when one is in full consciousness of Me by such devotion, he can enter into the kingdom of God.*

Krishna explains that we can understand Him in full only when we are thoroughly devoted to Him. Even Lord Ananta Sesa, the divine serpent upon whom Maha-Visnu resides in the Causal Ocean, cannot describe all Krishna's astounding activities, even though He possesses innumerable tongues that are constantly engaged in glorifying the Lord.

Krishna is present through His *bahiranga-sakti, tatastha-sakti,* and *antaranga-sakti*. We also have the opportunity to experience Him through His *samvit, sandhini,* and *hladini* potencies. The *hladini* potency consists of pure *prema*. It is manifested specifically in the *rupa* of Srimati Radharani, the Lord's eternal consort. We are not able to fully understand the Supreme Personality through *jnana, yoga,* or any other purificatory process, but only through *bhakti*. As Krishna emphasizes in this verse from *Bhagavad-gita*: *bhaktya mam abijanati*. "One can know Me only by pure devotional service." God makes Himself available in various religious systems according to the intensity of our desire to know Him. He also makes Himself available to Vaisnavas in variegated ways. Everything hinges upon the degree of our desire to know Him or to be with Him.

Previously, we discussed that many religious traditions do not offer knowledge of the Supreme Lord in full. Although Krishna consciousness offers the most profound understanding of the Godhead in the universe, we too can never know the Lord completely. Our limited minds cannot possibly grasp all aspects of divinity. After hearing that the Lord is incomprehensible even after the cultivation of devotion, some may ask, "Are we pretending, wasting our time as we attempt to understand this great knowledge inscribed in the Vedic scriptures and the writings of the *acaryas*? Have we been unfair to other faiths by saying that they give only half the truth, or less, when in fact, even in our tradition, so much more remains to be known?" One answer to this searching question lies in the realization that the Lord is by nature unknowable. As Yogesvara, the supreme mystic, He cannot be grasped completely by the mind. If our minds could fully comprehend the Lord, then we would be as great as He.

Mantra Four states unequivocally that "the Personality of Godhead is swifter than the mind and can overcome all others running." No one can capture Krishna. No one's activities, strength, perception, beauty, knowledge, intelligence, or renunciation can ever approach those of Krishna. Despite our limited capacity, however, we should be excited to know as much as we can about the Supreme Lord in order to experience more of His inconceivable love. This understanding will help us overcome our own obstructions in giving love to others. We will also increase our faith through the process of *bhakti*. The beauty of our tradition is that *the more we know, the more there is to be known*. A sign of an intelligent person is that he or she intuitively realizes that his or her knowledge

Mantra Four

is limited. A person who thinks that nothing else remains to be understood about the Lord exhibits a dull intellect. While intelligent people usually have access to a vast array of knowledge, they are always ready to appreciate new progressions and ever-deepening insights.

Endeavor or Mercy?

A frequent question arises in relation to effort versus mercy: what constitutes the most important ingredient in understanding Krishna? In this age, both are important as they are intimately connected. *Krpa-siddhas*, or those who become pure devotees of the Lord by His causeless mercy, are certainly more prevalent now than in other ages. Understanding Krishna begins with mercy. The Lord is so merciful that He has given us the free will to choose whether we wish to bond with Him or not. The process to attain Him varies according to the *yuga*, or age. For instance, in Satya-yuga, the golden age which lasts 1,728,000 years, human beings naturally had a higher *adhikari*, or capacity to comprehend God, than at present. Because their ability to engage in all kinds of austerities was more profound, their effort was concurrently more substantial. Similarly, in Treta-yuga, the silver age lasting 1,296,000 years, in which the authorized religious practice consisted of the execution of elaborate rituals, effort was foremost in bringing about the desired results. In Dvapara-yuga, the copper age of 864,000 years, a high standard of Deity worship was an absolute requirement. However, we are currently in Kali-yuga, the iron age, which lasts 432,000 years. In this age, people are most unfortunate and deficient in numerous ways. Lacking the ability to pronounce the *mantras* accurately, as well as other factors, we are simply unable to carry out the rituals prescribed in previous times flawlessly.

In the *Skanda Purana*, it is stated: *kalau sudra-sambhavah*. In the age of Kali everyone is born a *sudra*, or in the lowest class of human beings. Therefore, Srila Prabhupada gave us an abridged version of Vedic rituals. His aim was not just to make us *sastris*, scriptural scholars, or *panditas*, learned priests who emphasize intricate Vedic procedures. He wanted us to be *bhaktas*, or unalloyed devotees. Srila Prabhupada simplified the process of self-realization according to time, place, and circumstance, instructing us at times merely to carry out some very basic observances and essential ceremonies. These uncomplicated rituals are part of Vaisnava culture. If we simply execute them with sincerity, then the mercy will come—radiant and ready for us to absorb.

The way in which mercy interacts with endeavor can be clearly understood through the analogy of a drowning person who has fallen into a dark well. If somebody is drowning and another is trying to save him or her, contact between the two is needed, as well as some effort on the part of both individuals. The drowning person must reach out to the person who mercifully throws down a rope. The rescuer, in turn, must endeavor to pull the drowning person out of the water. In order for the rescue to be successful, the drowning person must grab onto the rope. Then he or she must maintain a strong hold on the rope as the rescuer pulls him or her to safety. However, if those in distress do not grab the rope tightly enough, then even though the mercy is being extended, they will not receive it. They will fall back into the well and perish. Similarly, some people may initially reach for Krishna, shouting "Help me, help me! Get me out of here!" However, they soon forget the dangers lurking in the dark well of material existence, and become caught up again in various mundane activities.

Making Excuses and Blaming the Environment
Although many call out for Krishna, when distinct help is given, they either fail to see it or refuse to take full advantage of it. Sometimes, they grab hold of the rope, and manage to get pulled up part of the way, but then they let go. When this happens, the person in the well will usually defend his or her failure by evoking all kinds of reasons. They might claim that the rope was not of good quality, the rescuing process itself does not really work, or the rescuer was not merciful enough and did not care for them in the right way. Perhaps they will try to rationalize their own shortcomings by saying to the rescuer, "Why did you not throw down a ladder instead of a rope?" Those of us who have been in the movement for a few years will notice that while some people take to devotional service for a certain period, sooner or later they drift away. When these devotees decide not to continue with the process, they search for a million different excuses to explain why they could not allow themselves to be rescued. As falldowns occur somewhat frequently nowadays, we should be careful not to be influenced by such a cheating mentality. Often people leave because they are not ready to see their own faults, weaknesses, or improper desires, and then defend their behavior by representing the genuine spiritual practices we follow as unhealthy.

We should be careful not to blame the environment for our predicaments. Bear in mind that Krishna facilitates each of us by arranging for the experiences we need to undergo. Sometimes, the spiritual master tries his best to rescue a disciple who is trapped in the deep well of material existence, but the disciple continues to shout for help while ignoring the rescuer standing patiently at the edge of the well, waiting tirelessly for him or her. This mentality is cheating and false. Such people want everything to be done for them. They want the mercy without any effort on their part. Such aspiring devotees miss the point of devotional service completely. As the years progress, difficulties will inevitably crop up that might disturb us and wear down our initial enthusiasm. We could start doubting the potency of the rope, and complain that help should come in some other way. We must, however, recall that Krishna arranges a particular type of assistance for each of us. He expertly arranges for our own personal battle of Kuruksetra according to the distinct types of issues and problems we have brought with us to this lifetime. Sometimes devotees get wounded, but if they do not attend to their wounds, or consult a qualified practitioner, then their fragile devotional creeper is at risk of wilting. In such times of difficulty, we should ask ourselves: Are we recognizing that divine mercy is already causelessly available to us? Do we do our best to grab onto it? And if we manage to grab the mercy, do we hold on tight until we are pulled out, or do we let go halfway?

It is evident that both effort and mercy are important. We must do our part and make the effort, just as we would in any situation in everyday life. Ultimately, however, effort alone is not enough. We must await the mercy eagerly. We should *position* ourselves through endeavor to get the mercy, and then take advantage of it, because Krishna has no favorites. As the Lord says about his pure devotee in *Bhagavad-gita* 9.29:

> *samo 'ham sarva-bhutesu*
> *na me dvesyo 'sti na priyah*
> *ye bhajanti tu mam bhaktya*
> *mayi te tesu capy aham*

> *I envy no one, nor am I partial to anyone.*
> *I am equal to all. But whoever renders service*
> *unto Me in devotion is a friend, is in Me, and I*
> *am also a friend to him.*

Pure devotees like the six Gosvamis are equally kind to everyone, regardless of their social status or level of spiritual advancement.

Why do Some Advance Faster than Others?

Although Krishna and His pure devotees have no favorites, we often notice that some advance much more quickly than others. This is due almost entirely to the ability to grab the mercy. Why are some very excited about their service, while others do not like their service at all and find any excuse to avoid it? They may claim that it is not their propensity or give some other excuse. This mentality is very unfortunate. We sometimes see a similar kind of negativity in those people who get married many times and still feel unhappy. A man married more than once or twice may think habitually about his current wife, "This woman is not attractive enough. She is too skinny—or too fat. She is too dull—or too talkative." Similarly, a much-wedded woman who is consistently dissatisfied with her present husband may reason, "I thought he was the one I was dreaming about from the time I was a girl, but now that I know him a little better, I realize that I don't really like him. I made the wrong choice." Regrettably, some people choose again and again, but still remain unsatisfied. This happens because nothing in the material world can ever completely fulfill a human being. If we were fully satisfied with any situation or person, then we would have no reason to be interested in transcendence.

We cannot be satisfied in a relationship with someone else until we ourselves connect completely to the wholesome, divine nature of the Lord. However, we can help one another work towards that goal. We can be excited about any opportunity to assist one another, whether we are associating amongst *brahmacaris* or *brahmacarinis*; whether we are in the *grhastha-asrama*, or regulated householder life; or in the *sannyasa-asrama*, or the renounced order of life. If we utilize these opportunities to work on ourselves and to grow together, then life becomes an exciting adventure.

A person with a cheating mentality thinks, "I want everything to be perfect. I must have the best situation in order to even think about observing this process seriously." They do not take into consideration that they themselves are imperfect and are not working on themselves sufficiently. Ultimately, such a person will be cheated. They want the greatest experiences, the best things in life, and all the mercy, but without any effort. A person with such a swindling attitude could get angry with Krishna and ask, "Krishna, why didn't You give me wealth? You are at fault, Krishna. It is not I who am imperfect. However, if I have any imperfection, it would be my husband, who is not very enthusiastic. He does not chant his rounds, read, or associate with the devotees, so what can I do? I am in *maya* also. It is Your arrangement!" Another may blame Krishna, thinking, "You could have given me a wife who is very vibrant and who likes to do service. But instead, You gave me a lazy woman. Look at her! She is dragging me down. It is your fault, Krishna, that I cannot engage in chanting or in devotional service." Such cheaters expect Krishna to do everything. If not, they remain miserable. The rope is there, but they will not grab hold of it. Consequently, they will be disappointed in many ways. We should remind ourselves that these transcendental potencies are all readily available, but if, when, and how we take advantage of them is entirely up to us.

Krishna Responds to Quality of Devotion

After Lord Damodara, or baby Krishna, stole butter from the elder *gopis*, or cowherd damsels of Vraja, mother Yasoda chased Him and, brimming with loving indignation, tried to bind Him to a wooden grinding mortar. Initially she was unable to tie Him up, but when Krishna noticed that her intense endeavor was filled with pure devotion, His heart melted and He allowed her to bind Him. This pastime illustrates that while effort is needed, ultimately we are dependent on mercy. Krishna responds to the *quality* of our devotion. In the *Bhagavad-gita* 10.2, Krishna explains His position:

> *ne me viduh sura-ganah*
> *prabhavam na maharsayah*
> *aham adir hi devanam*
> *maharsinam ca sarvasah*

> *Neither the hosts of demigods nor the great sages know My origin or opulences, for, in every respect, I am the source of the demigods and sages.*

Krishna cannot be captured or understood by the mind or even by the demigods. The Supreme Personality is not bound by their understanding or by ours, as no one can fully perceive or evaluate Him. However, as we endeavor properly, we will connect with more and more of His unlimited mercy.

Questions and Answers

Question: Does the *krpa-siddha* have to endeavor for the mercy of the Lord, or does it come to such a person causelessly, without any effort on his or her behalf?

Answer: The *krpa-siddha* is eager to seek out the mercy. A person does not become a *krpa-siddha* merely by sitting and waiting for Krishna to bestow mercy upon him or her. If we take up the mood of just waiting, it minimizes the fact that Krishna has arranged these fields of activity for our growth and unfoldment. By relying only upon His mercy, we ignore the fact that we have been deviant, and that we have a responsibility to make a change. It is our duty to prove that we are qualified and ready to receive the mercy. Unfortunately, due to the large amount of posturing and deception that takes place in our minds, we keep Krishna at a distance. We should look closer at ourselves and become more authentic in the way we relate to Krishna and to other devotees. We should endeavor to be responsible, working on ourselves in order to create quality interactions not only amongst *brahmacaris*, *grhasthas*, *sannyasis*, and *vanaprasthas*, or those retired from family life, but also among devotees of different economic, cultural, racial, national, and social backgrounds. If we sincerely strive to create more loving relationships with others, we will certainly experience Krishna's causeless mercy.

Mantra Five

tad ejati tan naijati
tad dure tad v antike
tad antar asya sarvasya
tad u sarvasyasya bahyatah

The Supreme Lord walks and does not walk. He is far away, but He is very near as well. He is within everything, and yet He is outside of everything.

Can We See God?

Initially, this particular *mantra* sounds like word jugglery alluding to the indefinable and indescribable nature of the Godhead. Certainly, many impersonalists would take great pleasure in hearing it! According to impersonalist philosophy, the Supreme Lord's energies pervade all things. The personalists also accept his all-pervading aspect, but understand that the Lord has transcendental form as well. Those who follow elementary religiosity may believe that we cannot see God and that He has no form. It is small-minded to think we can limit God, but, at the same time, we realize that God has definite forms in which He appears to His unalloyed devotees. Of course, we cannot confine God to a single *rupa*. Impersonalists, however, would consider it offensive to think that we can perceive God's form. Vaisnavas, or devotees of the Lord, agree with the impersonalists to the extent of acknowledging that an ordinary person cannot see the Supreme Lord. We will never be able to see Him by our effort alone. However, the Lord can make Himself available to us through His causeless mercy if we apply ourselves in the proper way. To really see the Lord, we must endeavor to clean our consciousness as we pray:

om ajnana-timirandhasya
jnananjana-salakaya
caksur unmilitam yena
tasmai sri-gurave namah

I was born in the darkest ignorance, and my spiritual master opened my eyes with the torch of knowledge. I offer my respectful obeisances unto him.

Nobody can see Krishna, who is both omniscient and omnipotent, with mundane vision. Our eyes must first be opened with the torchlight of knowledge. Wherever bona fide knowledge is cultivated, the darkness of nescience is banished. It is not difficult for the Supreme Lord to arrange for someone who loves Him to see Him, and also to take His association.

Unfortunately, some people will only accept God if they see Him first. They demand that He appears before them, but only under certain conditions. They might try to bargain with us by saying, "I will follow your philosophy and change my life if God first reveals Himself to me. Let Him appear in front of my house tomorrow at eight o'clock in the morning. If He shows up, then I will become one of His very best devotees. If somehow He decides to give me a pile of diamonds and gold, or some powerful *sakti*, then I will be even more willing to become His first-class servant." Those who demand the Lord's presence in order to believe in Him possess very little faith.

Nevertheless, at times devotees may question Krishna's apparent non-appearance as follows: "Why does Krishna hide Himself in so many ways, or make it so difficult for us to see Him? Why does He not manifest His universal form downtown, and then let it extend throughout the various continents? If everybody all over the planet could see Krishna, then of course they would become good devotees. All wars, drug abuse, prostitution, and other social ills would come to an end. Why, then, does He not show Himself? When Arjuna had doubts about following Krishna's instructions, the Lord personally revealed Himself. Why does He not take away our doubts similarly by appearing before us? After all, He needs to appear only once, playing a nice tune on His flute, in order for us to become enchanted forever. Did He not appear before Narada Muni, saying, 'You will never see Me in this life again, but here I am now. I want you to come back home. Stay fixed and focused, knowing that I am always there for you; know that you are loved. I have extended Myself in a very exceptional way. Although I will not appear again, you will spend your whole life hankering for this moment. Thus, you will return to Me.' If Krishna can appear before Narada Muni, why does He not do it for us, just once?"

Devotional Service Gives Us the Eyes to See

How does Krishna reveal Himself to His devotee? In our discussion on *Mantra Four*, we analyzed the different potencies of the Supreme Lord, which included His *bahiranga*, *tatastha*, and *antaranga saktis*. While the Supreme Lord is master of all these potencies, *Krishna Himself reveals that He can be understood fully only by pure love and devotion.*

When *bhakti* is practiced on the highest level, then, without doubt, those potent individuals who possess it will be given a chance to see, dance, speak, and interact with the Lord. In the neophyte stage, we have been given the *arca-vigraha*, or the Deity form of the Lord manifested through material elements. Krishna also appears through *sadhu*, *sastra*, and *guru*. The Lord appears to the extent that we connect with and absorb ourselves in Krishna consciousness. If somebody asks to see God, we should have no problem satisfying him or her, because God is present in all our wonderful Deities and pictures of His transcendental pastimes. If the inquirer still has doubts and says that nobody can know how God looks, we should feel confident in replying that *we know*. We know His intimate details; we have His cell-phone number, His fax number, and His e-mail address! In other words, the holy name is the direct connection to the Lord. When visitors come to our temples, we can introduce them to the knowledge of how to connect with the Supreme Lord. And we do not charge a subscriber's fee, either! The concept of personal reciprocation may seem strange initially to the general public, as it is only experienced by those who are suitably qualified or possess sufficient *bhakti*.

Prisoners cannot Make Demands

Bear in mind that even though the Lord appears in all these wonderful forms, we must endeavor to avail ourselves of the mercy. Our situation in the material world is often compared to that of a prisoner in a jailhouse. The prisoner may say to the prison warden, "Hey, officer, let me out of here! You hold the keys. Tell the jailers to let me go." However, any reasonably intelligent person knows that it is not so easy to be set free. Once incarcerated, convicted criminals might admit that they committed a crime. Declaring that now they have turned over a new leaf, some criminals may even demand immediate release. However, it follows logically that the criminals' declarations may or may not be true. Therefore, the warden and parole committee must evaluate each criminal to ascertain if, in fact, he or she has truly changed. It is highly possible that criminals may become even more degraded while in the jailhouse. Perhaps they were convicted for petty crimes only, but perpetrated subsequent offenses during their imprisonment. It is also probable that they could have become involved in serious illicit activities, such as drug trafficking. In this case, the criminal is in a worse situation in the present than before his or her imprisonment. However, if the authorities are convinced by their actions that they have reformed, then they are eligible for release.

Similarly, we have committed a crime against the Supreme Lord by desiring to enjoy separately from Him. Due to our deviation, the onus is on us to prove that we have transformed ourselves and that we are worthy to see the Lord. Krishna does not have to present Himself first. It is our duty to represent ourselves properly by changing our level of consciousness before we qualify to come into contact with the Supreme. If we want the experience of Godhead and the rewards without first paying the dues, then we have a cheating mentality. We must first be responsible spiritually before being eligible for the mercy. It is healthy to remind ourselves that we are deviants. We have entered into the prison house of the material world and we remain its prisoners. Although all kinds of arrangements are available to set us free, we have to measure up to certain standards first before we are eligible for parole.

The Limits of Mundane Scholarship

Many years ago, one of my services was to visit academic scholars from around the globe, scholars who were so-called experts in comparative religion and Indian philosophy. Although highly educated by material standards, these scholars often experienced extreme difficulty trying to understand Krishna. Their inability lay in resolving the great dissimilarity they discovered between the Krishna of *Bhagavad-gita*, the Krishna of *Mahabharata*, and the Krishna of Vrndavana. Some of them held the view that each Krishna in each scripture was totally separate from the other. Unfortunately, they could not grasp the fact that Krishna is the same Supreme Personality of Godhead in any historical location. The only difference is that Krishna extends Himself in diverse ways due to the level and the mood of reciprocation between His various devotees. If one lacks an understanding of how Krishna is Param Brahman, or the Supreme Spirit, then this explanation will bear no weight, however. Scholars generally do not understand the nature of *rasa*, of spiritual exchange between the Lord and His devotees, which constitutes the essence of the Lord's loving reciprocation. Furthermore, they refuse to recognize that a personal aspect of the Lord exists, from which everything emanates. On a mundane level, an approach to the Godhead through *bhakti* may seem confusing, but by developing the proper attitude of humility, Krishna allows us to grasp complex insights with ease.

Krishna is the original Personality of Godhead, who possesses all opulences in full: *krsnas tu bhagavan svayam* (*Srimad-Bhagavatam*, 1.3.28). Actually, there is nothing but Krishna. Taken at face value, such a statement could sound once more like impersonalist philosophy. Let us consider it in the light of this particular *mantra* again. All these supposedly contradictory attributes are concurrently present in Krishna because nothing can exist outside of Him. As discussed in *Mantra Four*, the world is a product of Krishna's different energies as they manifest in various ways. This is the vision of the *uttama-adhikari*; he or she is made totally cognizant by the *samvit* potency of the Lord.

Regardless of our philosophical inclinations, we all serve the Lord. Even those who think that they are atheists must serve Krishna, albeit in an unfavorable way. Impersonalists also serve Krishna, but they simply refuse to accept it. We ourselves are just parts and parcels of the Supreme Lord.

Understanding Spiritual Realities

Although we are fundamental parts of the Lord, we find ourselves in a condition of separation due to our captivation with the illusion that we can enjoy life independently from Krishna. We can look at this point from two perspectives: firstly, we can realize that any activity exists only because it has a counterpart in the spiritual world; and secondly, that these activities become perverted reflections of the spiritual world when they are centered on mundane enjoyment instead of on Krishna. Even events such as fashion shows, sporting events, and musical performances are found in the material world simply because they occur in the spiritual world. On any given day at an ISKCON temple, a guest may encounter singing, dancing, feasting, and perhaps the celebration of a festival. Newcomers may wonder what these activities have to do with spiritual life. While mundane events are really just distorted reflections of comparable spiritual activities, sacred activities mirror more accurately transcendental pastimes, which are taking place simultaneously in the spiritual world. All the different ways of relating with which we are familiar in the material world, such as romance and adventure, are found on this planet due to their existence in their purest state in the spiritual world.

Often, we try to understand spirituality by looking at it with material vision. Mistakenly, we think that somehow spiritual realities can be experienced through our physical senses. In essence, everything is spiritual; it is merely reflected in the material world in an unhealthy way. If we read the earlier verses of *Sri Isopanisad* with this spiritual truth in mind, the statement that the Godhead must contain everything will become further clarified for each of us. Nothing can exist outside of the *purnam*, the perfectly complete whole. Armed with the knowledge that all attributes and activities come from within the Godhead, we can develop our understanding of Krishna in a more profound way. Krishna consciousness is not as much about the avoidance of activity as it is about transforming our awareness. Ultimately, renunciation in and of itself is not helpful. It is more useful for us to shift our focus from our own bodies and senses to offering everything to Krishna. Srila Prabhupada said that the Krishna consciousness movement is a cultural movement for re-spiritualizing the planet. Culture is a holistic approach to life and encompasses everything, including how and why we eat, sleep, mate, and defend. All activities within a culture should be designed for re-spiritualization.

In one sense, the whole of creation consists merely of Krishna interacting with His different energies eternally. We are just aspects of Krishna. The impersonalists are correct in their implication that we are all God, in the sense that we are all servants of God—the same as God in quality, but different in quantity. As Krishna interrelates with His different energies continuously, we are always protected and loved by Him. We are always magnificent because we are parts and parcels of Krishna. We are His manifestations in different ways due to the exchanges between His various potencies. At different times and in various places, these interactions create an environment like this present *yuga*. Without much difficulty, we can turn Kali-yuga into Satya-yuga simply by shifting our consciousness. In our confidential scriptures, we read that although nobody can catch the Lord, He allows Himself to be caught by His pure devotee. He also allows Himself to be understood under certain

Mantra Five

circumstances. By His mercy, we can understand how the Lord walks but does not walk, and how He is within everything and at the same time outside of everything. This understanding is based on a high level of effort as it connects with tremendous grace. Beloved, let us do whatever is necessary for this grace to embrace us, to fulfill us, to devour us, and to reclaim us.

Questions and Answers

Question: How can we be part of the Lord, and at the same time different from Him?

Answer: In his purport to *Srimad-Bhagavatam* 2.1.39, Srila Prabhupada explains that the simultaneous oneness and difference between the individual soul and the Supersoul was propounded by Lord Sri Caitanya Mahaprabhu as the philosophy of *acintya-bhedabheda-tattva*. Mantra Five refers particularly to the phenomenal, seemingly contradictory nature of the Lord. Nobody can defeat Him in any area because He is the topmost. He is within everything as the Supersoul, while simultaneously He is outside of everything as Bhagavan, or the Supreme Person. Through the intersection of effort and mercy, understanding will naturally come about. In his purport to *Srimad-Bhagavatam* 2.1.38, Srila Prabhupada advises those who cannot grasp the simultaneous oneness and difference of the Lord to focus on any aspect of the material creation—whether it be a tree, a mountain, or a demigod—and to meditate on its connection to the Supreme Whole. He writes, "Everything being a part and parcel of the Complete Whole, the neophyte student will gradually realize the hymns of *Isopanisad* which state that the Supreme Lord is everywhere and thus he will learn the art of not committing any offense to the body of the Lord."

Question: Does it matter how one approaches Krishna? Is the result ultimately the same if one approaches Him as a demon, or if one approaches Him as a devotee?

Answer: Putana was a demon who approached baby Krishna with the intention to kill Him. Using her mystic powers to manifest the form of a beautiful *gopi*, she smeared her breasts with poison, and then entered the room in which baby Krishna was sleeping. However, instead of killing Krishna, she was killed by Him when He sucked her life airs. When Krishna annihilates the demons, they simultaneously receive some mercy, as they have come into direct contact with the Supreme Lord. Putana was a fortunate demon, because she chose to relate to the Supreme Lord as a mother. Her approach showed effort, even though her mood was perverted; therefore, she was blessed by Krishna, despite her evil designs. If Putana merely hated Krishna at a distance and did not endeavor to connect with Him, then she would not have received the same level of mercy. However, because she imitated the demeanor of a loving mother when she approached the Lord, she was elevated to the position of nursemaid in Goloka Vrndavana.

As Sukadeva Gosvami instructs Maharaja Pariksit in *Srimad-Bhagavatam* 2.3.10:

> *akamah sarva-kamo va*
> *moksa-kama udara-dhih*
> *tivrena bhakti-yogena*
> *yajeta purusam param*

> *A person who has broader intelligence, whether he be full of all material desire, without any material desire, or desiring liberation, must by all means worship the supreme whole, the Personality of Godhead.*

No matter how we approach Krishna, we will always derive benefit, regardless of whether we are devoid of material desires, whether we want to satisfy many material desires, or whether we are on the impersonal platform, desirous of liberation. We can observe this phenomenon also in the case of great devotees, whose chastisement, like Krishna's, brings benedictions. In actuality, what initially sounds like a curse attacks the material aspect of a conditioned soul's existence, while simultaneously enhancing his or her ability to become more serious in spiritual life. In this way, a curse can become a blessing. This is one of the ironic gifts of *bhakti*. When Krishna or His devotees seemingly attack, annihilate, or devastate us, in reality we become the recipients of the greatest mercy.

Mantra Six

*yas tu sarvani bhutany
atmany evanupasyati
sarva-bhutesu catmanam
tato na vijugupsate*

He who sees everything in relation to the Supreme Lord, who sees all living entities as His parts and parcels, and who sees the Supreme Lord within everything never hates anything or any being.

The Nature of a Sadhu

Mantra Six encapsulates the nature of a *sadhu* perfectly. Persons endowed with saintly qualities are exceptional because they do not consider those who act inimically towards them to be their enemies. Saintly people understand that an aggressor is merely captured by the modes of material nature. Instead of engaging in confrontation, they try to bring about transformation. In material life, it is natural to respond to negativity with a similar attitude. We rarely encounter anyone who does not react with anger in the face of provocation. However, when we practice seeing one another as allies rather than as enemies, we become stronger mentally. If we manage to maintain a state of compassion despite disturbing and disruptive people or situations, then we will find that our consciousness will become surcharged with spiritual energy.

The Lord's devotees are such *sadhus*. They do not become disturbed when they are provoked, but they do become disturbed when either the well-being of others or the spreading of the Lord's glories is endangered. As Lord Krishna says to Arjuna in *Bhagavad-gita* 10.9:

> *mac-citta mad-gata-prana*
> *bodhayantah parasparam*
> *kathayantas ca mam nityam*
> *tusyanti ca ramanti ca*

> *The thoughts of My pure devotees dwell in Me, their lives are fully devoted to My service, and they derive great satisfaction and bliss from always enlightening one another and conversing about Me.*

Sadhus become disturbed when they observe people denying themselves the opportunity to experience Krishna's love, which gives all living entities the highest pleasure. The residents of higher planets like Brahmaloka, on which Lord Brahma resides, do not experience the kinds of suffering we experience on this planet. Although birth and death, which cause everyone some degree of discomfort, exist even on Brahmaloka, generally distress experienced by beings in higher realms is due to the sympathy they feel towards other people in pain.

If we introspect, we may notice that we are often preoccupied with our own suffering. Contrary to the normal state of affairs on this planet, the main concern of high-level devotees is the anguish of other living entities. It is not that these advanced devotees are in denial about what is happening in their lives; rather, their tolerance of their own suffering springs from a deep understanding that whatever happens to them is not by accident. They realize that apparent suffering is merely a sign that Krishna cares and that He will provide for His devotees in all circumstances. At times, Krishna demonstrates His affection towards His devotees through His unpredictability. On occasion, He will give and on occasion, He will not. Krishna reciprocates with us as He sees fit.

For advanced devotees, whether Krishna seemingly reciprocates or not is unimportant, as they are always focused on their service to the Lord regardless of the external situation. When asked what he found to be most amazing about his *guru*, Hari-sauri prabhu, a senior disciple and personal servant of Srila Prabhupada, replied that what impressed him most was that Srila Prabhupada was always the same, regardless of whether he was in a hut in Bengal or in a mansion in Bombay. Srila Prabhupada was always fixed in glorifying and serving Krishna for the benefit of the conditioned souls. External inconveniences never interrupted his service to his own *guru*, Srila Bhaktisiddhanta Sarasvati Thakura.

The Importance of Environment

In the early days of the movement, we did not have a fraction of the facilities that we now take for granted. For instance, many of the first temples, like the one at 26 Second Avenue in New York, were no bigger than a large room. Despite the modesty of its resources, however, ISKCON New York had a major impact in that city. During the 1970s and 1980s, the movement grew into a society with many houses and large preaching centers filled with devotees. Now, wherever we go in the world, Krishna is visibly present. Bowing down in His beautiful presence makes it more difficult for us to become entangled in *maya*, because we see that Krishna is looking at us! Whenever others enter the devotional environment, they are reminded of our life focus and feel its impact.

I used to be part of a team of devotees who traveled around the world, distributing books to university professors. If the professors accepted the books, then they would usually make them available to the student population through the university libraries. This gave us opportunities to reach tens of thousands of people. As a result, we invested some of our time learning various techniques to increase the efficiency of our book distribution. One of the most effective techniques was to assess the environment of the person to whom we wished to sell the books. As we entered their offices, we would quickly peruse them, noting what types of books they had on the shelves, and what kinds of pictures hung on the walls. In this way, we could immediately understand how a particular professor thought and what was important to him or her. We would sell the books based on these indicators, clues we picked up from the immediate environment. In fact, it is easy to learn about anybody when entering their office or home. For example, people who are family-orientated will often have pictures of their children on their desks. Those who enjoy sports will frequently be surrounded by photographs of or books authored by athletes. Someone who considers him or herself 'an outdoor person' may have scenic pictures on the walls. Our personal environment not only reveals our state of consciousness, but also affects the mind in many subtle ways. Devotees, therefore, want to be surrounded by an environment that stimulates their Krishna consciousness.

Three Types of Devotees

The devotees of the Lord fall into three categories:

1. *Kanistha-adhikari*, or a person in the elementary stage of God realization.

2. *Madhyama-adhikari*, or a person in the intermediate stage of God realization.

3. *Uttama-adhikari*, or a person in the highest stage of God realization.

In *Mantra Four* and *Mantra Five*, we received indication of the inconceivable and all-encompassing nature of the Lord. Now, in *Mantra Six* we hear of how the *uttama-adhikari* constantly sees Krishna everywhere and in everything; for such a person, nothing is more important than Krishna. Any paraphernalia they possess, and anything they do always relates to Krishna. The opposite is true for the *kanistha-adhikari*, who relates only to Krishna as the Deity in the temple. Recently, I was confronted with this level of devotion when I visited a godbrother, who lives in Santa Cruz. When I arrived at the door to his house, he suddenly began to apologize profusely. Initially, I was puzzled because everything inside his palatial home was exquisitely beautiful. However, I soon discovered the problem—Krishna was missing! Not a single indicator revealed that the home belonged to a devotee. When I saw the absence of Krishna, I realized why my godbrother felt uncomfortable; he was living his private life separately from the Lord. One's house is a reflection of what is happening in one's mind. For some time, this devotee had been running away from Krishna. Therefore, perhaps he did not want to see Him. He did not want to see Krishna's *rupa* coming out from the altar or from the walls as a reminder that his lifestyle was improper. He would only think of Krishna when he went to the temple for festivals such as Janmastami or Gaura-purnima.

Characteristics of the Kanistha-Adhikari

Krishna reciprocates with us according to how we reciprocate with Him. *Kanistha-adhikaris* usually behave very deferentially when they are in the temple, but when they go outside that environment, they may have very little interest in or time for the devotees. Sometimes, while in the temple environment, these devotees are so fixed on the Deities that they will push other devotees out of the way in order to approach Them. On this subject, Srila Prabhupada writes in his purport to *Bhagavad-gita* 9.11:

> *The neophyte devotee gives more attention to the Deity in the temple than to other devotees, so Visvanatha Cakravarti Thakura warns that*

> *this sort of mentality should be corrected. A devotee should see that because Krishna is present in everyone's heart as Paramatma, every body is the embodiment or the temple of the Supreme Lord; so as one offers respect to the temple of the Lord, he should similarly properly respect each and every body in which the Paramatma dwells. Everyone should therefore be given proper respect and should not be neglected.*

If *kanistha-adhikaris* do not elevate themselves to a higher level, they may involve themselves in all sorts of nonsense when they leave the temple. Sometimes, after performing *yajnas*, *kanistha-adhikaris* may feel they have showed sufficient devotion, on the basis of which Krishna must reciprocate. Quite plainly, such a mentality does not indicate a high level of consciousness. Krishna is not at all impressed with such a state of mind. What He really wants is our hearts, our very selves as an offering. He does not care about how much money we give in donation. He is concerned about what happens when we leave the temple, which is even more important than what we do in the little time we spend in front of the Deity. Firstly, we should be in good consciousness and do quality service while we are at the temple, and secondly, we want to take that devotional mindset out into the world with us. By constantly reading, listening, chanting, and reminding ourselves who we really are, we can become connected to Krishna despite the fact that our surroundings may not be conducive for such. Once *kanistha-adhikaris* leave a place of worship, usually they allow their spiritual life to shut down until they return to the temple environment. The *kanistha-adhikari* platform is based on an elementary kind of religious posture, which is not spiritually advanced because it does not fully honor Krishna's presence everywhere and at all times.

Characteristics of the Madhyama-Adhikari

While the *kanistha-adhikari* sees the Lord only in the temple and is in the business of doing business with God, so to speak, the *madhyama-adhikari* discriminates between the various categories of living entities and relates to each category in a different manner. The *madhyama-adhikari* discriminates between the Lord, the Lord's devotees, those who are innocent, and those who are envious. Devotees on this platform relate to the Lord with great love, in a mood of service and appreciation. They associate with the devotees of the Lord with enormous enthusiasm because they realize that devotees not only represent the Lord, but remind us of Him as well. *Madhyama-adhikaris* are compassionate towards the innocent and therefore try to reach out to them, to assist them in reconnecting with God. However, they avoid the envious because they realize the importance of association and influence. Bad association is offensive and goes against their mood of glorifying and serving Krishna. Since *madhyama-adhikaris* are disturbed when they see others hurting themselves by shunning the Lord, they avoid association with such persons.

Characteristics of the Uttama-Adhikari

As opposed to the *madhyama-adhikari*, who discriminates between different levels of devotees, the *uttama-adhikari* is situated on such a high level that he or she views everything as Krishna's energies. These rare devotees are ready to offer obeisances even to an ant, because they see the Supersoul within. Since they are in this world but not of it, *uttama-adhikaris* must tune down the intensity of their devotion if they are to be able to deal with the material environment and to preach effectively. They are required to come down to the level of the *madhyama-adhikari* in order to understand how to approach different varieties of people, and to communicate their message successfully.

Healthy versus Unhealthy Discrimination

At various points in the *Srimad-Bhagavatam* and the *Narada-pancaratra*, Narada Muni describes the different ways in which devotees are to deal with superiors, peers, and subordinates. In a perverted sense, discrimination also exists in the material world, in which strong lines of demarcation often divide different groups of people. In most countries, social hierarchy is entrenched. Often, in the offices of big corporations, separate facilities are maintained for senior staff. Usually, executives will have access to a 'corporate lounge,' which has much more opulent facilities than the 'lunchroom' designated for juniors. In general, senior staff will enjoy superior office accommodation and special ablution facilities. Separation of corporate space communicates an underlying pecking order. It is a way of letting people know where they stand in the social scheme. Juniors are made to feel that perhaps one day, if they are lucky, they may advance to the point at which they may use the executive lounge or toilet. Frequently, this mindset is unhealthy and makes employees envious of one other. Proper etiquette and appreciation of seniors is essential, but it must be organic and natural.

Sometimes, in our own ISKCON society, we create unhealthy differences between generations. We should bear in mind that just because someone is a Prabhupada disciple, he or she is not necessarily more advanced. We would surely hope this to be the case, but sometimes it is not. Etiquette dictates that juniors should arrange things to honor senior disciples. By honoring them, we are also taking the opportunity to remind them to act as senior devotees. We are depending on our big brothers and sisters, on our uncles and aunts, to continue to advance and to maintain our wonderful culture of devotion. When culture is lacking, etiquette will also be absent.

Alternatively, when people experience too much imposed classification, they become disturbed and do not give their best. For example, if parents and teachers use fear to teach their children lessons, then the results will not be as deep or as long lasting as results which arise from encouraging children with love and understanding. Of course, if deviation occurs, then chastisement proportionate to the deviation is appropriate. In this sense, chastisement is part of loving discipline, which will enable the children to grow into healthy and happy adults. Therefore, etiquette and the honoring of seniors should be encouraged lovingly, but not heavily enforced. In this way, it will be genuine. We want to associate in environments where such authentic *sadhus* are to be found.

Genuine Respect

If senior devotees are not treated properly, it is very unfortunate, but it is just as unfortunate when seniors visit and demand to be honored. While it is true that seniors have a responsibility to train and instruct us, it should not be done with material consciousness. If a devotee thinks that he or she automatically qualifies as our *guru* just because he or she is more expert than us at applying *tilaka*, or more proficient at tying a *dhoti* or wrapping a *sari*, then that devotee is in material consciousness. Seniors should receive respect because they have been taking advantage of the process by genuinely chanting and serving for a longer period of time than we have. We should be eager to associate with these devotees in the knowledge that they have been engaged in austerity and have accumulated wisdom; therefore, their spiritual bank accounts have increased in value. In such cases, we must observe etiquette.

However, devotees who think they are advanced because they

have been around for two years, already play the harmonium wonderfully, can chant all the *bhajanas*, and know three-quarters of the *Bhagavad-gita* are sadly on their way out. If we hold onto this kind of mentality, Maya-devi, the personification of Krishna's illusory energy, will whisper, "You are doing very nicely! Keep on, and in another three months, you will be the temple president; in six months, you will be a GBC secretary; and in another two years, all these devotees will become your disciples." Such a person may be dedicated and work very hard in devotional service, but for all the wrong reasons. For them, disaster awaits. Maya-devi will find a way to take them deeper into confusion and illusion. In order to prevent such a downfall, we must take a closer look at ourselves. We should study the qualities of a high-level *sadhu* and try to genuinely emulate them as best we can.

As devotees, we are told that we should follow in the footsteps of the great *acaryas*. At the same time, we are warned not to imitate them. It is important for us to understand the difference between these two approaches, as it is possible to confuse them. This confusion is reflected by the secular world, in which so many books prescribing methods to become materially successful are available. Authors undertake research on achievers, and then write books on how they conduct their lives, which ordinary people buy in the vain hope that by reading them, they will achieve similar success. We need to understand where to draw the line between imitating and following, and how to avoid unhealthy imitation. Consciousness differentiates between them. For instance, if we follow an advanced devotee and at the same time think that we are of the same caliber, then we will inevitably experience problems, but if we take note of what constitutes a good standard, and then humbly attempt to absorb those principles, then we will achieve positive results.

Devotional Fraudsters

Occasionally, we encounter devotees in our movement who aspire to become determined *yogis* or *jnanis* devoted to austerity, rather than dedicated *bhaktas* who want to develop true love of God. Many years ago, the president of the Nairobi Temple presented himself as a very advanced devotee. This particular devotee went to Mayapura and attempted to imitate the *gosvamis* by living in a *bhajana-kutira*, or a small hut in which self-realized devotees traditionally worship the Lord in seclusion. He chanted over sixty-four rounds daily and ate only remnants from the plates of devotees residing at the nearby temple complex. Some of the devotees were amazed by his behavior—but not Srila Prabhupada. Rather, Srila Prabhupada used him as an example to warn us against the dangers of imitating great devotees like Haridasa Thakura and Raghunatha dasa Gosvami. Needless to say, later on this particular devotee fell down.

This is not an isolated incident. At one point or another during our devotional lives, many of us will observe a friend or an acquaintance who takes to a very austere lifestyle for a certain period, only to indulge in sinful activities shortly afterwards. The neophyte devotee may fast for a few days, then binge for a week. These kinds of austerity involve imitation without realization and proper consciousness. It may be helpful to keep these examples at the forefront of our minds in order to properly understand the correct spirit in which we are to execute our devotional service.

Another story comes to mind, which may serve to illustrate this point further. Once upon a time there was a *sadhu*, who was a devotee in some ways. People would come from far and wide for his *darsana*, or audience. When they were gathered before him, he would warn them against the sinful life of a prostitute who lived nearby. Over time, he became so disturbed by her sinful ways that he decided to take action: every time a customer went into her house, he would pick up a stone and place it on the ground. As the days went by, he sat outside her house, watching and waiting as the heap of stones beside him grew into a mound. Eventually, the prostitute received news that the saint was observing her. Filled with guilt at the thought that her lifestyle was disturbing him, she decided to change her ways, and became a saint herself. The so-called saintly man, on the other hand, became overwhelmed by material desires and fell down from the platform of a *sadhu*. Because his primary meditation was on the illicit affairs of the prostitute, his consciousness had become polluted, and now he longed to have various unhealthy experiences. The *sadhu* had a *kanistha-adhikari* type of mentality. He did not really have sufficient appreciation and compassion for the conditioned souls, but merely wanted to see himself as better than them. As a result, he was captured by *maya*, and lost his ability to maintain a strong spiritual platform.

Questions and Answers

Question: You mentioned that the *madhyama-adhikari* makes distinctions. How is it possible to discriminate between devotees without creating offenses?

Answer: Second-class devotees make distinctions in order to protect their own devotional creepers and to inspire others to come closer to Krishna. They do not discriminate in order to make people feel inferior. If the *madhyama-adhikari* made no distinctions and saw everyone as eternal servants of Krishna, then he or she would not be able to preach effectively. A lack of discrimination between those who are sinful and those who are devotional would create confusion. If we do not differentiate between various classes of devotees, then how can we reinforce positive behavior and discourage negative conduct? Distinctions are not made in order to abuse or misuse, but rather they are tools of assistance. By making distinctions, the *madhyama-adhikari* expresses thoughtfulness and a desire to help those suffering in this material world. Discriminating, in a material sense, means pushing one group of people down so that we can push ourselves up. Discriminating, in a spiritual sense, means that we are able to prescribe a specific remedy for the particular ailments of each living entity.

We should find high-level *sadhus*, associate with them, and try to absorb their qualities. But we should be careful to discriminate between true *sadhus*, and those who merely think of themselves as *sadhus*. On the one hand, we may feel someone is spiritually advanced because they are intelligent and have acquired so much knowledge in such a short space of time. On the other hand, if the person in question, although intelligent, considers himself or herself to be on a high spiritual platform, then we have made a big mistake. A sense of humility goes together with spiritual advancement. It cannot be otherwise. Intelligence in and of itself is not contrary to spiritual advancement. A devotee who is both humble and intelligent is a real *sadhu*, a true role model whom we can joyfully follow.

Mantra Seven

*yasmin sarvani bhutany
atmaivabhud vijanatah
tatra ko mohah kah soka
ekatvam anupasyatah*

One who always sees all living entities as spiritual sparks, in quality one with the Lord, becomes a true knower of things. What, then, can be illusion or anxiety for him?

A Higher State of Consciousness

Every living entity is connected with Krishna. *Mantra Seven* hints at the great potency which unfolds together with deep realization of this truth. Just imagine the power of being able to see Krishna everywhere and in all things, of being able to look at any environment and see that everyone is actually a devotee of the Supreme Personality of Godhead. Can you imagine the beauty of such a state of consciousness?

Our experiences of the environment and of other living entities are based on what is happening in our own consciousness. Many of us have come in contact with devotees who are always happy regardless of their health, material facilities, or type of service. Why are such devotees always blissful? At first, we may assume that they are either naïve or dull, but in actuality, they are most likely immersed in a higher state of consciousness. They take full advantage of any opportunity to offer their service to Krishna. Whatever happens, these devotees are vibrant and surcharged because they see Krishna everywhere and in all things. Others, who do not possess such an elevated level of consciousness, allow themselves to get caught up with the intricacies of their service. They ask, "How much work has to be done? How long will it take? Where is the facility to execute this service?" Appreciation for Krishna and His service gradually manifests as we raise ourselves to the *madhyama-adhikari* and *uttama-adhikari* platforms. We must ask ourselves, "How do I elevate myself to a higher level of transcendental experience?"

For certain devotees, such as our *acaryas*, an elevated state of consciousness is natural. The *acaryas* possess spiritual purity and many other wonderful qualities. Therefore, when they appear, we should be eager to associate, learn, and hear from them. It is difficult to aspire to become a *sadhu* if we cannot recognize the qualities of such a person. If we do not know what a diamond is, then any type of cut glass will fool us. It takes hard work, firstly, to understand the qualities of a real *sadhu;* secondly, to search out those people who manifest such qualities; and finally, to try to emulate those qualities ourselves.

Real *sadhus* use each and every occasion to give something back to Krishna. They are motivated by a deep sense of gratitude for whatever He has bestowed upon them. When we associate respectfully with such personalities, we benefit in many wonderful ways. They have the power to influence us positively by extending their consciousness. When we have an opportunity to be around such devotees, we should grab it with both hands. Many of us have experienced that we feel more Krishna conscious in the association of advanced devotees. It is very difficult to be around someone who is empowered by Krishna and not to be affected to some extent. Sometimes, devotees may even get angry because the *sadhu* may inadvertently expose their deviations, but this is also mercy! As *sadhus* act on behalf of Krishna, they possess the ability to influence the environment. They remind us that Krishna is ever-present in our daily lives, and that He plays an active role in the protection and growth of *bhakti*. At the same time, Krishna singles out nescience and deals with miscreants. He assists us in distinguishing clearly between devotion and deviation. As the Lord reveals to Arjuna in *Bhagavad-gita* 4.8:

> *paritranaya sadhunam*
> *vinasaya ca duskrtam*
> *dharma-samsthapanarthaya*
> *sambhavami yuge yuge*

> *To deliver the pious and to annihilate the miscreants, as well as to reestablish the principles of religion, I Myself appear, millennium after millennium.*

Therefore, we should eagerly search for such *sadhus*. When we find them, we should follow in their footsteps, while at the same time being careful not to imitate them.

Love: The Most Powerful Weapon

One technique we can adopt when trying to elevate ourselves spiritually is to think of others in a more devotional way. Simply recognize that in essence everyone is a pure devotee of Krishna. When we direct powerful, loving thoughts towards one another, we consciously uplift and inspire everyone. The opposite also holds true. When we direct negative thoughts towards others, we ourselves will feel uncomfortable as others sense our destructive judgments. In environments where negative energies are prevalent, people are often affected adversely.

Recently, someone wrote to me asking for advice concerning a spate of psychic attacks to which he was subjected. Desiring to defend himself against supernatural phenomena, the writer was desperate for practical help. Instead of advising him to conduct a series of complicated rituals, as he may have expected, I merely recommended that he should try to see everyone in a loving way and to carry that consciousness into all his daily interactions. Instead of anxiously meditating upon those who were bothering him, this person could focus rather on transmitting powerful, loving thoughts. Negative emotions such as terror and worry could not disturb his consciousness in the presence of loving vibrations. Just by sending out love, he was empowered to minimize any subtle, malicious transmissions.

Love is the most powerful weapon in existence. Unfortunately, however, we hear this word mentioned so much in magazines, newspapers, and in the movies, that sometimes it becomes emptied of meaning. Since people in general do not have a deep understanding of what real love is, they often confuse it with lust. Real love is only expressed in relation to Krishna. The *nitya-siddhas* and the *uttama-adhikaris* are the only ones who truly experience and understand this love. They are so madly intoxicated with love for Krishna that when they come into this world, they have to tune down the intensity of their adoration for the Lord in order to function within the material paradigm.

When Srila Prabhupada was wrapping up his pastimes on this planet before going back to Godhead, the tiniest incidents would trigger altered states of consciousness. The Vedic literatures describe that high-level devotees experience these states when they are in the stages of *bhava*, or preliminary love of God, and *prema*. Since circumstances had shifted, it was no longer so important for Srila Prabhupada to come down from the *uttama-adhikari* platform to the *madhyama-adhikari* platform for preaching purposes. He therefore often allowed the love he felt to ignite his entire being whenever he encountered something in association with Krishna. Previously, he had to relate effectively to the world of duality, but because he was preparing to leave his body, he could relinquish some of that involvement and immerse himself in his natural, blissful state of pure Krishna consciousness. Srila Prabhupada was barely eating and his body was not functioning on a normal level. Yet, his appreciation of Krishna's love was so intense that those around him could not figure out how his soul still remained in his body. We are not to imitate Srila Prabhupada, but we can follow his general mood of appreciating all of Krishna's energies.

A Story of Hope

Seemingly unfortunate things happen to all of us. At the time, most of us cannot understand why Krishna would allow these apparently disastrous events to occur in the lives of His devotees. We may even begin to question the depth of our faith. These feelings are natural. However, if we accept everything as the Lord's mercy, then our surrender will sustain us and enable us to carry on. We may even emerge from a difficult situation with stronger faith and deeper love for the Lord. Sometimes, when times get tough, I remember the following story. I hope it will inspire those of you who are going through difficulties to continue in Krishna consciousness—no matter what.

Once upon a time, a great king was given a magnificent sword as a gift. While examining the beauty of the sword's blade, the king, not anticipating its extreme sharpness, cut off one of his fingers by mistake. The king's advisor exclaimed that it was the mercy of the Lord! On hearing this, the king was enraged. How dare his advisor minimize the damage done to his royal body! The king immediately imprisoned the advisor for his 'foolish' interpretation of the situation.

A few weeks later, the king went out hunting. During the expedition, the king was captured by cannibals who planned to sacrifice and eat him. (Even today, places exist on the planet where people engage in human sacrifice). The cannibals dragged the king, bound and gagged, to their village, where their priest was preparing for the ritual. As the priest looked over his future sacrificial offering, he noticed that it had a glaring imperfection. It was missing a finger! The priest ruled that the king was not a suitable offering, and in disgust, let him go. The king wandered back to his kingdom, bewildered but nonetheless glad that his life had been spared. Safely within his royal palace, the king reflected on the events of the day. Sitting upon the throne that he thought he would never see again, he recalled the words of his advisor, describing his lost finger as the Lord's mercy. He summoned his guards to bring the advisor from the dungeon.

Seeing his advisor before him, the king was filled with remorse. As he apologized for acting harshly, the king admitted that only in hindsight could he see the wisdom of his advisor's words. However, there was still one part of the story that the king could not understand. If everything is the Lord's mercy, then how did the mercy of the Lord manifest for the advisor? After all, the advisor had spoken sincerely, but was thrown into jail. The advisor reminded the king that normally he was the king's companion on his hunting expeditions. If the advisor had been with the king on this particular outing, he would surely have been roasted alive by the cannibals.

This little story illustrates how everything happens for a reason. If we are endeavoring to serve the Lord sincerely, then without a doubt a higher purpose lies behind whatever difficulties we may experience. We can safely trust that Krishna has arranged them for our benefit. Krishna is always with us. Can we develop enough faith to become more aware of His presence?

Leaving the World of Duality Behind

One who sees Krishna in all things does not become disturbed. In *Bhagavad-gita* 6.30, the Lord confides in Arjuna:

> *yo mam pasyati sarvatra*
> *sarvam ca mayi pasyati*
> *tasyaham na pranasyami*
> *sa ca me na pranasyati*

> *For one who sees Me everywhere and sees everything in Me, I am never lost, nor is he ever lost to Me.*

One who appreciates that Krishna is present everywhere is ready to connect with the Lord, and He will reciprocate. We cannot imitate such a high level of realization, but, at the same time, we can absorb the spirit of it. Day by day, we can be mindful of the fact that whatever is going on in our lives is due to Krishna's personal reciprocation, which is why these events are happening to us, and not to someone else! We can introspect and see how we can apply our realizations to deepen our love for the Lord. Let us try to come to a point at which we can look on all devotees in a mood of love and affection. Let a loving mood become an integral part of our consciousness. In such a mood, we cannot help but move away from the platform of duality.

Questions and Answers
Question: Is it not perhaps dangerous to see everything simply as Krishna's mercy? If we adopt this worldview, then how do we avoid becoming lazy, insensitive, and even impersonal?

Answer: Seeing everything as Krishna's mercy means being exceptionally knowledgeable, alert, and always active, while simultaneously being very humble. One cannot be spiritually knowledgeable and humble while being lazy and insensitive at the same time. One of the qualities of the *sadhu* is that he or she is a well-wisher of everyone and is equal to all. In *Bhagavad-gita* 9.29, the Lord describes His own impartiality to all living beings, which does not preclude His mood of personal reciprocation with His devotees:

> *samo 'ham sarva-bhutesu*
> *na me dvesyo 'sti na priyah*
> *ye bhajanti tu mam bhaktya*
> *mayi te tesu capy aham*

> *I envy no one, nor am I partial to anyone. I am equal to all. But whoever renders service unto Me in devotion is a friend, is in Me, and I am also a friend to him.*

Similarly, a *sadhu*, while behaving with equanimity towards all, will not act impersonally because he or she does everything as a loving offering to Krishna, who is the Supreme Person.

Question: If the first-class devotee sees Krishna everywhere, then how can he or she experience *vipralambha*, or love in separation, which *sastra* describes as the highest form of unconditional, loving exchange?

Mantra Seven

Answer: Although a pure devotee sees Krishna everywhere, at the same time he or she feels the absence of the Lord. This phenomenon, which is part of Lord Caitanya's philosophy of *acintya-bhedabheda-tattva*, is made possible by the influence of *yoga-maya*, or the spiritual potency of the Lord. Through the agency of *yoga-maya*, the pure devotee experiences *vipralambha*, which includes ecstatic emotions that accompany loving separation from Krishna.

Let us always remember that when we are situated in our original *svarupa*, or our eternal, individual relationship with Krishna, we are all pure, first-class devotees. Actually, this is our most natural state. However, we have temporarily allowed ourselves to think and act differently. The illusion experienced by *suddha-bhaktas*, or pure devotees, is completely opposite in quality from that experienced by conditioned souls. While *suddha-bhaktas* are influenced by *yoga-maya*, conditioned souls are firmly in the thrall of *maha-maya*, the covering potency of the Lord.

When a pure devotee is separated from Krishna, transcendental emotions such as *sambhoga*, ecstatic meeting and togetherness, and *vipralambha*, characterized by loneliness and hankering, pour through his or her entire being simultaneously. The *acaryas* explain that Krishna is the ultimate *atmarama*, or one who is completely self-sufficient, unaffected by happiness and distress. At the same time, Krishna is also all-knowledgeable, fully aware of all the sufferings of His devotees. Not only is He fully cognizant of their anguish, but He is also truly empathetic. Normally, those who are empathetic will experience some suffering themselves as they identify with the pain of others. Krishna, however, is able to feel others' pain, but simultaneously to remain materially unaffected, complete, and perfect. This is another part of the wonderful, inconceivable potency of the Lord, which is described in detail in the invocation to this book:

om purnam adah purnam idam
purnat purnam udacyate
purnasya purnam adaya
purnam evavasisyate

The Personality of Godhead is perfect and complete, and because He is completely perfect, all emanations from Him, such as this phenomenal world, are perfectly equipped as complete wholes. Whatever is produced of the Complete Whole is also complete in itself. Because He is the Complete Whole, even though so many complete units emanate from Him, He remains the complete balance.

Mantra Eight

sa paryagac chukram akayam avranam
asnaviram suddham apapa-viddham
kavir manisi paribhuh svayambhur
yathatathyato 'rthan vyadadhac chasvatibhyah samabhyah

> Such a person must factually know the greatest of all, the Personality of Godhead, who is unembodied, omniscient, beyond reproach, without veins, pure and uncontaminated, the self-sufficient philosopher who has been fulfilling everyone's desire since time immemorial.

Gratitude and Reciprocation

Most of us are not unconditional givers. When we give, we expect some distinct reciprocation. Generally, people feel inspired to give when they feel valued, which is natural. For example, fundraisers who collect donations to support a cause will find it difficult to obtain funds if, firstly, the donors do not feel appreciated, and secondly, they feel that their donations will not be used in a proper way. Donors may give once, maybe even twice, but they will not continue to contribute if they do not experience a real sense of encouragement or self-worth as a result of their giving. Similarly, why should Krishna desire to reciprocate with us if we do not show gratitude for what He has given us?

In this *mantra*, the speaker of *Sri Isopanisad* explains that Krishna is *paribhuh*, the greatest. He has been fulfilling the desires of all the living entities since the beginning of *samabhyah*, or time. Ordinarily, if someone satisfies all of our needs, but we ignore him or her, then we are considered to be ill-mannered and insensitive. If someone gives us a gift, but we show no appreciation, then most likely that person will not want to give to us again.

Krishna, of course, is not a conditioned or a conditional person. He does not give based on such mundane considerations. He does not need someone else's support to help Him feel whole, to make Him feel good about Himself, or to enjoy what He does. From the example of mundane giving, we can see how rude it is to request something, but subsequently to refuse to honor the giver. Throughout the material universes, however, most living entities are behaving in this ungrateful manner. We desire all sorts of objects and experiences based on our consciousness, and Krishna facilitates them. Often, not only are we ungrateful, but we also become angry when what we receive is not exactly what we had in mind.

Impersonalists and gross materialists have no cognizance of Krishna. Those who are atheistic refuse to recognize that Krishna is the divine arranger. Underlying their lack of acknowledgement of the Supreme Lord is often disguised rage. Atheists may argue, "There is no God. If there is a God, why is there so much evil in the world? Either evil is greater than Him and He is out of control, or He is in control and allows wickedness to flourish. Therefore, how can I be excited about a God who stands aside while His subordinates undergo so much abuse? How can I have reverence for a God who controls my life, but will not show Himself?"

Krishna appears whenever we have the eyes to see Him. If we do not have transcendental vision, then so many wonderful things may manifest right in front of us, but still, we will not be able to see them. We understand that our perceptions are covered over, and that we are lacking in wisdom; consequently, we pray for the torchlight of knowledge to illuminate our minds and our consciousness. We are eager to have elevated vision. We want illumination to take place so that we can find our way. We have all experienced being in a dark room. Usually, we cannot see very well, but if someone turns on a light, then the darkness is pushed aside. The light shines, enabling us to see both what is in front of us and what is beside us. This is the nature of *sastra*. It helps us to place events in proper perspective. It gives us vision where normally there would be obscurity. When we find ourselves in nescience, our first consideration is to pray. Then, in turn, Krishna will arrange for us to see more clearly. However, we must take responsibility for what we have asked for, and thank the Lord for how He chooses to facilitate us, even though sometimes what we receive does not come in the way we envision.

Material Senses and Spiritual Senses

This *mantra* describes the Lord as "unembodied, omniscient,

Mantra Eight

beyond reproach, without veins, pure and uncontaminated." We are given this information to assist us in gaining a deeper understanding about the nature of the Lord. He is *paramesvara*, the supreme controller, and therefore His senses can interact in unlimited, amazing ways. He can smell with His eyes, see with His ears, and taste with His nose. If we meditate on the interchangeable nature of Krishna's senses, we will gain some insight into the limitations of the physical body. Our material senses surely do not function in a sharp and thorough way. The spiritual body, however, is not limited by the three-dimensional scheme of reality, by parameters of time and space. The spiritual body is not restricted to the stimulation of the material senses. In our original transcendental form, all the senses are in harmony and have the capacity to experience unlimited pleasure simultaneously. Although initially it may be difficult for us to truly realize how the senses can be interchangeable, we can gain some understanding of this transcendental state of being, firstly through an examination of psychic phenomena, and secondly through investigating the effects of some hallucinogenic drugs.

Sometimes, we hear of people who undergo altered states of consciousness by developing extrasensory powers. These individuals are able to transcend normal boundaries of perception and reach dimensions beyond the realm of the material senses. A few may experience clairvoyance, by which they can see beyond their immediate environment into the future or into the past. One type of clairvoyance is remote viewing, by which a person in one place is able to see a faraway event as it unfolds, even though it may be happening in another country. It is as if he or she is watching a movie on a screen. We find an example of this phenomenon in *Bhagavad-gita*. Sanjaya could view the battlefield of Kuruksetra and explain what was taking place to Dhrtarastra, just like a modern newscaster who describes events occurring in a remote land for television viewers. Some may also experience clairaudience, by which they are able hear voices in other dimensions or sounds of incidents occurring in locations far removed from their immediate environments. From a careful examination of these phenomena, we can appreciate how little we normally experience, and how much more is actually accessible. Many *yogis* and mystics possess these kinds of power, which exceed the limitations of ordinary human capability.

Although perverted, some kinds of extrasensory perceptions arise from the use of psychedelic drugs. It is not recommended for anyone to experiment with drugs, as they are harmful to the body and mind, as well as detrimental for spiritual life. Under their influence, however, users have reported that sometimes their senses become interchangeable—they claim to see with the nose or smell with their ears. They are able to experience the world in a subtler, though distorted, way. Sometimes there is a rush of interaction amongst all the senses; the user experiences many sensations simultaneously. Psychic and hallucinatory experiences allow us just a small glimpse into possibilities of perception that far exceed the regular attachment of the senses to sense objects. In the spiritual body, extraordinary extrasensory experiences are always occurring, because this is the normal way in which it functions.

Following the urgings of the mundane senses often spells death for the living entity. At various points in his writings and lectures, Srila Prabhupada gives examples of the behavior of the firefly, the deer, the fish, and the elephant to illustrate this line of reasoning. The firefly is an insect which is attracted to light because it desires to experience through the eye. Seeing illumination, it becomes overwhelmed and plunges into a fire, or onto the blazing surface of a light bulb. Similarly, the deer is attracted to the sweet sound of the flute. The hunter, who knows the weakness of the deer, will play a flute to entice it. As the deer's ear becomes agitated, it emerges from its hiding place in order to relish the musical experience. Exposing itself to the hunter's arrow or rifle, the deer loses its life. The fish is vulnerable to allurement through the agitation of its sense of taste. When fishermen go fishing, they sometimes use worms as bait. The fish sees the worm and thinks, "Oh, something nice to enjoy, something good to eat." Because of the excitement of its tongue, the fish swims to bite the worm, but instead finds itself pierced by the fisherman's hook.

Likewise, the male elephant's desire for sense enjoyment makes him vulnerable to traps laid by ivory hunters. Hunters often place a female elephant in heat behind a hole in the ground, which is covered over. Attracted by the scent of her genitals, the male elephant charges towards her with the intention to mount her. Instead, he falls straight into the hole, and is captured. In each of these cases, whether it is the eye of the firefly, the ear of the deer, the tongue of the fish, or the genitals of the elephant, agitation of the senses proves fatal.

In the human form of life, we are subject to the intense demands of not just one, but of all five senses. Often our senses pull us in different directions simultaneously. The desire of one sense to enjoy separately from the others is a perverted reflection of the

Mantra Eight

spiritual world. In Vaikuntha, the eternal planets of the spiritual world, which are characterized by an absence of suffering and anxiety, all the senses work together to produce the experience of *prema*. Presently, however, we find ourselves situated in *kuntha*, a place full of anxiety and misery due to the constant disturbance of our minds and senses.

While it is true that uncontrolled urges for sense gratification invite death, at the same time the living entity is naturally pleasure-seeking. As we progress through the verses of *Sri Isopanisad*, Srila Vyasadeva gives us more detailed information concerning the Supreme Personality of Godhead by elucidating why He is Krishna, the reservoir or storehouse of all pleasure. By hearing how the Supreme Lord has been supplying everything since time immemorial, we are enlightened about Krishna's *guna*. As Krishna says to Arjuna in *Bhagavad-gita* 7.7:

mattah parataram nanyat
kincid asti dhananjaya
mayi sarvam idam protam
sutre mani-gana iva

O conqueror of wealth, there is no truth superior to Me. Everything rests upon Me, as pearls are strung on a thread.

As Krishna is the supplier of everything, all things rest upon Him. If we truly understand this concept, we will behold our entire lives with gratitude. We can see that the desire of our senses to enjoy the material world is only a perverted reflection of our soul's craving for an ecstatic loving relationship with Krishna. The hankering for material sense enjoyment can only lead to death, whereas the yearning for spiritual pleasure results in eternal life. The senses are interchangeable in our spiritual bodies, as well as in Krishna's *rupa*. Therefore, experiences are not limited to one sense as it makes contact with its object. *Sambandha* is so much more powerful on the spiritual platform because the *jiva* is totally absorbed in its experience.

How to Strengthen Memory

Even on a mundane level, multisensory encounters are much more powerful than single sensory ones. Both David A. Peoples, in his book *Presentation Plus*, and William Glasser study this phenomenon in connection with the ways in which we remember information.

Peoples and Glasser both conclude that, in general, people retain approximately:

- 10% of what they read
- 20% of what they hear
- 30% of what they see
- 50% of what they see and hear
- 70% of what they discuss with others
- 80% of what they experience directly
- 95% of what they teach

According to these statistics, one of the better ways to learn is by direct involvement and interaction. However, even better than direct experience is engagement in teaching, because when we teach, we are prompted to think about the subject matter in a deeper way. Many years ago, I read *Sri Isopanisad* a number of times, but when I decided to write this book, I was driven to reflect on its words and themes more intensely than I did previously.

When we prepare to give class, we read the purport with the view of having to explain it to others. As a result, it enters the consciousness on a more profound level. For this reason, it is beneficial for all devotees to give class. Even if we are not in a position to give class, then at least when we study we should try to read in the spirit of having to explain what we are reading to someone else. We should think, "How am I going to share this?" Occasionally, devotees are very scholarly and intelligent. They have excellent memories which enable them to fix whatever they hear or read immediately within their minds. One of the qualities of a *pukka brahmacari* is that he can remember just by hearing. Unfortunately, such a high quality of memory is not common in Kali-yuga. Our memories have become degraded and our intelligence is not so sharp. In previous ages, everyone could immediately remember whatever they heard, but not today. Therefore, Srila Vyasadeva compiled the Vedic literatures for us.

In general, most of us have to study actively, finding ways to get the mind to reflect on the subject matter in order to increase our mental retention. As scientists have proved, one way to retain more knowledge is to involve more of the senses in the learning experience. The greater the number of senses engaged, the greater the likelihood that a person will remember, understand, and appreciate transcendental information.

Mantra Eight

Vaisnavas, and spiritualists in general, place enormous trust in the oral tradition because, under favorable circumstances, it is the best way of transmitting knowledge. Regrettably, in this age of hypocrisy and quarrel, people often retain only a superficial reflection of what they hear. During lectures, the mind often becomes restless and does not retain much. Therefore, throughout the Krishna consciousness movement, workshops are available for most devotees to attend on a regular basis. Even when I speak outside of the devotee community, I choose to give seminars rather than speeches. The workshop format enables me to share knowledge, to ask for feedback, and to engage those listening in interactive activities. In this way, everybody walks away understanding the essential message on a deeper level.

The Greatest Sense Gratification

Engaging people in interactive activities is in harmony with *svarupa-jnana*, or knowledge of our original constitutional position, for the workshops help us to engage more of our senses in a complimentary way. In our spiritual bodies, all our senses work together to produce a variety of different sensations. Even in our physical bodies, we strive to employ all of our senses in serving Krishna through *sadhana-bhakti*, or the practice of devotional service. As we engage our senses more in serving the senses of Krishna, He makes Himself more available to us. Initially, we do it out of duty. Then gradually, we integrate our *sadhana* with our desire, which results in *ruci*, or a taste for devotional service. *Ruci* matures into *asakti*, or deep attachment to the service of the Lord, leading in due course to an experience of true pleasure and ecstasy in the state of *bhava*. The process culminates in *prema*, in unalloyed love of God. In one sense, attaining *prema* is simply a matter of reconditioning, revitalizing, and reorienting the senses so that they can return to their original state.

In real terms, Krishna consciousness offers the greatest possible sense gratification we can ever experience. It is not only about austerity and strict DO'S and DON'TS, but also about anticipating and undergoing the most pleasing experiences possible. The spiritual world is not a place of *yogis* meditating in caves. It is a continuous festival of wonderful association that endures perpetually. It is a life of never-ending enthusiasm, of constantly creating wonderful arrangements for the thrilling *lilas* of Radha and Krishna.

The Importance of Arca-Vigraha

In his purport to *Mantra Eight*, Srila Prabhupada explains the importance of worshiping the *arca-vigraha*. Through the Deity, Krishna makes Himself available by allowing us to absorb our material senses in His transcendental form. In this way, we can engage in reciprocation with the Lord as we address His senses by feeding Him, putting Him to rest, waking Him up, and singing to Him.

A compelling example of the power of *arca-vigraha* is contained within the story of Mukunda Kaviraja, a famous doctor who came from a very devotional family, and His son, Sri Raghunandana. They were happily engaged in the service of Gopinatha, their family Deity of Krishna as the proprietor of the *gopis*. Sri Raghunandana's mother would prepare the *bhoga*, while his father would cook, do the offering, and the *puja*. Eventually, Sri Raghunandana came of age to become a *brahmana*, or priest. He took *diksa* from his father in a joyful mood, pleased to have the opportunity to serve Gopinatha directly. Soon afterward, Mukunda Kaviraja needed to leave the house for a while. He asked his son to do the *puja* and to arrange for the *bhoga* offering to Gopinatha. Sri Raghunandana's mother affectionately prepared many dishes and gave them to her son to offer to the Lord.

Sri Raghunandana did not have much experience of Deity worship. Previously, he had merely watched the same scenario daily. His mother would lovingly give his father Gopinatha's special plate on which she had laid out the dishes, after which his father would go behind the curtain, ring the bell, and give the food to the Lord. Sri Raghunandana attempted to copy what he had seen. He closed the curtain (as we do when we make our offerings to the Lord), and he started to ring the bell. After he recited the required prayers, he looked up, but all the items were still on Gopinatha's plate. He could not understand what was happening. He made an offering to the Lord, but the Lord was not eating. Again, with more intensity, he repeated the prayers, but nothing happened. He became very anxious, meditating as follows: "I am a *brahmana* now. My father has gone, giving me the chance to do some service. Unfortunately, my effort has resulted in dismal failure. Krishna will not reciprocate." Sri Raghunandana thought that on his return, his father would be very disturbed because his son could not carry out his duty properly. He tried again, for a third time, with even more sincerity. He begged the Lord, "Please, my dear Lord, please come and eat. Please do not let my mother and father become disappointed. I am doing this for the first time; therefore, I plead with you

Mantra Eight

to overlook my immaturity and my offenses. Please be so kind as to accept this offering." Then he rang the bell again, chanting the *mantras* and prayers. As he looked up, he noticed that all the items had disappeared off the plate. Happily, he brought out the empty dishes and gave them to his mother.

When she saw that Gopinatha's plate was bare, his mother was so disappointed that she almost collapsed. She said nothing, thinking it best to wait until her husband arrived home. Eventually Mukunda Kaviraja returned. His wife told him how their son had made the offering, but had returned with an empty plate. She lamented that despite following the *samskaras*, or ceremonies prescribed for rites of passage, despite adhering to the principles set forth in the scripture, and despite offering respects to saintly people, she had given birth to such a rascal son. The father heard the events of the day and became distressed. He thought, "How can our son go onto the altar and eat the offering meant for the Lord?" He asked Sri Raghunandana to explain what had happened.

Sri Raghunandana told his father how he had tried to offer the foodstuffs. At first, he prayed, reciting the *mantras*, but the food remained uneaten. He tried a second time, but again the Lord did not accept. The third time, he really pleaded, "Please, dear Supreme Personality of Godhead, come and eat Your food! Overlook all my faults and offenses." After that the Lord came and ate. Mukunda Kaviraja suspected his son was not telling the truth. He had not trained his son up to be a liar, and he surely did not give his son *brahmana* initiation only for him to turn out to be a big cheater! He asked his son to make an offering again, to prove to him what had occurred. While Sri Raghunandana did the offering, his father watched and saw for himself that the Lord took the food away. Sri Raghunandana did not understand that because Krishna eats with His eyes, He did not need to remove the material aspect of the food. However, as his desire was so strong and his devotion was so pure, Krishna reciprocated by swallowing the foodstuffs.

In our temples and in some congregational homes, *pujaris* place foodstuffs before the Deity form of the Lord, and then invite Him by *mantras* to come, sit down, and accept the offering. The Lord then takes the *bhakti* in the foodstuffs, and we later reciprocate with Him further by honoring His remnants. However, unlike Sri Raghunandana, often our tendency is to be impersonal and take the Lord for granted. From this story we can learn that when the *bhakti* is pure, Krishna Himself will go out of His way to serve His unalloyed devotees, whose only desire is to serve His senses.

Questions and Answers

Question: I understand from reading Srila Prabhupada's books that all devotional experiences, such as reading and association with devotees, are powerful, but are they equally so for each individual? Can two people do the same service yet obtain varying levels of benefit?

Answer: Spiritual benefit is dependent on both action and consciousness. For example, a devotee who undertakes a service begrudgingly will not gain the same benefit as one who is genuinely inspired to do the same work. A *bhakta* who cuts up vegetables in the morning in a grumpy mood, while meditating morosely on the amount of work to be done, does not gain as much spiritually as a devotee who cuts the same vegetables while thinking how fortunate he is to assist in preparing an offering for the Lord. While the same action is present, one devotee is a little more advanced than the other in terms of consciousness, and therefore he derives greater blessings. Similarly, if a devotee distributes *prasadam* while reflecting negatively on the customers, concerned only with how much money they are paying, she will not receive the same benefit as another devotee who dishes out the preparations with love and devotion, feeling happy that she has been given such a wonderful opportunity to help facilitate people in their spiritual life. The same action is present, but it is executed with different levels of awareness.

Krishna consciousness is not as much about learning a vast array of things as it is about deepening our realization of the knowledge we already have. Sometimes, devotees get caught in the trap of pursuing knowledge without understanding properly how to apply it. Increasing our knowledge is beneficial if it assists us in controlling our minds and in preaching more effectively. Real understanding is not just a matter of information processing, but rather one of more profound realization.

Mantra Nine

> andham tamah pravisanti
> ye 'vidyam upasate
> tato bhuya iva te tamo
> ya u vidyayam ratah

> *Those who engage in the culture of nescient activities shall enter into the darkest region of ignorance. Worse still are those engaged in the culture of so-called knowledge.*

Does Knowledge Mean Sorrow?

Usually, we consider the possession of knowledge to be a wonderful condition. Initially, therefore, we may feel bewildered when we read this *mantra*. After all, knowledge is one of the opulences of Krishna. He is known as the most intelligent being, because He is full in all knowledge. As Krishna states in *Bhagavad-gita* 10.8:

> aham sarvasya prabhavo
> mattah sarvam pravartate
> iti matva bhajante mam
> budha bhava-samanvitah

> *I am the source of all spiritual and material worlds. Everything emanates from Me. The wise who perfectly know this engage in My devotional service and worship Me with all their hearts.*

One of the signs of those who are in true knowledge is that they dedicate themselves to Krishna, as opposed to those in so-called knowledge, who dedicate themselves elsewhere.

Sometimes, secular philosophers claim that knowledge is sorrow. When they notice that the more of the material world they experience, the more sorrow they encounter, these philosophers frequently conclude that ignorance is bliss. Rather than develop true knowledge of their constitutional position, they resort to denial. Mundane religionists, too, sometimes accept knowledge as entangling. They think it is best not to see, hear, or know, because they sense that with knowledge comes not only the inclination but also the responsibility to respond to reality. Often, they feel that they do not need to worry about what they do not know.

Sincere people in all spheres of life realize that they should act upon any knowledge they acquire. Once a person has knowledge, he or she will have to make changes; that is, if he or she is an honest person. For those who are not very honest, having access to knowledge makes no difference. Devotees approach knowledge from a spiritual perspective. Being the recipient of immense wisdom comes with a price, however. If we do not act on the knowledge we have been given regarding what is proper, then we will experience great pain. When we do something deviant out of ignorance, the mind and the intelligence do not become bothered, even though we will still have to suffer karmic consequences. But when devotees get into *maya*, they suffer more than materialists who commit the same activities. While devotees possess the knowledge that they should not deviate, sometimes they choose to do it anyway. By breaking the principles, they may obtain some *capala-sukha*, or flickering happiness, but later the mind will beat them, and beat them, and beat them to such an extent that any so-called pleasure is practically cancelled out due to the extensive internal suffering. Further pain will come as a result of offenses stemming from the deviation, a pain far more intense than the karmic reaction suffered by the ordinary materialist.

Breaking Spiritual Laws

Many spiritualists are impersonalists because they really do not want to go deeper into spiritual life. Actually, they do not want to know Krishna. Unconsciously, they avoid higher knowledge because they sense that if they allow themselves to know more, they will be obliged to follow higher laws. Thinking of God as energy, as love, as everything and everyone is a part of the cheating mentality of refusing to know. Sometimes impersonalists even become angry when devotees preach to them about the fact that the Lord has form, because they intuitively understand that the more they hear, the more they will be held accountable to spiritual principles.

In civil and criminal law, penalties exist for breaking regulations and statutes. However, if it can be proved that the accused was either unaware of breaking the law, or had not intended to break it, then his lack of awareness or intention may become a mitigating circumstance. For example, if somebody commits a serious crime such as murder, but it happens extemporaneously, out of passion or for self-defence, then it is not considered as severe as if that same crime was premeditated. If the perpetrator was fully in control, planned to kill, and subsequently acted upon his plan, then his crime is considered to be a far more ruthless one. Similarly, as this *mantra* and the subsequent one explain, those who break spiritual laws enter the darkest region of ignorance. But an even worse fate awaits those who deviate in knowledge. In his purport to the verse, Srila Prabhupada writes that *Mantra Nine* "offers a comparative study" of *vidya*, or knowledge, versus *avidya*, or ignorance (*Sri Isopanisad*, 63). Ignorance means not to know. To act out of ignorance is still a sin, but to commit a crime knowingly is a much greater one. Therefore, it follows that the consequences will be much more severe.

In fact, it is dangerous to hear from *sadhus*, to read *sastra*, and to receive so many benedictions, but then to put it all to the side. It is extremely hazardous to take initiation, whether it is first initiation, second initiation, or even *sannyasa*, and then to engage in deviation after receiving the mercy.

The Higher the Knowledge, the Greater the Consequences

Often when a *sannyasi* falls, he leaves the movement. The Vedic injunction is that a fallen *sannyasi* should take his own life. Such an injunction conveys the heavy consequences of not honoring principles which such a person is supposed to represent. When an abundance of blessings, knowledge, and mercy are dishonored, then the karmic reaction is severe. In many cases, unless he receives very special mercy, a fallen *sannyasi* will have tremendous trouble just trying to be an ordinary devotee, because he is carrying such intense karmic weight. Therefore, we have to try and protect our *sannyasis*, to protect our leaders, and to protect our presidents, because the higher the position they hold, the more serious the consequences for deviation. Devotees who pretend to be spiritual while they abuse others, or who use religion to mask deviance, fall into this second category of deviation within knowledge.

Currently, fanatics are perpetrating violence in the name of religion. Such persons are actually much worse than ordinary sinners. They are going to have to endure much greater misery than those who do not even believe in or talk about God. Somebody who is commissioning others to go out and kill in the name of the Bible, to kill in the name of the Koran, to kill in the name of the Hadith, or to kill in the name of the Muwatta, will have to deal with extremely heavy karmic reactions. They will go to some of the darkest regions of the material universe because they possess spiritual knowledge, yet at the same they have chosen to abuse it.

We can also analyze sinning by comparing the difference between sinning in ignorance and sinning intentionally. The worst type of falldown is a philosophical falldown. Sometimes, devotees may fall down because of inattention. If they fall down because they cannot control their senses, then at least such a falldown is clear both to them and to others. Everyone can acknowledge that they are weak, and that a deviation has occurred. However, the consequences of a philosophical falldown can be far worse, as the devotee propagating the subtle pollution is often not aware that anything is amiss, while others become polluted easily because they are less vigilant in his or her presence. For example, when we are acquainted with people who smoke cigarettes and take drugs or alcohol, naturally we feel a little uncomfortable in their association. It is obvious to us that they are in *maya*, and therefore we are able to resist them consciously. However, when devotees alter the philosophy but at the same time pretend that they are spiritually fixed-up, their association becomes much more dangerous, because we let our guard down around them. Our devotional creeper may be ravaged by such persons before we realize what is happening.

Insider Deviation

In his writing, Srila Prabhupada repeatedly cautions us against different kinds of personalities who could threaten our tender devotional creepers. He warns us, of course, against the gross atheists. He warns us against the cheating materialists. He warns us about getting caught up with the speculation of material scientists. He helps us to see the danger of the *smarta-brahmanas*, or the hereditary priestly class, who demand respect based on casteism, but whose leaders do not follow the injunctions of the Vedas properly. He also cautions us against the impersonalists and the voidists. However, Srila Prabhupada issues some of his most severe warnings against the *sahajiyas*, or mundane devotees who think of themselves as intimate associates of Krishna.

Mantra Nine

At first, we may view Srila Prabhupada's emphasis as somewhat unusual, because the *sahajiyas* are participating in Vedic culture, after all. They recognize Krishna's *nama, rupa, guna,* and *lila.* Sometimes, just like the *jnanis,* they may even know more than the *bhaktas,* but their *vidya* is problematic. *Sahajiyas* appear to know much, but their understanding is not deep, for they are cheaters. They want the experience without the proper commitment. It is as if they want the salary without the proper work. They are not paying their spiritual dues sufficiently. This class is most dangerous because they are on familiar terms with important confidential aspects of devotional service, but they approach them in a perverted way.

Since these deviants are insiders, devotees are less likely to defend themselves against the negativity which they transmit. It is possible to compare insider deviation to a coup d'état, or a sudden, illegal change of government. In many countries, the most successful coup d'états happen from within. They are executed by parties who were close to the leader previously, but then turned against him or her. Because these subversive parties have inside connections, they are more likely to be successful. Insider deviation may similarly be compared to domestic violence. Frequently, the worst arguments occur between friends and family. When people are close to one other and share intimately, an intense situation arises when they become disturbed. In America and other countries, one of the worst calls that a policeman can receive is to attend to a domestic argument. When people who live with one other experience a conflict, they can become very vicious. Similarly, when a very close friendship between two people breaks down, these former best friends may become the greatest of enemies.

A relationship between close friends is analogous to the bond between the mind and the spirit soul. The mind can be our greatest enemy or our greatest friend. The mind is our enemy because it knows us the best; it is our greatest friend because it knows us the best. Similarly, those who are close to us present corresponding advantages and disadvantages. Since they know us well, they can hurt us more than someone who does not, but for the same reason, they can also provide us with the greatest understanding and affection. The danger of *vidya* lies in knowing just how to hurt somebody because we are aware of his or her weaknesses. Knowledge is dangerous when it is misused, just as powerful information becomes destructive when it is applied in an unhealthy way.

A Cobra Decorated with a Valuable Jewel

In his translation of the *mantra*, and in his purport, Srila Prabhupada uses the word "so-called" to describe a perverted culture of knowledge (*Sri Isopanisad*, 63-64, 67). Quoting *Bhagavad-gita*, Srila Prabhupada refers to those who misuse knowledge as *veda-vada-ratas*, or supposed followers of the *Vedas* (2.42) and *mayayapahrta-jnanas*, or those whose knowledge has been stolen by the illusory energy (7.15). Studying Vedic knowledge, terminology, and culture, these classes of people have nevertheless failed to put their learning into the proper perspective. *Veda-vada-ratas* and *mayayapahrta-jnanas* engage in varieties of conjecture about sacred truths. Since these people are insiders, they can present their philosophy as authentic, while in actuality it is merely a replica. Because it looks like the real thing, however, people are easily tricked.

In his purport, Srila Prabhupada describes that a "cobra decorated with a valuable jewel is more dangerous than one not decorated" (*Sri Isopanisad*, 65). He refers to a verse in *Hari-bhakti-sudhodaya* (3.12), in which the advancement of education by godless people is compared to decorations on a dead body:

> *bhagavad-bhakti-hinasya*
> *jatih sastram japas tapah*
> *apranasyeva dehasya*
> *mandanam loka-ranjanam*

> *For a person devoid of devotional service, birth in a great family or nation, knowledge of revealed scripture, performance of austerities and penance, and chanting of Vedic mantras are all like ornaments on a dead body. Such ornaments simply serve the concocted pleasures of the general populace.*

Decorations entice, drawing people's attention closer, and in this way the innocent become vulnerable to exploitation. Sinister people behave in this manner: they attract people by tricking them, and then they attempt to destroy them. In the international arena, one of the main problems right now is the abuse of knowledge in the forms of misinformation, espionage, and propaganda. People are fooled into believing that this adulterated information is sound knowledge. However, *Sri Isopanisad* states that such people will go to the darkest regions because they have abused deeper understandings.

Sri Isopanisad Is a Powerful Weapon

Since time immemorial, the Lord has been giving His shelter and His knowledge to all of us. And since time immemorial, we have been doing our best to avoid it. Thus the cycle of *samsara* is perpetuated. *Sri Isopanisad* is a very small book, but, at the same time, it is an extremely powerful book for clearing up nescience. The impersonalists are very frightened of this kind of book. As *Mantra Five* says, "The Supreme Lord walks and does not walk." He can do anything and everything, but He is not controlled by the laws of material nature. He has many *rupas* full of variegatedness. Similarly, we have eternal forms. Together with these eternal forms come eternal senses with which we are to enjoy eternally. The *tapasvis*, the *yogis*, and sometimes the *jnanis* have trouble understanding these transcendental truths. We realize that spiritual life must be all-encompassing. Desires to enjoy the material energy stem from our natural propensity for pure enjoyment, pure sensory absorption, and pure interaction.

Questions and Answers

Question: Why does Krishna sometimes not give us the knowledge we need? If He did, then we could act in a more bona fide way.

Answer: He will and He does if we want it. Krishna gives us knowledge according to our level of desire. We must question the purity of our desires. The impersonalists want to be in ignorance because the more they know about Krishna, the more they are obliged to serve Krishna; consequently, the more they will feel bound to orient their lives in a very specific way. If a person wants to know Krishna ten percent, twenty percent, or fifty percent, then He will arrange for certain theologies to give that person the exact degree of knowledge he or she wants. Therefore, we really need to take a closer look at the nature of our innermost wishes. We must learn how to align our desires properly. When we have proper desires, then we will receive higher knowledge or deeper understanding.

What affects our desires? What we hear, what we read, and most importantly, whom we associate with. Our association dominates our experience and so affects the quality of our deepest needs and wants. By reading and hearing, we become aware of greater possibilities. When we become more aware of these possibilities, we become more enthused and stimulated to obtain and experience the higher realms. But if we are not aware of greater possibilities, then we receive less stimulation to yearn for something more elevated. Sometimes we think, "Why doesn't Krishna give us the intelligence so that we will never deviate?" In fact, to think like this is an escapist mentality or a form of denial. We are same in quality as the Lord; therefore, we also possess freedom of expression and free will. Notice how we use that free will. Sometimes when we do not use it well, we want to blame Krishna. Internally, we chastise Him, "Why did You arrange this, why did You arrange that?" It might sound harsh, but everybody is responsible for everything that ever happens to them. People sometimes say, "Oh, you Krishna people, stop all this nonsense talk about *karma*!" However, it is a fact that we are indirectly responsible for everything. Therefore, if anything is happening in our lives that we are not comfortable with, we should look closer to see how to change our consciousness, so that our lives can also change. Depending on our priorities, Krishna is making certain arrangements, or allowing the demigods to arrange on His behalf. As we think and request differently, different things will happen to us and around us. There is so much power available if we truly want it.

Question: If we always have free will, is it possible that even after we go back to the spiritual world, we could again begin to desire to enjoy separately from Krishna?

Answer: This is an interesting concern. Sometimes, we may think that if free will is still a factor in the spiritual world, it may manifest in a tendency to explore independently again. However, Srila Prabhupada explains that once we go back to Godhead, we relinquish such desires. We learn from the process of being in hellish places and in hellish bodies; therefore, we are able to give up any wish to be separate from the Lord, or to master the realm of limitations. In this world, there is also some *lila* we are trying to engage in, but it is perverted. Our Vaisnava understanding is that once we return, we never come back unless we return specifically to serve Krishna by helping to reclaim others. Srila Prabhupada also explains that most entities never even leave the spiritual world. Only a minority go into the material prisons. Even for the prisoners, however, so many rehabilitation facilities are available. In some cases, it takes many, many millions of lifetimes, but in other cases, correction occurs faster.

The *uttama-adhikari* does not distinguish between those who go back faster, and those who go back more slowly, because he or she sees that everybody is going to return, and that everybody is still connected to Krishna. We merely think that we lack this connection. Everyone is still in the spiritual world. The only difference is that a number of us are covered by the *mahat-tattva*.

Mantra Ten

anyad evahur vidyaya-
nyad ahur avidyaya
iti susruma dhiranam
ye nas tad vicacaksire

The wise have explained that one result is derived from the culture of knowledge and that a different result is obtained from the culture of nescience.

Light Always Dispels Darkness

"Godhead is light. Nescience is darkness. Where there is Godhead there is no nescience," reads the motto on the cover of *Back To Godhead* magazine, the official journal of ISKCON. Through Srila Prabhupada's penetrating insight, nescience or moral darkness is instantly linked to a lack of knowledge about Krishna. In his purport to *Mantra Ten*, Srila Prabhupada lists eighteen different methods, based on *Bhagavad-gita* 13.8-12, which assist us in understanding knowledge. He writes emphatically that besides these eighteen methods, all others are considered to be irrelevant, a mere distraction to our spiritual lives. Thus, *Mantra Ten* may be read as an investigation into or an analysis of Krishna's definition of knowledge in *Bhagavad-gita* 13.8-12:

amanitvam adambhitvam
ahimsa ksantir arjavam
acaryopasanam saucam
sthairyam atma-vinigrahah

indriyarthesu vairagyam
anahankara eva ca
janma-mrtyu-jara-vyadhi
dukha-dosanudarsanam

*asaktir anabhisvangah
putra-dara-grhadisu
nityam ca sama-cittatvam
istanistopapattisu*

*mayi cananya-yogena
bhaktir avyabhicarini
vivikta-desa-sevitvam
aratir jana-samsadi*

*adhyatma-jnana-nityatvam
tattva-jnanartha-darsanam
etaj jnanam iti proktam
ajnanam yad ato 'nyatha*

Humility; pridelessness; nonviolence; tolerance; simplicity; approaching a bona fide spiritual master; cleanliness; steadiness; self-control; renunciation of the objects of sense gratification; absence of false ego; the perception of the evil of birth, death, old age and disease; detachment; freedom from entanglement with children, wife, home and the rest; even-mindedness amid pleasant and unpleasant events; constant and unalloyed devotion to Me; aspiring to live in a solitary place; detachment from the general mass of people; accepting the importance of self-realization; and philosophical search for the Absolute Truth—all these I declare to be knowledge, and besides this whatever there may be is ignorance.

Various traditions suggest diverse ways of triumphing over *maya*, of differentiating knowledge from ignorance. In certain understandings, the mystic Sufis are similar to the *bhaktas* in their approach to challenging illusion. The Sufis use the analogy of confronting a thief to suggest the best way of dealing with nescience. These days, thieves can be very vicious. Nevertheless, most of them will exercise some discretion about how to react to circumstances at the scene of the crime. Imagine, for instance, that we are upstairs when a thief comes into our home. According to the Sufis, we can respond in various ways. We can run downstairs with a hammer or a knife, or pick up the closest chair. However, we may find that when we confront the thief with a knife, he or she may have a gun. If we run down the stairs with a regular gun, the thief may wield a machine gun. If we arm ourselves with a machine gun, we may find that we are outmatched by three thieves bearing three machine guns. Sufis maintain, therefore, that the best way to confront a thief is to turn on the light. When the thief sees the light, he or she will realize that somebody is awake in the house and will run away—a rational thief, that is. Some thieves may turn to violence regardless of the situation. A clever thief, however, will prefer to avoid a confrontation.

Similarly, one way to address any intrusion of *maya* is to illuminate our own consciousness by increasing the potency of our devotion. When Maya-devi enters our personal space, we can best confront her by ensuring that we take shelter of role models who set proper examples. The behavior of role models indicates clearly the standard of any environment. In any type of spiritual community, we will always find members with different levels of spiritual consciousness. Role models form a strong nucleus, reminding us of what kind of conduct is required to raise consciousness. This is especially necessary when there has been stagnation in our spiritual lives (for example, if we have temporarily stopped honoring certain vows).

Building Community

In *Bhagavad-gita* 7.16, Krishna explains to Arjuna that *catuhvidhah*, or four types of people, come to devotional service out of a variety of motivations. Once we are in the process, we also address challenges differently according to the quality of our *sukrti, ajnatasukrti*, as well as our *sadacara*, or good character. Clearly, we bring our past with us to the devotional process. We will experience varying levels of spiritual advancement, depending upon the interaction between the following factors:

1. The quality of devotional service to the Lord that we bring with us from previous lives

2. Our level of spiritual greed, and the special mercy of the Lord

3. Our environment, which has a profound impact on the strength of our spiritual desires

Devotees associate in order to help one another go back to Godhead. One way to strengthen a community is by creating a nucleus of devotees who are very dedicated and serious, and who are able to work well together as a team. In most cases, the formation of a good team automatically causes others to approach a higher standard. In a few instances, however, the formation of a strong devotional nucleus will cause others to move away from that environment because they may feel uncomfortable. This is especially true when the forces of *maya* are very strong. Some are not ready to change. Therefore, we should not be surprised when an intensely devotional environment repels stagnant devotees away.

We often reiterate that Srila Prabhupada has built a house in which everybody can live. However, we should remind ourselves that Srila Prabhupada built a wonderful house—not a circus. In a circus, everybody is acting wildly, and freak shows are considered part of the normal flow of events. A wholesome household, however, is an organized one. Members fulfill specific roles to assist in the maintenance of their home. Although their roles may differ, the family members bond, work, and share together. Similarly, we should always try to increase the level of our own consciousness in order to please our father and mother, and to uplift our brothers and sisters. Quality service is most important.

Diversity and Dedication Result in Victory

Endeavoring seriously to defeat the culture of nescience is similar to engaging in warfare. War takes many different kinds of weapons and soldiers. When many sincere and dedicated soldiers each fulfill their specific roles, great victory is assured. Diversity combined with dedication results in success, protection, and progress. If we are genuine and committed, our devotional encounters will be similar to the attainment of on-going victories. Some of us embrace Krishna consciousness fully, while others make only a half-hearted attempt. However, even if the quality of our devotional service is poor, we will nevertheless make some spiritual advancement in this lifetime. Merely by chanting the Lord's holy names, our consciousness receives amazing stimulation. Devotees of the Lord regularly perform *harinama-sankirtana*, or the public chanting of the *maha-mantra*. Just the sight of the *harinama* party is often enough to attract others to Krishna consciousness. *Prasadam* will also nourish the *bhakti-lata-bija*, drawing whoever serves or eats it closer to his or her true spiritual nature.

Mantra Ten

Recovering from Amnesia

The experience of being in the material body is similar to that of suffering from amnesia, or loss of memory. Medically, it is known that certain encounters will stimulate the memories of amnesiacs by reminding them of their true identities. Recall is more likely when amnesiacs see a person from their past, for instance. Sometimes, by reading a book, visiting former environments, seeing previous associates, or watching a film, the memory of the amnesiac will suddenly be rejuvenated. Similarly, we may become attracted to devotional service by visiting spiritual communities, meeting a *sadhu*, hearing the holy name, taking *prasadam*, or reading even a single passage of *sastra*. Since we desire to share Krishna consciousness, we must assess our own environment in order to make it as conducive as possible to refreshing the memories of other amnesiacs who are still bewildered. We must make use of all methods available to us to enable people to come forward.

Since we are individuals, the awakening of our real identity will naturally occur in different ways. For example, some of us read regularly, but if we are approached by someone on the street with a book, we may not buy it. However, if we find the same book in the bookstore, we may very well purchase it. In fact, not only may we buy the very same book, but we may pay more for it in the store. Similarly, some people might refuse to visit a temple, but if they hear about a similar program at a home, a school, or at some other venue, they may attend and listen with great attention. This is the nature of the process—different environments allow us to make the connection and to produce auspiciousness.

Eighteen Methods for Developing Real Knowledge

Let us now turn to the eighteen different methods of developing real knowledge as defined by Srila Prabhupada in his purport to *Mantra Ten*.

1. One should become a perfect gentleman and learn to give proper respect to others.

Srila Prabhupada emphasizes that a devotee is to be polite, thoughtful, and kind to everyone as a first principle. Most importantly, giving proper respects to others also applies to women and children. We should be nice people and seen as such. Since we are followers of *sanatana-dharma*, we may ask whether becoming perfect gentlemen or gentlewomen is really of importance to devotees. Unfortunately, sometimes devotees maintain the misconception that there is no place for *dharma* in the process of devotional service. However, if we do not honor *dharma*, we cannot properly embrace *sanatana-dharma*. We cannot attempt to be transcendental unless we become good people first. We cannot acquire transcendental knowledge if we refuse to acknowledge the qualities that constitute elementary knowledge. In fact, the qualities that help us to be well-behaved people connect us to the mode of goodness. It is very natural to progress from goodness to transcendence. Sometimes, the reason why we experience so much trouble in our lives is because we are deeply captured by the modes of ignorance and passion. Therefore, each time we try to connect with transcendental knowledge, we fail because the lower modes bind our consciousness.

The qualities of the mode of goodness include truthfulness, cleanliness, wisdom, and other pious traits. Aggression, pride, attachment, and greed represent some of the qualities of the mode of passion. Those dominated by this mode are energetic with a fruitive orientation, selfish, overly concerned with their own sovereignty, and lusty. Those predominated by the mode of ignorance lack cleanliness and respect, and are foolish and illusioned. Whether they engage in work, worship, or austerity, they do the wrong thing at the wrong time in the wrong way. If we become comfortable with the attributes of the two lower modes, we will find it difficult to become transcendental. However, if we endeavor to become more pious, kind, and polite in our activities, we will connect more easily with devotion. It is practically impossible to jump straight from either the mode of passion or ignorance to transcendence. One predominated by these lower modes will reflect some of the qualities of nescience, like duplicity and deviation. Therefore, developing real knowledge entails cultivating the qualities of a good person.

2. One should not pose himself as a religionist simply for name and fame.

Generally, when someone desires to be famous, he or she tries to become a rock star or an actor. Initially, we may ask ourselves why a person would consider religion as a means to attract adoration, but when we reflect on this question, we realize that religion holds a large amount of power. Only a few years ago, the Catholic Church was exposed as one of the world's biggest financiers. People in general would be shocked if they could see how much finance is

Mantra Ten

invested in religious institutions, and how much manpower, womanpower, and influence they are able to wield. In some countries, religious lobbies affect the national policy. Often, what is accepted as standard is based upon the views of the dominant religion in that society. Even today, religious institutions cast a major influence on world affairs. Religious fanaticism is one of the negative by-products of this phenomenon. At times, people hide behind religion in order to engage in highly irreligious activities.

I once had a personal experience of this underhand inclination. One day, while I was at a small preaching center, a restaurant in Washington D.C., an old roommate from my college days suddenly appeared. Although we had studied together at Princeton, I had not seen him for a long time. He had graduated with Honors and continued his studies at Cambridge, at Yale, and at Harvard. He dabbled in various disciplines and received many degrees. Now, years later, he started to visit the restaurant frequently and would stay for hours. My old roommate would listen to philosophy, talk to different people, and ask many questions. While I knew that he was not very spiritual, I reasoned with myself that anyone could go through amazing changes in the association of devotees of the Lord. After a little while, however, he revealed to me the real reasons for his frequent visits. He was studying the process of becoming a *guru* in order to use the role for business purposes! I remembered that he was always clever in business. He analyzed the situation and concluded that one can obtain real money by becoming a spiritual leader. He thought of becoming an evangelist, an *imam*, or a *guru*, or occupying any type of spiritual leadership position in which he could have access to power and influence. He then intended to create his own quasi-religious organization for no other reason than to make money.

People like my old college roommate hold strange conceptions about religion. They view it as a tool with which they can easily exploit others for name, fame, and wealth. This is a very dangerous phenomenon. In some countries, institutions which train Christian ministers instruct their students in mind-control techniques such as neuro-linguistic programming. In this way, ministers are taught to wield power over crowds of people. These institutions guarantee that the size of their congregations will triple, or even quadruple in two years. They guarantee that their assets will double in six months. In essence, they turn religion into a performance. The ministers are taught to instruct the organist to play certain hymns in particular chords in order to manipulate the mood of the worshipers. They are trained to create strong feelings of guilt among those present. Subsequently, they ask those assembled to donate money. During specific points in the ceremony, the minister will stand at the podium, speaking about the need for the congregation to give more. Once people have given more money, another song is played and the collection plate is passed around again. Sometimes, the ministers play music with subliminal messages through the sound system, and even adjust the air conditioning to an optimal level to affect peoples' psyches. They treat religion as a marketable product, or as if it were some kind of game.

Certainly, all religious movements, including our own, are trying to convince other people to adopt their views to some extent. A desire to convert others is not necessarily bad. But we must ask ourselves, "What are we offering and what are our intentions?" Recently, the Catholic Church had a problem concerning the decline in the number of priests and nuns who wanted to join. In many monasteries and convents, the average age of the residents is sixty years old. Senior members of the Catholic Church realize that with the passing of time, preaching will become more and more problematic as every year many of the older renunciates retire or die, while fewer volunteers decide to join. This realization has spurred some religious institutions to use very sophisticated marketing companies to recruit new members. They advertise on bulletin boards and in magazines. Sometimes, they advertise a retreat, and then offer those who attend a chance to experience the church environment for a few weeks or months. They reason that a certain percentage of those who experience life in a monastery or convent will want to remain. Occasionally, the intention behind these attempts to influence others is basically good; that is, to inspire people to dedicate themselves to a genuine community of faith.

Unfortunately, however, people often simply create their own religions. By building a power base for themselves through the façade of faith, these con artists merely create confusion. Some bogus religious leaders purposely endeavor to maintain fragmentation, because they know that if warring factions come together, their own power base will be lost.

3. One should not become a source of anxiety to others by the actions of his body, by the thoughts of his mind, or by his words.

We are to be very kind and polite to others, even when we are faced with situations that may be distressing to ourselves. If we cause people anxiety, then they often become angry not only with us, but also with ISKCON and with Krishna. When this happens, we add to their suffering instead of helping them. When we represent ISKCON, we are engaging in devotional service and therefore we automatically carry some potency with us. When people assist us, they receive benefit and blessings. If they harass or offend us, they suffer a karmic reaction as a result. Even if somebody is a little uptight, we should try to be cordial and interact with him or her tactfully. We are to take a humble position so as not to hurt them.

4. *One should learn forbearance even in the face of provocation from others.*

A devotee always maintains a sense of equilibrium in order to reduce anxiety in others, even though he or she may have legitimate reasons to be disturbed. Sincere devotees meditate continuously about how to assist everyone in their environment. If they are not able to help, they will at least refrain from doing anything to worsen a problematic situation. Genuine devotees cultivate tolerance. They will study a situation to see what actions they can take to assist in a constructive way.

5. *One should learn to avoid duplicity in his dealings with others.*

It is very important to be straightforward in our interpersonal relationships. Duplicity means double-dealing. When we are duplicitous, it means that we do not honor and respect others. We are demonstrating that we do not fully accept Krishna as the ultimate witness. By engaging in deceit, we also show that we do not view other devotees as our masters. We address each other as *prabhu* in order to train ourselves in the position of servant. In the *Narada-pancaratra*, Narada Muni expands on this philosophy:

- When a devotee is senior to us, we should listen, serve, and try to get his or her mercy.

- When a devotee is our peer, we should seek his or her friendship, desiring to serve together and help each other.

- When a devotee is a subordinate, we should reach out and assist him or her in spiritual life.

There is no room for duplicity in Narada Muni's scheme of devotee relationships. In whatever way we approach devotees, service should always be central. When there is a lack of open communication and a presence of deception and dishonesty, the environment becomes one in which people do not trust each another. Lack of trust breeds speculation, fear, and overreaction. Eventually, due to the absence of strong love, trust, and appreciation, everyone in that environment suffers. Therefore, when problems arise, they should be discussed in an open and honest way.

In the Govardhana Hill pastime related in the Tenth Canto of *Srimad-Bhagavatam*, one of the pivotal themes is that saintly people do not keep secrets. At the beginning of this pastime, Krishna asks Nanda Maharaja why he was preparing to make elaborate offerings to Lord Indra. In His conversation with His father, Krishna explains that saintly people have neither enemies nor friends. They understand that all their associations are to benefit all parties involved. Likewise, in the devotee community, it is unhealthy to hold secrets. If we do have to keep certain information classified, we should regret that we have to do so for some unusual reason, but this should definitely not be our normal mode of operation. Some issues are naturally private; however, an organization which consistently operates on secrecy is a dysfunctional one. A culture of secrecy is indicative of a society riddled with faults, dishonesty, ambiguity, poor communications, lack of accountability, and great interpersonal distrust. No one can be a serious *bhakta* or *bhaktin* without considering his or her life to be an open book. We should say what we mean, and mean what we say. Whatever we say and do should always lead to quality association and relationships. If we are wrong, we should be ready to hear how to improve ourselves.

Cultivating healthy association among devotees is similar to building relationships within a family. A healthy family is one in which the children, the husband, and the wife openly discuss and resolve their issues. When problems arise such as sickness, anxiety, or fighting between siblings, they should be discussed openly so that they can be addressed and solved. In this way, peace will prevail in the home, as the family members understand their roles clearly. However, if the parents and the children are secretive or withdrawn, independently engaged in their own activities, communication will ultimately breakdown, and chaos will result. Similarly, in devotee interactions, genuine communication is essential for strong unity with diversity.

In whatever environment we find ourselves, we all have choices available to us. Sometimes, devotees are so secretive that nobody knows their real identity. Whether we go to college or to work, if our fellow students or colleagues do not have a basic understanding of our lifestyle, they will approach us in unhealthy ways. This is unavoidable because they are unaware of our principles or what constitutes our everyday life. However, if at least they understand that we do not eat meat, we do not engage in promiscuous activities, we do not gamble, and we do not take drugs, then they are less likely to entice us into such activities. But if, in reply to an invitation to visit a bar, we tell them, "Actually, since I drank a lot yesterday, I have decided to abstain for a while," they will naturally consider that we will drink alcohol at some time in the future. They will therefore present intoxication to us again. If we say, "I am on a diet right now, so I cannot eat hamburgers," they will think that in other circumstances, we will eat meat. They should clearly understand that meat-eating, intoxication, gambling, and illicit sex are not a part of our lifestyle. We do not place bets on horses, we do not play roulette, and we do not entertain extra-marital connections. Our associates must see that we have principles. If we are secretive about our ethics, however, then we should not be surprised when they expect us to engage in forbidden behavior. We must show them from our conduct that we will not involve ourselves in degraded activities. People will then honor our practices and, in many cases, will be very respectful. Although we may worry about being different, generally others will admire our high level of ethics and spirituality. They will be in awe as they observe how determined we are to maintain our principles. Occasionally, they will even want to change themselves because they will feel embarrassed about their conduct while in our presence.

6. One should search out a bona fide spiritual master who can lead him gradually to the stage of spiritual realization, and one must submit himself to such a spiritual master, render him service and ask relevant questions.

Much of the process of *bhakti* is based on guidance and mentorship. We learn by listening and watching those who are more astute than ourselves in devotional service. The bona fide spiritual master also studies his or her disciples in order to best ascertain how to encourage them in honoring *sadhu* and *sastra* according to time, place, and circumstance. By the rendering of selfless service to the *guru* and through making submissive inquiries, the disciple will make steady progress.

7. *In order to approach the platform of self-realization, one must follow the regulative principles enjoined in the revealed scriptures.*

Notice that Srila Prabhupada uses the word 'must,' thus conveying that abiding by the four rules and regulations is a non-negotiable requirement for the attainment of transcendental knowledge. However, it is not that by adhering to the rules and regulations alone we will receive true love of God. It is not that we can purchase the Lord in any mechanical way. These regulations act as mere prerequisites, setting the stage for us to receive the mercy of Krishna. Basically, the four rules and regulations assist us in becoming healthy human beings. They facilitate our absorption in the mode of goodness, but we do not necessarily become transcendental by adhering to them alone. First, we must be situated in the mode of goodness if we want to attain transcendence. If we do not abide by the regulations, then we cannot progress further in our spiritual lives. It follows logically that a student who has not completed his or her undergraduate studies successfully cannot achieve an advanced degree. Conversely, it holds true that simply by achieving the basic degree, we do not automatically become specialists. The principle is that by not completing the basic studies, we surely will not obtain the chance to become a specialist. The requirements for obtaining a general degree are different from those needed for specialization. Similarly, regulations merely serve as prerequisites to further our spiritual objectives.

Sometimes, we presume that all we need to do in order to go back to Godhead is to adhere to these four rules and regulations, especially in Kali-yuga. It is true that due to the difficulties associated with obtaining perfection in this fallen age, we all have the opportunity to become *krpa-siddhas*, which means attaining perfection not by our own efforts, but by the mercy of a great soul. If our spiritual master is sufficiently pleased, then he will complement what is deficient in us because we have been loyal. Srila Prabhupada promised that Lord Nityananda will reach out and shed His mercy on the soul who is faithful and sincere. Therefore, we should try to follow the rules and regulative principles very strictly, indicating by our efforts that we are really serious about receiving help. By this process, assistance will surely come. However, we should neither be like *karma-kandis*, who engage in fruitive activities, considering spiritual life to be merely a schemata of rituals, formulae, and axioms; nor like *karma-mimamsas*, who believe

Mantra Ten

the results of action take place automatically without the Supreme Lord; nor like *veda-vada-ratas,* who merely mouth the words of the scriptures without understanding them; nor like *mayayapahrta-jnanas,* who appear to be learned scholars, but who misunderstand the essence of *Vedanta.*

We cannot engage in spiritual activities without the proper consciousness and still expect full benefit because we are externally following prescribed rules. Krishna will not respond to that kind of business mentality. We must follow the rules because they help to elevate our consciousness, but more importantly, we must be available to receive Krishna's mercy. In one sense, following the rules and regulations is simply a token effort in attaining the true level of purity necessary to go back to Godhead. If we sincerely endeavor, Krishna will say, "Yes, you are Srila Prabhupada's devoted child. Come home to Me," or "Yes, you are Srila Prabhupada's sincere grandchild. Therefore, I will open the door to the spiritual world for you." In this way, we avail ourselves of the opportunity to receive the mercy.

8. One must be fixed in the tenets of the revealed scriptures.

In all our activities, we should always consult *sastra,* as the process of devotional service is understood through these holy texts. Study of the bona fide scriptures is foremost. *Sastra* enables us to comprehend the teachings of Krishna with clarity. When we minimize the *sastra,* we minimize the rules and regulations. Diminishing *sastra* causes *vinasyati,* destruction of our devotional creeper. Srila Rupa Gosvami confirms this in Text Two of his *Sri Upadesamrta,* adapted by Srila Prabhupada as *The Nectar of Instruction*:

> atyaharah prayasas ca
> prajalpo niyamagrahah
> jana-sangas ca laulyam ca
> sadbhir bhaktir vinasyati

> *One's devotional service is spoiled when he becomes too entangled in the following six activities: (1) eating more than necessary or collecting more funds than required; (2) overendeavoring for mundane things that are very difficult to obtain; (3) talking unnecessarily about mundane subject matters; (4) practicing*

> *the scriptural rules and regulations only for the sake of following them and not for the sake of spiritual advancement, or rejecting the rules and regulations of the scriptures and working independently or whimsically; (5) associating with worldly-minded persons who are not interested in Krishna consciousness; and (6) being greedy for mundane achievements.*

Sastra clearly defines those activities which help us advance, as well as those which stunt the growth of the devotional creeper.

9. One should completely refrain from practices which are detrimental to the interest of self-realization.

How do we know which activities are favorable and which are not favorable for our devotional service? This can be quite a complex problem, because sometimes what is favorable or not is relative to both the situation and to the conditioning of the individual devotee. If we simply speculate on what is favorable, we will certainly run into difficulties. One devotee might approach another, saying, *"Prabhu,* as you know, we are supposed to accept things that are favorable for our spiritual lives. Well, it is favorable for me to eat three helpings of *prasadam*; therefore, you should offer whatever is on your plate to me. Furthermore, the scripture explains that no one is the ultimate proprietor. Do you think that you are the real owner of your car? You should become more renounced, and let others use it—like me. One should live a simple life." Another devotee might say, "Krishna revealed to me in my heart that I should have a tape recorder because I need to hear more in order to advance faster. The Supersoul has informed me that you have the best tape recorder in the temple. In fact, He manifested that tape recorder simply so that you can make it available to me." We can rationalize any situation in this manner.

Many followers of the New Age movement make comparable types of proclamations, based on speculation. There is nothing to substantiate them because their movement has no spiritual mentor and no *sastra*. Everyone looks at the world through their own spectacles, which are distorted by their own contaminations and ambiguities. Therefore, we should see through the eyes of *sastra* when accepting that which is favorable and rejecting that which is unfavorable for our devotional lives. Taking the advice of the spiritual master and senior devotees when approaching *sastra* is indispensable.

It is important to gauge in a measurable way whether an activity is beneficial or detrimental to us. One method of measuring the spiritual worth of an activity is to honestly assess its result. We know that certain experiences exert a positive influence on our devotional lives when we:

- think of Krishna more often
- want to engage more in service to Krishna
- want to chant Krishna's name more frequently
- desire more association of the devotees
- have greater appreciation for the devotional process
- find that our attachment to material life drastically reduces

We know that experiences exercise a negative influence on our devotional lives when we:

- lose faith in Krishna
- find reasons to escape service
- feel less desire to chant
- want to avoid the association of the devotees
- feel embarrassed to come before the Deities of the Lord in our house or in our temple
- experience an increase in our material hankerings

We hear at the Sunday program that Krishna takes away whatever is not favorable to our Krishna consciousness. Throughout this life and throughout many past lives, we have been wandering the three worlds, desperately searching for some type of magic or miracle that can resolve all our problems. We pursue wealth, pray for our boyfriend or girlfriend to love us again, or escape into drugs and other addictions. Often, when we hear that Krishna will take everything away, we do not fully realize the power and beauty embedded in this principle. It is a sign of tremendous auspiciousness when unhealthy material desires and objects are taken away from us, because it means that Krishna is being particularly merciful. Krishna takes away many obstacles that may interfere with our devotion. Sometimes, He helps us in ways that catch us unprepared. We may look back on the past and see that even at a time when we may not have been interested in Krishna, He suddenly intervened in our lives. Even now, we may not anticipate His help. Frequently, we fail to realize that we are in fact the extremely fortunate beneficiaries of His unlimited munificence.

10. One should not accept more than he requires for the maintenance of the body.

What constitutes a healthy quota for each individual may be judged by the degree to which it has a constructive impact on that individual's Krishna consciousness. In order to avoid renunciation in the mode of ignorance, we must be honest with ourselves about how much material facility we need in order to progress optimally in spiritual life. Simultaneously, we should also avoid accepting unnecessary things in the mode of passion. As *Mantra One* of *Sri Isopanisad* states:

*isavasyam idam sarvam
yat kinca jagatyam jagat
tena tyaktena bhunjitha
ma grdhah kasya svid dhanam*

Everything animate or inanimate that is within the universe is controlled and owned by the Lord. One should therefore accept only those things necessary for himself, which are set aside as his quota, and one should not accept other things, knowing well to whom they belong.

The principle explained in this *mantra* is very significant in today's world, where many individuals, groups, and nations consume amounts of material goods which exceed what is healthy for them. Over-consumption inevitably causes many problems on the planet.

11. One should not falsely identify himself with the gross material body, nor should one consider those who are related to his body to be his own.

Great power may be derived simply by following this principle. When I give courses on loving relationships, I emphasize cultivating a deep understanding that everything belongs to Krishna. Krishna consciousness is a powerful, groundbreaking philosophy: it implies that even our children are not to be seen as our own. If we know that everything belongs to Krishna, we will treat everything in a way that will please Him. Therefore, items like shoes, a house, or a car—all sorts of paraphernalia—are to be dealt with properly. If Srila Prabhupada discovered a running garden-hose or a dripping tap when he went about his walks, he would immediately turn them off, because he saw everything as Krishna's energies. He would become disturbed when he saw us dishonoring Krishna's energies in some way. If we constantly see Krishna in all things and always think of Him, then we will never mistreat any of His energies or other living entities, who are His children. In *Bhagavad-gita* 9.34, Krishna says:

*man-mana bhava mad-bhakto
mad-yaji mam namaskuru
mam evaisyasi yuktvaivam
atmanam mat-parayanah*

Engage your mind always in thinking of Me, become My devotee, offer obeisances to Me and worship Me. Being completely absorbed in Me, surely you will come to Me.

If we always think of Krishna, He constantly manifests for us in different ways.

12. One should always remember that as long as he has a material body he must face the miseries of repeated birth, old age, disease and death. There is no use in making plans to get rid of these miseries of the material body. The best course is to find out the means by which one may regain his spiritual identity.

We have to undergo certain experiences due to our acceptance of a material body in this world. Instead of allowing this realization to overwhelm us, we can turn our attention instead to finding a permanent solution. We can achieve this by strengthening our devotional lives. Recognizing that we are in the age of Kali, we should not lament, but instead strive to tolerate the constant duality of the material world.

13. One should not be attached to more than the necessities of life required for spiritual advancement.

We have to be careful not to overendeavor in both our spiritual and material activities, as when we try to force things, we find ways to justify our ignorance and passion. If we persist despite the fact that our plans are not materializing as we anticipate, we reinforce the controller mentality. When Krishna does not allow certain events to take place in our lives, we should be alert to the fact that He is probably sending us a message to go in a different direction. We are to do our best, but if somehow our efforts do not bring us the desired result, we should not continue to strive unnecessarily. When Krishna is pleased, amazing things happen with just a little effort, even beyond what we could have planned. Conversely, when Krishna is not pleased, our repeated endeavor merely results in disappointment. When we receive such indications from Krishna, we need to change our behavior, and to work hard in some other areas. Depending on Krishna, we must always remember not to be attached to the ultimate results of our efforts.

14. One should not be more attached to wife, children and home than the revealed scriptures ordain.

When we are more attached to anything other than Krishna, it is extremely likely that we will take birth in another material body. Whether we are attached to our computer, new car, house, son, daughter, husband, or wife, if we do not identify them as agents of Krishna, then we are dangerously under the influence of *maya*. However, such relationships, when maintained in proper spiritual consciousness, can be very helpful. We can protect one another, compliment one another, and engage in *dharma*, while at the same time cultivating proper *sanatana-dharma*, our eternal occupation of devotional service to Krishna. When undertaken with proper consciousness, our day-to-day activities create auspiciousness. However, it is inauspicious to cultivate deep material attachments that are not healthy to spiritual advancement.

Family relationships cannot be neutral. Relationships incarcerate us when they distract us from keeping Krishna in the center of our activities. If we focus primarily on Krishna, however, all relationships immediately become auspicious. They then assist us in our endeavor to think of and serve Krishna more often. Creating auspicious relationships is a delicate undertaking because when we become involved with other conditioned souls, we risk allowing *maya* to entertain much of our consciousness. As a result, we may become distracted from our real spiritual identity. Therefore,

Mantra Ten

we must be careful not to be overly attached to our husbands or wives, children and homes, as advised by the revealed scriptures. We should aim to be *grhasthas*, not *grhamedhis*. A *grhastha* way of life pertains to a healthy domestic situation in which the family is taken care of materially, emotionally, and spiritually. A *grhamedhi* existence occurs when material demands and priorities push out basic spiritual concerns.

We should endeavor to structure our lives in such a way to ensure that we can maintain both the body and the soul. It is not easy to accomplish this balance successfully in Kali-yuga. *Grhasthas* must continuously check in with themselves to see whether they are jeopardizing their spiritual commitments. We must always ensure that our activities bring auspiciousness by being attentive in our chanting and in worshiping the Deity. We should always ask, "How can I be more focused on Krishna? Am I reading with rapt attention? Or am I drifting further and further away from *sravanam kirtanam visnoh smaranam*, namely, hearing, chanting, and remembering the Lord's glories, which are part of the ninefold process of *bhakti*?" Each of us has to be honest with ourselves. Sometimes, the nature of our occupations imposes negatively on our consciousness. If our work environment is destructive, we might have to consider changing to another type of job in which we can more easily place Krishna at the center of our activities.

15. One should not be happy or distressed over desirables and undesirables, knowing that such feelings are just created by the mind.

We should not get too disturbed by either happiness or distress. Rather, we should take shelter of transcendental knowledge, which will enable us to truly understand what is illusory and what is genuine. When we realize what constitutes genuineness, transitory events will not overly bother us. We will be able to bounce back from any negative experience quickly, instantly recognizing that we should not allow it to demoralize us.

16. One should become an unalloyed devotee of the Personality of Godhead, Sri Krishna, and serve Him with rapt attention.

Becoming an unconditional, loving devotee of the Lord means letting go of all fruitive motivations. We should strive to be free of all *misra*, or mixed intentions in our devotional service, as well as other activities that weaken our *bhakti-lata*. Mixed devotional service falls into three main categories: *karma-misra-bhakti*, when *bhakti* is disturbed by fruitive concerns; *jnana-misra-bhakti*, when devotional service is tainted by a fascination with knowledge based on mental speculation; and *yoga-misra-bhakti*, when it is contaminated by an infatuation with psychic phenomena. *Jnana-misra-bhaktas* are more captivated by what they can know than by what they can become. They pursue the course of *bhakti* while simultaneously striving to stimulate the intelligence. With rapt attention, we must become *suddha-bhaktas*, or pure devotees whose most important activity is the loving service of Krishna and His parts and parcels.

17. *One should develop a liking for residence in a secluded place with a calm and quiet atmosphere favorable for spiritual culture, and one should avoid congested places where nondevotees congregate.*

The key message here is the avoidance of excessive nondevotee association. When activities which do not include Krishna bombard our mind and senses, it becomes much easier for us to deviate from spiritual principles. We should therefore be selective about being in congregations of nondevotees. A devotee wants to use his or her time wisely by seeking out environments in which good devotee association and discussions about the Supreme Lord are to be found. On hearing this principle initially, some of us may think that it is acceptable to hide out in our rooms, in the attic, or in a special place that we designate as our *bhajana-kutira*. However, this kind of behavior is not recommended either, as very few devotees in the age of Kali are qualified to perform *nirjana-bhajana*, or solitary worship. Instead of meditating on Krishna, we may meditate on acquiring money or engaging in sex life. Therefore, spiritual practice in the association of other devotees is recommended for healthy spiritual life.

18. *One should become a scientist or philosopher and conduct research into spiritual knowledge, recognizing that spiritual knowledge is permanent whereas material knowledge ends with the death of the body.*

Srila Prabhupada concludes his purport on *Mantra Ten* with a discussion of *vidya* versus *avidya*. One who misuses *vidya*, or

Mantra Ten

knowledge, is worse than one who is in *avidya*, or ignorance. Srila Prabhupada writes that for us to really understand that we are not the body, we should associate with *dhiras*, or those who are steady, determined, and situated in transcendence. *Adhiras* are those who are not fixed, who tend to become distracted and drift away from Krishna. Although an *adhira* may attempt to embrace transcendence, without the shelter of a bona fide spiritual master, he or she courts nescience, ignorance, and passion. To become situated in transcendence, we are to be very clear about our spiritual goals, about what constitutes *siddhanta*, and about what is necessary to obtain the goal.

As Sri Caitanya Mahaprabhu instructs Sanatana Gosvami:

veda-sastra kahe – 'sambandha', 'abhidheya', 'prayojana'
'krishna' – prapya sambandha, 'bhakti' – praptyera sadhana

> *The Vedic literatures give information about the living entity's eternal relationship with Krishna, which is called sambandha. The living entity's understanding of this relationship and acting accordingly is called abhidheya. Returning home, back to Godhead, is the ultimate goal of life and is called prayojana*
> Sri Caitanya-caritamrta, Madhya-lila 20.124

If we sincerely desire to obtain the love of the Supreme Lord, then *sambandha*, *abhideya*, and *prayojana* must be understood with steady, rapt attention. We should meditate on these eighteen methods of obtaining knowledge given to us by Srila Prabhupada. As Srila Bhaktivinoda Thakura says, any methods outside of these are in the realm of nescience. To obtain real knowledge, we must engage in devotional service. Real knowledge sets the stage for us to understand the source of knowledge and nourishes the *bhakti-lata-bija* in the heart. Nescience causes us to think that we are God, and therefore we do not desire to take shelter of Krishna. Those activities that take us away from Krishna are rooted in nescience, while those that bring us closer to Krishna are situated in real knowledge.

Questions and Answers
Question: Maharaja, earlier you stated that saintly people should not have secrets, but according to *Caitanya-caritamrta*, Lord

Caitanya sometimes associated with His devotees in secret. How do we reconcile these two seemingly contrary pieces of information?

Answer: Yes, it is true that Lord Caitanya and His eternal associates sometimes held confidential *kirtanas*. Confidentiality was enforced, firstly, in order to prevent bewildering those who were not ready to behold the potency of love emanating from Lord Caitanya, and secondly, because these meetings were intimate and therefore kept genuinely private based on proper observance of etiquette. It is important to distinguish between confidentiality and keeping secrets. Some activities are righteously done in private and are not for public view. They are not a secret; they are simply confidential, because they constitute an intimacy between a certain group of people who have a special relationship. Secrecy, however, means an acceptance of the material duality. Mahatma Gandhi explains that secrecy is actually an act of violence, because secrecy implies that we are not ready to fully share with and trust one another. From time to time, we may find ourselves in circumstances in which we cannot fully reveal our mind and actions. This is unfortunate. We should be secretive only when it is absolutely necessary and with a sense of genuine regret.

It is a leadership principle that secrecy cuts down trust, and a lack of trust destroys synergy. Distrust also erodes the presence of love. As secrecy causes speculation, an environment in which secrecy is prevalent will naturally be filled with insecurity and anxiety. People in such an environment might overreact or fail to act when they should. Secrecy also results in poor communication. It breeds emotional distance, conscious or unconscious, which is not healthy. When we have a low-trust culture, all kinds of issues surface. There is posturing, and ultimately we are not really sure what is going on. This slows down many devotional activities. Is it not better to cultivate open communication and feedback instead?

What essentially produces a healthy family? A family is healthy when the children and parents communicate openly, lovingly, and sweetly. However, if a son keeps secrets, how can his parents possibly give him their full help? If a son has a problem and feels disturbed, his parents and his siblings want to be aware of the situation so that they can support him. Conversely, when he is happy and balanced, they want to rejoice with him and congratulate him. This is a healthy family.

We should not reveal our minds only when everything in our lives is going well. Actually, when we are struggling, we have even more reason to share because we are most in need of help at this time. When we cannot open up, we convey the message that we cannot trust one another. However, we must create an environment based on the spiritual world. Although this suggestion may sound idealistic, it is possible. Creating a transcendental atmosphere will help us to keep the goal of increasing our Krishna consciousness foremost. We must continue to work toward our goals or we will never reach them. We often think that keeping secrets is the norm, because this is how life works in the material world. Even as devotees, we often act under the material energy, reinforcing an unhealthy status quo by allowing negative situations to prevail. If we go along with the crowd, we will simply stagnate, engage in posturing, and create artificial relationships. Even if we are in the wrong, we should express our inner thoughts. Our heartfelt admission should be seen as a genuine offering to our peers or to our community, and consequently, we should be received with affection and care. Whether we offer or receive this type of honest exchange, we are to do it tactfully, with humility and with honesty. For example, if we know that a fellow devotee smokes a cigarette after *tulasi-puja*, then it is our duty to find some way to approach him or her and offer help with humility. Otherwise, it might become 'just our secret' or somebody else's secret if we discuss it with others without openly discussing it with the devotee in question.

Question: Is it not perhaps unrealistic to think that we can trust everyone, even in the devotee community?

Answer: Rupa Gosvami explains that it is natural for devotees to have certain idiosyncratic tendencies and to connect more intensely with specific types of association than with others. Because we are not impersonalists, we acknowledge that in particular kinds of relationships, a stronger chemistry is present, and that some relationships are smoother and run deeper than others. Actually, this is also true in the spiritual world, in which over three hundred thousand *gopis* align themselves differently even in their intimate services to Radha and Krishna. The *gopis* in Radharani's camp play the role of transcendental rivals to those in Candravali's camp. Some *gopis* are always on Krishna's side, others are always on Radha's side, while still others emerge in favor of Krishna sometimes, and Radha at other times. The spiritual world is amazingly variegated in terms of relationships, groups, services, and alignments. Similarly, we experience different levels of intimacy as we serve together. It is natural to share a more intimate relationship with some than we do with others.

It is unfortunate, however, when a devotee never really reveals his or her mind to anybody. Friendless devotees will fall down at some point, because nobody can survive in spiritual life by him or herself. We all need assistance. This is the main reason why we have association. When devotees experience problems, but do not reveal them to anybody, it means that they do not trust Krishna. They do not trust the Lord because they cannot see Him in anybody, nor do they perceive that He can offer them much assistance from within their own environment. Due to their weak faith, they create unhealthy mindsets for themselves. Of course, we may be selective in deciding with whom to open our hearts. But if we do not have an open relationship with a least one *sadhu*, then automatically we place ourselves in an unfortunate position. Our lack of relationship signifies that we do not feel surrounded by people who care about us, nor do we care about others, because our fear blocks us from giving.

In almost all societies of today, people cannot trust and have trouble with honesty. Some of these people become devotees. Frequently, they carry issues from previous lives, or this life, and feel too intimidated to communicate sincerely, afraid of reactions which they believe may come upon them. Also, they may find the environment too hostile. Due to our past conditioning, many of us maintain certain fears. Perhaps in the past, there were times when we tried to be revealing and people did not honor what we shared. Perhaps they did not appreciate our confidences, or even used them against us. Many of us carry immense psychological wounds. Sometimes, we have been disappointed by someone for whom we had respect, or who was an authority in our life. In America, one out of every three girls and about one out of every five boys is sexually abused. This type of abuse usually has quite a lasting effect on the consciousness. When someone who is supposed to offer a girl genuine affection, care, and protection is the same person who exploits her, she will naturally develop a mistrust for authorities. It will be extremely difficult for her to be fully trusting, because she has been wounded so deeply. A woman who has been sexually abused as a young girl may be so scarred emotionally that she will even continue this mood of distance with her own husband. However, as we go deeper and deeper into the devotional process, we find that we are able to deal with so many of these issues. Since so much of the mindset of the adult is formed from childhood

Mantra Ten

incidents, and even experiences in the womb, it is imperative that those devotees who have children try their best to give them all protection and care.

Of course, we should not be overly idealistic, and just trust anybody. We do not have to tell everything to everybody. The idea is simply that devotees should bond genuinely with one another. Then, when a problem arises, we will be able to talk it out. For instance, in so many places in the world, the divorce rate among devotees is very high. However, by addressing genuine problems with honesty and humility, divorce can be minimized, especially if the couple is ready to share their issues with a third party. There are times when a relationship needs the intervention of someone who cares about both parties involved. Often, each person in a relationship just sees his or her own point of view. A caring third party can assist the couple in clarifying the issue, in reaching some sort of compromise or understanding, and in determining how they can work together better on an ongoing basis. This is why fostering a strong culture of support is so important. For example, when the families of both the bride and the groom have participated in bringing the couple together initially, then everybody has a vested interest in seeing the marriage work. When problems arise, a support system is naturally in place to help the couple. And because both parties have faith in and affection for those who are able to assist them, they are much more ready to hear and appreciate any advice.

Unfortunately, nowadays couples who have issues usually try to work them out by themselves, but often they end up living under the same roof either tolerating or hating each other. Sometimes, they decide to consult a marriage counselor whom neither of them knows, and who sees them in exchange for a fee. As long as their clients pay for the consultation, most marriage counselors will not care if they never see the couple again. The counselor is often insensitive to the final outcome of the therapeutic process. However, when we have proper culture, the couple is able to approach an elder, someone who genuinely wants to see their relationship flourish, and who empathizes with their pain. This person will feel immensely happy if they can assist in resolving the relationship. When both parties appreciate the sincere intention of the elder, they are more likely to listen to any advice offered. When both parties are ready to listen to each other, it becomes easier to reach a resolution.

In our society, many cases occur in which both *grhasthas* and renunciates experience problems, but do not feel comfortable enough to share them with anybody. Problems fester like cancer, and then one day, we find that those devotees are no longer with us. It is a big loss to everyone if a devotee begins to have doubts in some areas, but we lack an open culture of sharing. Perhaps a devotee may think, "How is it possible for Lord Brahma to have four heads? In the morning, we dance around a little plant. Just by dancing around her, all my sins will be relieved? Everyday, this philosophy seems more and more obscure to me." If devotees consistently meditate in this way without being able to clarify their doubts with a sensitive authority, one day they will leave because they will think, "I cannot continue with this *bhakti-yoga* any longer because it is all mythology."

In general, when we have good intentions and aspirations, then whatever we share helps everyone. Healthy openness helps people feel positive because it communicates that the goals are genuine, the process is real, and the support system is bona fide. We want to continue to clarify the goals of Krishna consciousness month after month, year after year. We want to examine how we can honor the process as a transcendental one, while bringing less and less duality into it. When duality is pushed further and further away, then we align ourselves in genuine practice for what we are to do eternally. We must practice sincerely now for what will be our perpetual occupation. A culture of love cannot flourish in an atmosphere of secrecy. Secrecy rests on fragmentation, not wholesomeness. Secrecy is about hiding instead of giving, communicating, and sharing.

Mantra Eleven

*vidyam cavidyam ca yas
tad vedobhayam saha
avidyaya mrtyum tirtva
vidyayamrtam asnute*

Only one who can learn the process of nescience and that of transcendental knowledge side by side can transcend the influence of repeated birth and death and enjoy the full blessings of immortality.

Making Healthy Distinctions

In *Mantra Eleven*, the speaker of *Sri Isopanisad* places the culture of nescience in a parallel relationship with that of transcendental knowledge. He writes that by understanding these two aspects simultaneously, we can experience the full blessings of immortality. Nevertheless, we must be aware of the danger that lies in misunderstanding this statement. This *mantra* may be misinterpreted to mean that there is nothing wrong with nescience, deviation, and offenses as long as they are accompanied by transcendental knowledge. When Lord Brahma constructed this universe, he first created aspects of nescience, such as false ego, bodily identification, and attachments. Only after he manifested these nescient factors did Lord Brahma create the knowledge factors such as *tapasya* and the various systems of *yoga*. Since nescience is indeed part of the universal design, various philosophical and religious thinkers sometimes interpret this fact to signify that deviation is an acceptable part of life on this planet.

People who are influenced by this conception of ethical behavior sometimes approach devotees, saying, "What do you folks mean, that it is unhealthy and non-spiritual to eat flesh? God created animals and plants so that we can have dominion over them. We are obviously made to rule over other life forms. God is good; therefore, all that God creates is also good. We do not see any problem with eating meat." In such a situation, devotees may seize the opportunity to defeat this kind of deceptive argument by replying, "God also created poisonous snakes, diseased rats, and cockroaches, so why not eat them as well? Yes, God is responsible for the creation of all forms of life, even the various aspects of the human species. God has created your sons, daughters, and friends. They are also good, so why not eat them, too?" Clearly, we need to make distinctions between what is appropriate and healthy, and what is inappropriate and unhealthy in particular situations.

Life is about making distinctions and acting according to what is proper. A healthy life is one of accountability rather than one of exploitation, in which we use whatever exists in an improper way. *Mantra Eleven* implies that in order for us to attain the full blessings of immortality, we must cultivate an understanding of nescience together with transcendence. To comprehend this concept properly, we need to look a little closer at what it truly means. Does it indicate that it is acceptable to engage in sinful activities as long as these activities are accompanied by some sort of penance? For example, a devotee may engage in sinful activities and then chant some extra rounds to counteract the offense. Ultimately, this behavior is unacceptable; it will weaken the devotional creeper because it involves the seventh offense, committing sinful activities on the strength of chanting the holy names of the Lord. It is offensive to possess knowledge, to engage in sinful activities, and then subsequently to perform another pious activity to counteract that sin.

To knowingly commit sin minimizes the importance of a proper lifestyle. In fact, this type of conduct is worse than *bhoga-tyaga*, which Srila Prabhupada describes as a "vicious cycle of alternating sense gratification and renunciation" (*Srimad-Bhagavatam* 11.5.33, purport). Essentially, engaging in these kinds of activities communicates the message that we wish to play mind-games with God. We may attempt to bargain with Him. "Okay, God," we may think, "I know You are the great autocrat and You are going to chastise me for my wrongdoings. Therefore, I will try to please You and flatter You so that You will leave me alone! I know what I did was sinful, but take these austerities and penances, which I give as a little bribe to You." On the one hand, we know that this behavior is not proper, but, on the other hand, *Mantra Eleven* appears to indicate that this sort of duality may be permissible. How do we understand duality as Vaisnavas? We should understand what constitutes sinful life in order to know which activities to avoid, and ultimately to gain liberation from repeated birth and death.

Mantra Eleven

Liberation via Material Indulgence?
Certain philosophies point the way to liberation via a mountain of material experiences. One theory proposes that by engaging in material enjoyment, we will eventually burn out and hence be freed from attachment. It is based on the hypothesis that in order to become liberated from worldly bondage, a person must first become extremely attached to the objects of the senses. The professed result is that one will become so frustrated by engaging with such objects that renunciation will follow in due course. The Osho movement of Bhagwan Sri Rajneesh (1931-1990) is one such organization which propagates this type of contaminated Eastern philosophy. Sometimes, people live out their lives cultivating bad habits in the hope that by going wild, eventually they will become disgusted. Logically, it follows that if this kind of consciousness gave liberation, then the pig would be the most elevated species. The pig, whose body is geared towards sense gratification, will eat anything, including stool. They enjoy wallowing in mud, and are so lusty that they will even enter into sexual liaisons with their own little piglets. They have no sense of restriction.

Medical science has shown repeatedly that free indulgence in drugs, whether prescribed or illegal, leads to dependence rather than to aversion. Normally, when a person takes addictive substances, his or her body requires increasingly larger doses to achieve satiation. Eventually, the addict imbibes the drug simply to avoid sickness. Clearly, by absorbing ourselves in sinful acts, an automatic disgust and disengagement usually will not occur. Educating ourselves about the dangers of taking drugs, however, is not the same as experimenting with them. We cannot advance simply by identifying what is to be done. This knowledge is only partial. If we know only what is proper, we will eventually encounter problems, as we will not have a clear understanding about what is improper. Inappropriate situations can then sneak into our life space and bewilder us because we lack realization concerning what should be avoided on the path of Krishna consciousness.

The Vedic scriptures supply us with a catalogue of what constitutes both proper action and inappropriate conduct. *Pravrtti* and *nivrtti* form the building blocks of *sadhana-bhakti*, or devotional service in practice. *Pravrtti* are those activities in which we should engage in order to achieve the goal of devotional service, while *nivrtti* are those which we should avoid. In the *Bhakti-rasamrta-sindhu*, Srila Rupa Gosvami lists sixty-four principles which will help us achieve *bhava* and subsequently *prema*. The sixty-four principles include both positive and negative injunctions. With such principles as a basis for our spiritual practice, advancement will naturally occur. We should always be aware of the *siddhanta*, but, at the same time, we need to be cognizant of how Maya presents herself so that we will not be captured. We do not need to experience flesh-eating, intoxication, gambling, or illicit affairs to understand that these will short-circuit our spiritual lives. However, it is imperative that we understand *why* we are to shun such activities. When we can clearly distinguish between what is right and what is wrong through transcendental knowledge, then we have access to a very powerful catalyst for spiritual advancement.

Discernment Strengthens Determination

While we must be mentally lucid about the various steps for accelerating devotional service, we also have to be wary of some of the hindrances. In this way, we will be able to attain immortality. This verse does not mean that sinful life and devotional life go hand in hand. It means exactly the opposite—that sin and piety are conversely related. Maturity of consciousness is required in order for us to progress; progression means knowing what is to be done and acting accordingly, as well as knowing what should be avoided and why. If we know what is to be done and what is to be avoided without understanding the reasons behind these injunctions, eventually we will lose our impetus for spiritual life. If someone simply tells us to avoid an activity without explaining the deeper reason behind the sinful behavior, we will still fall prey to illusion. We grow by engaging in *sadhana-bhakti* in the proper way, and by rooting out the weeds, or offenses. In the scriptures, we find many descriptions that will help us identify the weeds, which can strangle our devotional creepers. Once we know what the enemy looks like, then we can stand guard.

As we begin to appreciate what the goal entails, we will find the determination to keeping moving towards it, because it will become clearly delineated in our consciousness. If we do not have the goal in mind, then how will we know what direction to take? A well-known proverb succinctly elucidates this point: "If you don't know where you are going, any road will do." If we do not identify the goal vividly, then we will not be able to gauge whether or not we are advancing towards it and to what degree. If we lack understanding, then a person can be fully or partially engulfed by nescience and not even be aware of it!

Another dimension to the principle of knowing described here concerns the degree of potency with which we undertake our devotional service. The more we understand why certain activities are to be performed, the more spiritually potent they become. Although individuals can engage in the devotional process without being aware and still receive some credit, understanding evokes exponential benefit. For example, if guests at a festival purchase *prasadam* with the primary goal of satisfying their hunger, then they will not attain the same benefit as those who buy with the understanding that the food is a manifestation of the Lord's mercy. Those who act in knowledge attain far greater blessings than those who act out of ignorance.

Another example relates to the benefit derived from purchasing one of Srila Prabhupada's books. If someone buys a book from a book distributor in order to read about fantastic mysteries and war stories, they will receive some blessings, but if the same person purchases the book in order to read about God and our relationship with Him, then the transaction becomes even more potent. Our daily worship of Srimati Tulasi-devi, a pure devotee of the Lord who manifests in this world in the form of a plant, serves as another good example of this principle. If visitors at a temple water Tulasi merely because the *pujari* prompts them to do so, they will profit spiritually even though they may not understand her true identity. However, if we realize that Tulasi is a pure devotee of the Lord, and we wish to serve her by bathing her, then we gain tremendously. We should understand clearly the reasons for our activities in order to draw more potency from the experience. It is also important that we explain our activities properly to others. As we deepen our understanding, our motivation to continue in the devotional process increases. If our understanding does not grow, we will lose our conviction in spiritual life and may even find ourselves leaving the process.

Sometimes, when a new devotee joins the movement, they end up feeling harassed rather than blissful because they cannot seem to do anything right. They are told not to leave their bead bag on the floor; not to enter the restroom while wearing a *harinama cadar*, or a shawl decorated with the holy names of the Lord; or not to turn their backs to the Deity. As a result, the new *bhakta* or *bhaktin* feels self-conscious, as if everyone is against him or her. The new devotee should not be made to feel as if they are under attack, but rather they should be educated nicely in what is proper. If we explain why we enforce so many rules, new devotees may begin to see for themselves the necessity of maintaining a particular code of conduct in the devotional environment. Because Krishna consciousness is such a fertile culture, everything must be done in such a way to facilitate our service to Krishna. When we attempt to train new devotees, we should keep in mind that education, or specifically explaining the reasons for certain observances, is far more effective than mere chastisement.

Should Indulgence Precede Renunciation?

When the movement first started in America, most of the people who joined came from the upper middle-class or the middle-class economic strata. For such people, renunciation was not too difficult because they were aware of the complexities that accompanied the materialistic way of life. These people understood that an opulent lifestyle did not make them or their families happy, and were consequently open to exploring alternative lifestyles which included austerity. Conversely, in many of the less developed parts of the world in which we preach today, many find it more difficult to embrace austerity. When we tell people who have never experienced many of the trappings of the material world to renounce it as an illusion, they feel that this request is premature. Often, these people need to experience firsthand the allurements of *maya* before they can take to spiritual life seriously. Indulging in the material energy is a dangerous activity, however, because it may bewilder us to such an extent that we may fail to reconnect with spiritual life later on.

Often, it is difficult for a person to renounce activities of sense gratification if the mind is always meditating on missed experiences, wondering what they would have been like. For example, individuals who have never indulged in sexual activity are usually curious. While the position of a *naistika-brahmacari*, or a lifetime celibate student, can be very exalted, sometimes it is easier for someone to genuinely renounce material life after they have indulged in sexual experiences. Generally, those who have never experienced sex life will be fascinated by it, but after their curiosity is satisfied, they may find that it no longer holds such excitement for them. This situation is similar to that of a weary traveler, who, through various sojourns, realizes that one place is much like another. After having reached countless destinations, the traveler finds his or her travel-lust quelled. However, the abatement of desires for either the traveler or the sexual adventurer is not guaranteed. By nature, the senses are meant to bewilder the living entity. Our tendency is to succumb to pleasurable experiences, and, as we become habituated to them, we desire more.

Maya-devi will not leave us alone even after we have surrendered to her attractions. Tempting us to indulge in drugs, meat, gambling, and illicit sex, this pure devotee of the Lord will not admit defeat. On the contrary, once we yield to her, she pushes us more. Maya whispers, "What is your problem? Why do you now refuse to take intoxication? Don't you remember the rush you felt, the ecstasy? Why are you abandoning me? Although you are wearing a *dhoti* or a *sari*, I'm not fooled. You're the same person you always were, so why are you trying to ignore what brings you pleasure? We both know you would like to experience it yet again." The more we give in to sense gratification, the more Maya kicks us, but by cultivating the side-by-side knowledge suggested in this verse, we can gain an understanding of how she works without having to indulge in sinful experiences. Situated firmly in knowledge, *we can say NO and really mean it.*

Developing a Higher Taste

Even though most of us have succumbed to sense gratification in the past, Krishna enables us to develop a higher taste through the power of devotional service. By engaging in service, we acquire realization. Shifts in consciousness occur within us, causing allurements that would have attracted us previously to lose their appeal. For instance, most devotees feel repulsed by the scent of cooking flesh, which frequently bombards us as we walk past a restaurant. If acquaintances invite us to eat a hamburger with them at McDonald's, we will usually have no desire, for two reasons: firstly, we have acquired a higher taste, and secondly, we understand the reasons for not indulging in meat-eating with our intelligence. However, desire will become a problem if either philosophical understanding or a genuine replacement for the lower taste is lacking. If we have knowledge, understanding, and an alternative situation into which we can repose our energies, then there will be no problem. Understanding the karmic perils of meat-eating, we become more motivated to search out a replacement, such as a 'veggie burger,' which is many times more enjoyable than the ground body parts of cows sandwiched between two slices of bread.

Despite the fact that we may have developed a higher taste and a proper philosophical understanding, renunciation can sometimes still be difficult when attachments to sense gratification are present in the consciousness, and when the seeds of sin exist despite access to higher knowledge. Occasionally, individuals come to Krishna consciousness who have already lost the taste for sinful activities. Even though they have not undergone many experiences of sense gratification in this lifetime, they tackle spiritual life with a certain focus as the result of past-life indulgences. Because previously they experimented with the material energy and were disappointed, such people find that they are naturally motivated to adhere to austerity.

We do not necessarily have to experience nescience in this life or in a previous life to become discouraged, but often, this is the case. However, if we cultivate sharp intelligence, we can distinguish between what is truly beneficial for us and what is detrimental to us by hearing from *sadhu, sastra,* and *guru,* without needing to come into direct contact with the illusory energy. By clear mental vision, we can evaluate certain indicators to determine that improper actions produce unhealthy results. We understand that if we commit a certain action, a specific result will occur. If we commit a sinful act, then we will have to experience an inauspicious reaction. The dull child has to be punished several times to realize that if he or she does something wrong, suffering will follow. More intelligent children will be able to understand simply by listening to the reasoning of their parents that they are to refrain from certain activities. Intelligent children consider that their parents are acting out of love for them; therefore, they understand that any instruction they receive is for their own benefit. These children will abstain from harmful activities on their own accord, because they realize that the advice of their parents is an expression of care and concern, and that following it will produce auspiciousness. When there is proper dedication and attention, proper behavior automatically follows.

Dodging Death Is Futile

In his purport to this particular verse, Srila Prabhupada emphasizes the Sanskrit word *amara,* meaning 'immortal,' and explains it in connection with the story of Hiranyakasipu. Hiranyakasipu was a powerful demon who, by dint of his great austerities, was able to request any boon from Lord Brahma. Desiring initially the benediction of immortality, Hiranyakasipu was unable to obtain it directly because Lord Brahma himself is mortal. Subsequently, Hiranyakasipu sought a number of guarantees from Lord Brahma that he thought would safeguard him from death indefinitely. He obtained blessings which prevented him from being killed by any mortal being, at any time of the day, and within any of the five elements. Although Hiranyakasipu cultivated only nescience, and not transcendental knowledge, he nevertheless was convinced that he could counter the laws of material nature by his own intelligence. Ultimately, however, all the benedictions he extracted from Lord Brahma failed to protect him from death, as he was ignorant of both the true significance of immortality and the means to attain it. Hiranyakasipu was ultimately defeated by Lord Nrsimhadeva, the form of the Lord as half-man, half-lion who bifurcated the demon with his long, beautiful nails. By hearing this pastime, we can learn that worshiping the demigods is not a very elevated activity, as any boon they may grant us can be superseded very easily by Krishna's desire. No matter how intelligent we may be, in due course of time inauspiciousness will certainly occur if we do not connect with transcendence.

In his purport, Srila Prabhupada explains that people in general think they are not going to die. Since time immemorial, most cultures have offered myths, which engage the imagination in pursuits for eternal life within the physical body. Many have searched for the mythical 'fountain of youth,' or have attempted to manufacture certain potions which ostensibly help to slow down the ageing process. Governments and scientists also participate in undertakings of physical preservation. Around the world, different regimes build bomb shelters in the hope that, if a war occurs, their people will survive. Nowadays, we are confronted with genetic manipulation on a widespread basis. Sometimes, people who are terminally ill spend millions of dollars for their bodies to be frozen in the hope that in the future, when a cure is found for their illness, they will be able to regain their life again. However, the hard truth is that all entities in the material world have to give up their physical bodies at some point. Even when spiritually elevated beings come into this world, usually they leave in the same way as conditioned entities—by quitting the material body. In some rare cases, elevated beings leave in the self-same body, but in most cases the physical body is given up. The material body is essentially composed of ignorance and passion; therefore, it is destined to deteriorate, and eventually, it will be destroyed.

Advice from the Expert Preacher

Many years ago, when Srila Prabhupada was still on the planet, I used to be part of a traveling preaching team consisting of two *sannyasis* and a group of *brahmacaris*. We used to visit colleges and universities in various parts of the country and stage preaching programs. Once, we wrote a letter to Srila Prabhupada expressing some of the frustrations we encountered. We would visit many different schools throughout the day and do *harinama*, pass out flyers, distribute books, and invite people to attend evening programs, which we would usually hold in a local hall. Although we would distribute flyers and books for hours on end to hundreds of people, only a handful would actually attend the programs. Sometimes, half a dozen *brahmacaris* would preach the entire day, but only three of four people would arrive that evening. Even among the handful of people who did attend the meetings, none of them would turn up regularly. As a result, we wrote to Srila Prabhupada and asked him if our efforts were really worthwhile. Srila Prabhupada wrote back telling us that even if nobody came, we should preach to the walls. The lesson was quite clear. We had received an order and we should execute it, relinquishing the fruits of our endeavor to Krishna. If only one or two people attended and became serious, or even if we managed merely to plant the seed of *bhakti* in their consciousness, then our mission was successful. There was no need to expect guests to renounce everything and join us after they had attended two meetings; neither should we feel discouraged if they did not return.

Srila Prabhupada expertly advised us how to go about preaching at the universities and colleges. He emphasized that we should tread lightly when mentioning the activities from which devotees are meant to refrain. I specifically remember him saying, "Do not go and preach only rules and regulations to the students." His mood was that we should simply stress the depth of the Krishna consciousness philosophy. If we just sermonized, saying "Don't do this," and "Don't do that," students would think that we were fundamentalists and bureaucrats. They were already repulsed by the idea of organized religion. If they only heard "DON'T!", then they would close off their minds completely and leave. They would have no desire to be favorable to our movement if, for example, we said, "Oh, you eat flesh? Then you are on the road to hell, and will take a very low birth. You are trying to be intelligent, Mr. Scholar, but just wait and see! You will come back as a simple donkey who won't be able to read or write." However, if we created in them an understanding of how the philosophy can give insight into life and higher realities, they would become more encouraged. If we highlight the positive by communicating the real mystery connected with religion, then naturally people will be attracted to our movement.

Mantra Eleven

Avoiding Extremes

Consider what happens to a child who is constantly told, "Don't do this," and "Don't do that." A dysfunctional child is created who is consequently so nervous about every little action that he or she is even afraid to do the right thing. Such children cannot really understand what is proper, because they are so hurt and bewildered. Alternatively, if knowledge is exchanged in a mood of love and affection, then the result will be a healthy child. In the early days of the movement, we were too restrictive with our children. All they heard was "DON'T!", and as a result, when they became a little older and more independent, they wanted to experience all the things we told them not to do. As a young *sannyasi*, occasionally I would take some of the younger boys who used to attend the *gurukula* traveling with me. One of the *gurukula* boys who accompanied me rejected the philosophy of his parents due to the negativity with which it was communicated. During our travels, I would usually give *Bhagavad-gita* class in the evenings. This young boy would attend the classes, but by the time I had finished chanting *Jaya Radha-Madhava*, I would discover that he had disappeared. He would always arrive back just in time to catch the end of the class. One day, I asked him what he did while he was absent.

He told me that, while growing up, he felt he had been deprived of a whole world out there. All he knew about life was chanting *slokas*, playing harmonium and *mrdanga*, and hearing about the evils of this world. Since he had only heard about the nescience of materialism, he felt that he should explore it for himself to discover whether or not it was true. As we traveled throughout America, he would go to the drugstores in order to leaf through magazines, and then he would go out onto the street and just observe the people talking, smoking, and cursing. He would simply sit there and observe. As the result of only being told what *NOT* to do, this boy had acquired an unhealthy attitude towards Krishna consciousness. A form of education which just emphasizes negative instruction is immature; we must find a proper balance between discipline and experience through which knowledge can be conveyed in a positive way.

Parents, as caretakers of their children's lives, naturally desire to protect them. However, using scare tactics is ineffective. Rather, we should explain to children why they should avoid deviant behavior in a way which will sound reasonable to them and will not be interpreted as just another imposition. As discussed, if we revert to citing DO'S and DON'TS, it is highly probable that our children will do the opposite. At the same time, we cannot allow them complete freedom to do exactly what they want in the spirit of letting them learn from their own mistakes. Srila Prabhupada sometimes recounted a story about a son who ended up going to jail because his parents gave him too much freedom. It seems the parents did not care enough to set guidelines or to discipline him when he was a child. As a result, he engaged in all sorts of sinful activities, and ended up in prison on death row. Before he was executed, he called for his mother. Leaning over, as if to whisper something confidential, he bit off her ear in retribution for the lack of guidance he received while growing up.

To let children do whatever they want is like placing them in a boat without a rudder. Inevitably, they will drift into all sorts of calamities. Sending children out into the world without any kind of guidance and without endowing them with an ability to steer themselves properly is disastrous not only for them, but for society in general. It is sad that this kind of upbringing has become popular in recent years, because it leads to an unhealthy type of freedom which cannot fail to produce problems.

Srila Prabhupada educated us to avoid extremes. On the one hand, we were told to steer clear of engaging in unrestricted freedoms which lead to nescience, while on the other hand, we were instructed not to force transcendental knowledge on people without invoking clarity, understanding, and appreciation. It is a fairly well-known phenomenon in the material world that sometimes the children of church ministers and judges become the most degraded of people, because they naturally rebel against rules which are heavily enforced upon them all the time. If the children of a minister grow up under the continual threat of hell and the Devil, they will probably lose the desire to adhere to moral principles. However, if knowledge is imparted to them in a healthy, balanced way, then they will be motivated to follow accordingly. *Mantra Eleven* conveys the profundity of understanding the essence with proper balance.

Institutional Knowledge or Misinformation?

The year I received my degree from Princeton, all the graduates were asked to make statements, which were to appear next to our photographs in the annual yearbook. These statements were supposed to serve as mementoes by which alumni could remember one another. When the yearbook editors asked me what I had to say about Princeton University, I told them that I felt so indebted to the institution because it had assisted me in perceiving what I did NOT want to do with my life and what I did NOT want to become. From my experiences there, I knew very definitely that I desired to become neither a materialist nor an academic. As a student, I noticed that while my professors possessed so much material knowledge, their lifestyles were base and immoral. Many of them were alcoholics and chain-smokers, who resorted to substance abuse because they were keeling over from the pressure to perform. In academic circles, the expression 'publish or perish' is used to convey the demands placed upon professors to write articles and books. These people were considered to be some of the best educators in their fields in America at that time, but in actuality, they were struggling and miserable.

Nowadays, the fees to attend institutions such as Princeton are exorbitant. A single year's tuition may cost up to $40,000 dollars. A four-year undergraduate degree costs on average at least $160,000. A person could spend the rest of his or her life simply trying to pay back the student loan. Perhaps by the time he or she reaches old age, the fees may be repaid. Finally, the individual may even be able to afford to return for postgraduate studies. By this time, however, it may be too late. It is unbelievable that people actually pay so much money to learn misinformation. Princeton was and still is one of the most expensive schools on the planet. On completing my studies, I felt so happy due to the realizations I attained from undergoing that experience. Subsequently, I became more fixed in my determination to take up spiritual life. My experience demonstrates that there are times when suffering a certain degree of nescience can help us to move forward by deepening our spiritual convictions.

Many people who have not had the opportunity to attend university may be infatuated with the mystique surrounding that environment. However, Srila Bhaktivinoda Thakura explains that the longer one is convinced by misinformation, the duller one is. Some people have to attain many degrees in material knowledge before they begin to appreciate that there is more to life than textbooks. If we are able to understand the futility of this system of acquiring knowledge earlier on in life, then we can count ourselves fortunate. When university education is used in Krishna's service, however, it becomes a spiritual asset. If we have been educated, then we should engage our skills in His service. We should bear in mind that the simultaneous cultivation of an understanding of nescience and transcendence is recommended by this *mantra*. Therefore, if we attend university merely to cultivate relative knowledge, then that is to our dishonor. Conversely, if we believe that there is no value in material knowledge, we may be doing ourselves a disservice, also. As we have material bodies and are situated in the material world, we will often be faced with the need to utilize the material energy to connect more intensely with spirituality. In my experience, preaching is often enhanced when it is undertaken by devotees who have attended university, and who apply what they have gained materially to assist in spreading Lord Caitanya's mission.

The Illusion of Wedded Bliss

Another institution in Western society, which is shrouded in myth, is that of marriage. While marriage offers some positive benefits, it is also fraught with difficulties and challenges. Despite this reality, most devotees need to undertake marriage at some point. One of the most powerful advantages of marriage lies merely in undergoing the experience. Once they have been married, devotees often acquire a sense of having 'been there and done that.' Thereafter, the ideas and desires surrounding mundane romance no longer bother them to the same degree. If we have committed ourselves to a marital situation, we must use the experience to keep focused on serving Krishna. To concentrate on the goal of life in this *asrama* is not always so easy, but, at the same time, it does not have to be so difficult. The difficulty of keeping Krishna in the center arises when people are narcissistic and not really ready to communicate and to understand each other's needs and concerns.

Most people should marry in order to attain the realization that *wedded bliss is an illusion*. As a result of undergoing this experience, devotees' minds become less agitated because they appreciate that no perfection can be found in this material world, and that no other conditioned soul can make us as happy as we were perhaps anticipating. Once we realize this truth, we can go on with our lives, or as Srila Prabhupada puts it in his purport, "To make the best use of a bad bargain" (*Sri Isopanisad*, 80). Srila Prabhupada evokes this expression to describe material life in general, as usually most things that we do in this realm leave us feeling cheated. It is natural that at some stage we will become overwhelmed, discouraged, and disappointed by this world. At this point, we have a choice—we can either develop a defeatist mentality and become dysfunctional, or we can recognize that the world is indeed a bad bargain, but still try to see how to minimize its complexities in order to concentrate on Krishna.

One of the reasons why marriages often fail is an over-romanticized view of the conjugal relationship held by one or both partners.

When problems arise, they will seem insurmountable if the couple thinks that there were not supposed to be any problems in the first place. This phenomenon also occurs when people enter our devotional communities with the assumption that everyone around them is a pure devotee. However, soon they will see that some devotees possess large amounts of what is colloquially called 'attitude.' Subsequently, these new members experience personal conflicts and anxieties due to their prior misconceptions. Before joining, they were idealistic, but when they see the realities of the devotional environment, problems start to arise, and they may even leave.

When people are unnaturally euphoric about an institution such as ISKCON or a relationship like matrimony, then it becomes very difficult to build healthy relationships. However, when we understand that certain challenges will arise and that misunderstandings will occur, then we can be prepared to see how we can work through them. Again, we must cultivate knowledge of the positive aspects alongside an appreciation of the problems. Keeping a healthy balance brings about a great sense of well-being.

Studying the Experiences of Others

While exploring this *mantra*, we have seen that mixing nescience with transcendence is not recommended. Rather, it communicates that a person must acquire an *understanding* of nescience. The experience of nescience may or may not be required, but understanding is so vital. As discussed previously, in the early years, most of those who joined the movement came from so-called successful and wealthy backgrounds. Since they knew that an opulent lifestyle did not necessarily make them happy, it was not difficult for them to take to Krishna consciousness. It is easier to renounce that which one understands to be not very wonderful.

Nonetheless, experience is not always necessary for renunciation. An understanding of nescience can come from previous lifetimes or through study. By observing the effects of certain situations on others, we can logically infer that if we were to enter a similar situation, we would experience comparable suffering. In this way, we can avoid going through particular material experiences. What is certain is that we cannot avoid death and have eternal happiness without aligning ourselves with transcendence. We can be as clever as possible in our dealings with the material energy, but ultimately we will run into obstacles if we do not surrender to Krishna. Hiranyakasipu, for example, was most intelligent. He was so clever that he was able to extricate benedictions from Lord

Brahma himself, which appeared to protect him from all angles. He thought, "Now, I am immortal." But because his mindset was dominated by nescience, his attempts failed wretchedly.

Gratitude Is Essential

At the end of his purport, Srila Prabhupada quotes a verse spoken by Suta Gosvami as he instructs the sages gathered at Naimisaranya, in which he summarizes the culture of *vidya*:

> *tasmad ekena manasa*
> *bhagavan satvatam patih*
> *srotavyah kirtitavyas ca*
> *dhyeyah pujyas ca nityada*
>
> *Therefore, with one-pointed attention, one should constantly hear about, glorify, remember and worship the Personality of Godhead, who is the protector of the devotees.*
> Srimad-Bhagavatam 1.2.14

Krishna consciousness is a constant growth process; we will never reach a point at which we cannot become more serious or gain a greater understanding. We should never come to a point at which we feel that we do not have to work on ourselves anymore. As a matter of fact, the more we become involved in Krishna consciousness, the more we see *anarthas*, or unwanted desires in the heart, that we need to work on. As we appreciate the devotees more, and as we attribute greater value to what it really means to become Krishna conscious, then automatically we will have more gratitude about all aspects of devotional service. In the end, it all boils down to gratitude. Krishna has given us an amazing amount of mercy, which has allowed us to take to devotional service. If we can maintain an attitude of proper gratitude, then we will not become cynical and depressed. Even when we are faced with serious challenges in our lives, we will use them as opportunities to grow.

Once we lose our gratitude, however, and start to think that Krishna owes us something, or that He has not delivered the goods, we are on our way down. When there is sufficient gratitude, it is as if we are saying, "Thank You, Krishna. Thank You for taking care of me, and thank You for arranging for my well-being in every situation. Whether events are materially good or bad, I understand that they have been lovingly arranged by You in order to bring me home.

Thank You!" In this way, we offer ourselves more to Krishna. When we lose our gratitude, we are saying the opposite. Therefore, it is important to have the right mindset. It can be very dangerous if we do not.

I highly recommend that we all pay more attention to our self-talk; that is, to what we say to ourselves in our minds. Our external actions are secondary to our internal dialogue. We identify more strongly with what goes on inside of us than with what happens on the outside. Even though outwardly we may execute our duties properly, inwardly our minds may be filled with mental garbage, such as low self-esteem or a self-defeating mood. If this is the case, then negativity is what will manifest in our lives. Research has shown that between eighty to ninety percent of the time, our self-talk is negative. We meditate upon what we cannot do, what we do not have, how somebody did not speak to us in the right way, how somebody else looked at us askance, or how yet another person mistreated us.

I suggest that we all take a couple of hours just to observe our thoughts: we will be amazed at the result. By listening carefully to our self-talk, we can catch ourselves and realize that our minds are really monsters. Internal dialogue is constant. From thought comes speech, and from speech comes action. It follows that what we think, feel, and will must gradually fructify into external deeds. Therefore, we should be more careful about what we think. As a result, our actions will be of a higher quality. Just watch the mind. By doing so, we will quickly realize why sometimes we have so much trouble in our devotional lives.

The nature of the mind is cynical and negative. It is continually mistrusting and faultfinding. When we see people, do we not size them up and look for faults? Often, we even criticize physical imperfections, thinking, "His nose is too long. Her feet are so big! He is balding, while her neck is too long for her body." The mind dwells on all these irrelevant things. Even when we come to see the Deities, the mind is often all over the place. Our bodies may be in the temple room, but our minds are frequently far away. Even while doing Deity worship, the mind of the *pujari* may not be fully present. If this is so, then he or she will not receive the same benefit as one who is fully focused on the Lord. The deeper the quality of devotional culture and the absorption of the mind within it, the more powerful all spiritual experiences become, and the greater the degree of transcendental reciprocation.

Questions and Answers

Question: How can we keep the memories and lessons of past experiences in the front of our minds, so that we can avoid having to undergo the same experience again and again?

Answer: You have raised a complex and important point. If we reflect on our past behavior, we will notice that periodically we undergo certain experiences which become very prominent within our consciousness, but then, within a very short space of time, we forget the negative results that accompanied them. We can all remember times when something traumatic happened in our lives and we thought, "Now, I am really going to become serious about my spiritual life." However, within a few weeks or even a few days, we found ourselves back to 'business as usual.' One technique that I find effective in dealing with such a problem is to revisit such an event mentally while reflecting on our convictions.

In order to make optimal advancement in spiritual life, it is important to make vows that assist us in focusing on our desired goal. Simultaneously, we should take life one day at a time, and view each day as a fresh opportunity to renew our vows. Every now and then, it is immensely healthy for devotees to rejoin the Hare Krishna movement. It is important for us to constantly remind ourselves why we joined. In this way, we can maintain our convictions in spiritual life. When most of us decided to join the movement, we faced so many challenges, including those from many people who advised us not to become a Hare Krishna under any circumstances. In spite of it all, however, *we said YES*. Similarly, by rejoining the movement, we are directed to consider the different variables in our lives and why it is important to continue. If we do not strengthen our commitment, then inevitably there will be times when environmental and institutional issues will cause us to lose our equilibrium. We risk becoming demoralized and distracted by some of our immediate experiences, forgetting why we have come and where we are going. However, when we center our awareness on our reasons for becoming Krishna conscious, then we become rejuvenated and keep on at it. Remaining Krishna conscious is a science in the sense that it entails a constant revisiting of the philosophy in order to remind ourselves about our motivations and convictions.

His Holiness Tamal Krishna Gosvami recently left the planet. As a result of the sad passing of Gosvami Maharaja, the whole movement in general became quite serious—for a while. Devotees started to think more deeply about their relationships with their *gurus*. They became more self-critical, looking closer at themselves to see what kind of disciples they had become. As the leaders considered the fact that any one of them could be next to leave the body, a mood of greater appreciation for one another permeated dealings at that time. Some devotees maintained this heightened sense of urgency regarding the way they related to one another, but others had already lapsed back to their former ways a few days after the event. In order to maintain the impact of a learning experience on our consciousness, we must be reflective and allow the lessons we have absorbed to continue to act as motivating factors in our lives.

Question: Maharaja, at what point during your university career did you come across Srila Prabhupada and his books? Did you join the movement straight after obtaining your degree, or did you work for a while before joining it?

Answer: Actually, I have always been involved in spiritual activities of some kind. I grew up in a devoutly Christian environment, and became a child evangelist. By the time I was nine years old, I was preaching on radio and television, and at penal institutions and homes for the mentally challenged. Later, when I went off to university, I tried to forget anything that was connected with spirituality. I could not manage to accomplish this, fortunately. Krishna was kind to me and did not allow me to forget. While at university, I dabbled into various metaphysical subject matters. Every time I saw a poster advertising the public appearance of any sort of spiritualist, I would attend the event and try to learn something. At the same time, I was also a student leader at Princeton and became involved in revolutionary politics. I have always been quite an outrageous person, and in this field I proved to be no exception. During this period, I also met certain spiritual mentors, and took initiation from them. In my senior year, I undertook a dissertation which explored meeting points between Western Psychology and Eastern Philosophy. Through hypnotherapy, I regressed people not only to earlier events in this life, but also sometimes to their past lives.

One day during my junior year, I came in touch with the Hare Krishna movement. At that point, I was undergoing a big shift in my life. I was living with a group of men who were living a very unhealthy lifestyle, but a few months later, I decided to move into my own place and became almost like a hermit. I read and meditated almost all the time, as I attempted to make decisions concerning what I would do with my life after graduation. It was a real pivotal point, as I had grown up in a poor family. I was the only one who went to university, because I was the only one who had managed to obtain a scholarship. I was fortunate enough to have many contacts from my involvement in student leadership. The president of the university took a liking to me, and stepped forward. Despite the fact that I was not going to continue my studies at that particular school and probably not even in America, the president had arranged for one or two alumni to finance the rest of my education. In this way, I was presented with the most amazing dilemma.

I had planned to begin a career in International Law and to work at the United Nations. Generous financiers had manifested, and it seemed as if everything was laid out for my future in a materialistic sense. I had arranged to go to Jamaica and then to Tanzania, where I would work with the Chief Justice. After that, I planned to go to China and to apprentice at the United Nations. All the right people had been contacted, facility had been arranged, and the money had been organized. Maya was bending over backwards in order to entice me. I hesitated to forge ahead with my plans, however, because I had begun to get involved in the Hare Krishna movement. I knew that I needed to make a choice between the material and spiritual worlds. I am essentially an extremist; therefore, I knew that whatever I chose to do, I would undertake with all my energy and determination.

After I graduated, I decided to take a year off. I did not go back into my studies, nor did I join the temple. Instead, I worked for the Office of the Public Defender in the state of New Jersey. I was appointed to oversee all the penal reform programs in that state. I took the job mainly to earn a little money so that I could be by myself. It was a period of introspection. I bought a house and lived there alone. I went to work, came home, and chanted and prayed for the rest of the day. I did that for a year, praying to God to let me know what I should do. Part of me believed that the plans for my material advancement must be in alignment with God's desire; otherwise, why would I have access to so much money? Why were all these things arranged for me? However, another part of me was saying, "Don't get involved in this kind of bureaucratic stuff! You know that life is all about consciousness. Why don't you involve yourself more in consciousness studies and go deeper into your spiritual life? If you want to bring about change, dealing with political issues will not help. Spiritual transformation yields the only real results." From a very young age, I had always been concerned about

Mantra Eleven

what was happening in the international arena. I wanted to try to make a difference in the world. Therefore, for a year I considered whether I could make more of an impact in the world through being a typical bureaucrat in the realm of politics and International Law, or whether I could do more by taking the spiritual path. Towards the end, it became clear that the real goal of life was to become a spiritualist.

When I became completely sure of what I wanted to do, I got rid of the house and told the Public Defender that I had to leave immediately due to some emergency. I caught up with some old friends, and invited them to come to my house to take all of my suits and other possessions. When I told one of my friends to take my hi-fi or my record player, he started crying. Formerly, I had been very attached to my hi-fi. My friend said, "Well, if John (my name was John, then) can give up his suits and his house, that's one thing, but if John wants to give up his hi-fi, that's a sure sign that he has gone crazy." Nevertheless, he took the hi-fi. After my friends had taken everything away, I visited the store, bought some cloth, entered the bathroom, shaved my head, packed a few lecture tapes into a suitcase, and bought a ticket to Dallas, Texas where I joined.

I abandoned my next degree, the money, and all those material opportunities without looking back. Lately, I have been feeling regretful that I did not write a letter to the university president thanking him for his endeavors, and apologizing for any difficulties that I created for him and the donors by my choice. In retrospect, looking back through the lens of twenty-nine years come and gone, I think that I should have at least requested that they give the money to somebody else. However, at the time it was crystal clear in my mind that if I did not abandon my material life without delay, then probably later I would find some justification not to surrender. I knew that if I really wanted to help the suffering people of the world in a meaningful way, then I needed to work on myself first by sincerely trying to understand spirituality. I was one of the first minority graduates at Princeton. Then I went on to join the Hare Krishna movement in Dallas, where I ended up washing pots. That is the austerity of Krishna consciousness. The Dallas temple was where we started our first *gurukula*. One of my first services was to assist His Holiness Satsvarupa Maharaja, who was in charge of the school at that time. Later, I began to travel in the capacity of a preacher. I have never looked back.

When I left university, I was so happy. I was happy to leave material life, and happy also that Krishna had arranged for me to undergo that particular type of experience, which convinced me totally that I did not want to be a materialist. My first roommate was so rich that when he turned twenty-one, he automatically received hundreds of millions of dollars. He was so wealthy that on weekends he would fly off to Switzerland for a skiing trip, or to Mexico to catch some sun. He could do practically anything in the material arena, because he had so much money. However, like many other very wealthy people, my roommate was also very miserable. He was depressed, and hated his parents for placing him in exclusive boarding schools when he was younger. He felt that he had neither a mother nor a father. His parents were preoccupied with traveling around the world, making money. While all the children were given a good education, they felt abandoned, as if they were just pushed away. It was not only the majority of students at Princeton who were despondent, but also most of the professors. While I was there, I spent most of my time with my professors, which gave me the opportunity to study their lives. As I was a very inquisitive person, I could not help but notice how unhappy they were.

I have expanded somewhat on my earlier life largely because it serves as a suitable example of what it means to cultivate a deep understanding of nescience, together with the acquisition of spiritual knowledge. The realizations I gained from these experiences helped me to appreciate Krishna consciousness on a more profound level.

Mantra Twelve

andham tamah pravisanti
ye 'sambhutim upasate
tato bhuya iva te tamo
ya u sambhutyam ratah

> Those who are engaged in the worship of demigods enter into the darkest region of ignorance, and still more so do the worshipers of the impersonal Absolute.

The Destination of the Worshiper

In *Mantra Twelve*, the speaker communicates interesting information about the destination of the worshiper, based on the object of worship. Those who pray to the *devas*, as well as the worshipers of the impersonal Brahman, will arrive at specific destinations at the time of death. Both destinations, however, are situated in the regions of darkness. Initially, we may wonder what is wrong with worshiping the *devas*, who are, after all, empowered and bona fide representatives of the Supreme Lord. The *devas* have distinct personalities and reciprocate personally, just as Krishna has a unique personality and relates to every living being in a particular way. Nevertheless, we worship Krishna as the Supreme because *krsnas tu bhagavan svayam* (*Srimad-Bhagavatam*, 1.3.28) which means that Krishna is the original Personality of Godhead, who possesses all opulences in full. While we are all similar to the Lord in quality, we are different in quantity.

The *devas* usually obtain their positions as the result of certain *tapasyas* they have performed based on the Vedic system. Therefore, we may ask, why should they not be worshiped? There are thirty-three million types of *devas*, who control every aspect of our being, such as respiration, defecation, and mobility. Certain scriptures emphasize that if a person wants benedictions such as intelligence, beauty, longevity, or a good spouse, then particular *devas* should be worshiped. But at the same time, *Sri Isopanisad* states that those who worship the *devas* ultimately experience inauspiciousness; they go to the darkest regions of ignorance. How do we reconcile these seemingly juxtaposed scriptural injunctions?

The *Bhagavad-gita* explains that whomever we worship determines our consciousness, and that ultimately whatever we put our energy into is what we become. *Devas* exist on different moral levels: there are pious demigods and also impious demigods, *suras* as well as *asuras*. All carry a certain *sakti*. But while we acknowledge that the demigods are empowered, we also need to inquire into the category of that power. What is the *siddhanta* of their influence? Nothing can happen effectively without some *sakti*. Intention without *sakti* is merely sentiment.

Is Sastra Subject to Interpretation?

In his purport to this verse, Srila Prabhupada discusses the worship of the *devas* by evoking the potency of *sastra*. Through the use of *sastra*, as it aligns with *sadhu* and *guru*, we are able to understand what is *vidya* (true knowledge). All three are important spiritual resources, but in many ways *sastra* is most significant. If we reflect carefully, we see that it is *sastra* that helps us to identify a proper *sadhu*. *Sastra* lists the qualities of the *sadhu*, enabling us to properly understand how to both emulate and appreciate them. It is also *sastra* that assists us in comprehending what constitutes the different levels of spiritual mentorship, or what defines *guru*.

Ultimately, however, even *sastra* can be quite confusing, because *sastra* is subject to the understanding of the reader, to the ear of the listener, and to the enunciation of the speaker. Bewilderment may occur despite the fact that we are following the *parampara* system. As Krishna says to Arjuna in *Bhagavad-gita* 4.2:

> *evam parampara-praptam*
> *imam rajarsayo viduh*
> *sa kaleneha mahata*
> *yogo nastah parantapa*

> *This supreme science was thus received through the chain of disciplic succession, and the saintly kings understood it in that way. But in course of time the succession was broken, and therefore the science as it is appears to be lost.*

Although we understand that everything within the universe is placed systematically within Krishna's divine arrangement, we must still endeavor to make a proper evaluation of *sastra*. If not, Krishna's instructions may be codified differently to His intention, or perhaps applied in an unhealthy way. According to the *Chandogya Upanisad* 6.14.2, *acaryavan puruso veda*: one who approaches a bona fide spiritual master can understand everything about spiritual realization. As the Lord instructs Sri Uddhava in *Srimad-Bhagavatam* 11.17.27:

> *acaryam mam vijaniyan*
> *navanmanyeta karhicit*
> *na martya-buddhyasuyeta*
> *sarva-deva-mayo guruh*

> One should know the *acarya* as Myself and never disrespect him in any way. One should not envy him, thinking him an ordinary man, for he is the representative of all the demigods.

The Exploitation of Religion

In a recent radio interview in Cape Town, South Africa, I spoke about how religion has become one of the most threatening aspects to human civilization and to a peaceful world order. That is, the *exploitation* of religion. This exploitation stems from the abuse of *sastra*, engendered by improper *sadhus* who do not have a genuine connection with *acarya*ship or with *guru*. When materially motivated people project themselves as *acaryas*, and in so doing stimulate so-called saintly people in the wrong way, the religion that is supposed to be a harmonizing element for humankind produces chaos and pandemonium.

Since religion is so powerful, intense devastation and fragmentation occur when it is perverted. Employed properly, religion results in amazing and auspicious effects. When it is employed improperly, however, it becomes the cause of widespread distress. Vedic culture is a potent force. Therefore, when it is misused, it gives rise to the greatest inhumanity in the form of insensitive tyrants, casteism, and chauvinism. All bona fide scriptures, whether the Torah, the Bible, the Koran, the Hadith, or the Vedic texts, testify that humans are supposed to exercise dominance over creation. Dominance means occupying a superior position in order to caretake and to facilitate others. But abusive domination does the opposite, and will invariably lead to manipulation and exploitation.

How to Research the Goal

Just as Krishna appears from time to time in the material universes through various plenary expansions and incarnations to perform His numerous *lilas,* so too does He send certain representatives and make particular scriptures available according to time, place, and circumstance. Although these various types of scriptures, saints, and *acaryas* may be involved in completely different religious systems, they may all be bona fide but offer dissimilar benedictions. When we evaluate any theology or philosophy, the first question we need to ask is, *"What is the siddhanta, or the ultimate goal of this process?"* If I follow this religion perfectly, what is the highest achievement that is attainable?" Many people who adhere to certain systems actually have no clue of what the precise goal of that particular system is. If they were to find out what the final goal is, they might become disinterested in following that system.

For instance, there are bona fide teachers whose mission is to assist their followers in attaining a more pious mood on the earth planet, to create a type of heaven on earth. Other *acaryas* are qualified to teach the development of *saktis* through mystic processes such as *astanga-yoga* and *kriya-yoga* which, when practiced correctly, empower the practitioner with some of the qualities of God. Additional bona fide systems help followers become detached from matter, resulting in an experience of *nirvana,* or the absence of botheration from the activities of duality, which is a central principle of Buddhism. Yet other authentic systems exist which aim to lead the sincere adherent into an encounter with the all-pervading effulgence of the Lord. If we pursue any of these systems very deeply, then these different results will be within our reach. Of course, there are also *acaryas* who would like to connect us with Krishna, the Supreme Personality of Godhead, whether in His *aisvarya* aspect in Vaikuntha, or as Govinda in Vrndavana, the land of lawless love.

Once we become educated in what the goal of a particular system is, and we find that we are comfortable with it, then we have to ask ourselves the second question: *"What do I need to do to achieve the objective?"* Once we have that information, and we conclude that we are ready to do what it takes to attain our goal, then we must ask the third question: *"Where are those who have achieved the goal? Let me hear from them."* Once we accept the goal together with the process required to attain that goal, and we see that people exist who have already reached the goal (and we desire to become like them), then we may choose to go full steam ahead.

Every bona fide spiritual teaching has its own *sastras*, *sadhus*, and *gurus*. And every *guru* is connected to an alignment of saintly persons. As bona fide scripture, saint, and teacher become aligned, so a genuine strong unity within diversity becomes possible. Religions are amazing methods which allow their followers to acquaint themselves with God to varying degrees. The depth of knowledge available is based on the level of our surrender and desire. What is causing fragmentation in the world at the present moment is not the existence of different religious systems. What is causing destruction are those people who do not follow bona fide systems in a bona fide way.

At present, many Jews exist who are not spiritually connected in a tangible way, as well as many Christians who are not bona fide Christians, many Muslims who are not authentic Muslims, many Buddhists who are not true Buddhists, and a large number of Vaisnavas who are not genuine Vaisnavas. Therefore, we are encountering both intra-group and inter-group problems. So much dissent has arisen as the result of the misuse of religion that many people now think, "Do away with all this religious stuff because it just brings confusion." There is nothing wrong with spirituality and deep religion, per se. There is something wrong with devious people who try to hijack religious teachings. Since time immemorial, people have existed who will exploit anything for ulterior motives, including religion. However, applied properly, bona fide religion is extremely powerful.

Scripture: Literal or Allegorical?

Srila Bhaktivinoda Thakura explains that even though scripture is most important, no scripture on its own will be able to provide a practitioner with full attainment of the goal. Scripture can supply total knowledge, but not complete realization. Scripture is not just to be read, but also to be practiced and experienced. In the beginning, the aspiring spiritualist is meant to accept scripture in its entirety, because scripture points us in the right direction. When we begin to evolve spiritually, however, we understand that even though scripture is essential, it merely supplies us with clues to the possibilities available. In some of the higher material planets, so many more volumes of the *Bhagavatam* are available than we are able to find here on this planet, and even they do not describe the entire potential of the spiritual world. Similarly, although devotees derive great bliss from talking about the pastimes of Krishna, it is impossible to discuss them in their entirety.

Devotees are animated when they hear *hari-katha*, narrations about the pastimes of the Lord. However, there is so much more to be heard and understood. Srila Bhaktivinoda Thakura explains that, in the neophyte stage, one should accept scripture as it is. But as our spirituality starts unfolding, we begin to realize that scripture is alive and vibrant. If we think that scripture is dead and take it strictly as it is, then our mood can result in fanaticism. Although it is correct, on the neophyte level, to take scripture only literally, on a more mature level, it is not sufficient. For example, the story of King Puranjana in the *Srimad-Bhagavatam* (which appears in the Fourth Canto, Chapters Twenty-five to Twenty-nine) is an allegory, or what may be described in the Christian tradition as a parable: a story that did not occur historically, but one that has been manufactured in order to convey a moral message.

It will be problematic, however, if we begin to think that every scriptural narration is simply a parable or an allegory. This is where the guidance of proper *guru* and *sadhu* is essential in order to assist us in our understanding. Srila Bhaktivinoda Thakura addresses this point by explaining the difference between *artha-prada* and *paramartha-prada*. *Artha-prada* are concepts or traditions within a religious system that are subject to change or to challenge. They should be looked at and studied in terms of their validity for the day and time, and for their ability to bring us to the goal. *Artha-prada* refer to relative knowledge connected with material nature, as codified by theoretical systems such as history, anthropology, sociology, and science, which do not form part of the categorical essence. They are normally details, secondary understandings which help us approach the primary. Sometimes, the secondary must be changed so as not to alter the primary. However, if we change some of the secondary, but those changes do not help to maintain and reinforce the essence, then they are *maya*.

Srila Prabhupada was once asked about these concepts, about how we should understand them. He said that it is not easy and it takes realization. Often it is better just to be conservative, but a conservative position does not necessarily bring massive expansion to any philosophy or movement. Conservatives can play an important role in maintaining, but not in expansion. In the past, great teachings were spread to the masses, but they did not really take off until they were accepted by the élites. For instance, Christianity was a small religious sect until Constantine the Great (275

Mantra Twelve

CE - 337 CE) was converted. Buddhism was in the same category until Emperor Asoka of India (270 BCE - 230 BCE) was convinced of its validity. While spirituality has to be relevant to time, place, and circumstance and to the masses as well as to the élites, if the essence is taken away, then it becomes watered down and causes confusion rather than elevation and liberation.

The *paramartha-prada* are those activities that are essential to our identity as Vaisnavas, essential to the soul, essential to love of God, and which therefore are not meant to be changed. What constitutes our position as *sadhus*? Essentially honoring scripture and taking shelter of the bona fide *acaryas*. We see that every major *acarya* makes many changes, but never loses the essence. So if people genuinely follow the great *acaryas*, such as Sri Ramanujacarya, Sri Madhvacarya, Sri Nimbarkacarya, and our own Srila Prabhupada, they will make serious advancement based on what the goals of their teachings are. This is applicable also to *acaryas* not in our Vaisnava line. If people would follow the actual words of Moses, the real instructions of Lord Jesus, the genuine teachings of Muhammad, or the unadulterated directives of Buddha, then there is no doubt that they could attain the objectives offered by these spiritual systems.

Various Types of Study Lead to Different Goals

Sometimes, we make the mistake of assuming that if all these teachers are bona fide, then following any of them will get us to the same place. If a student is attending high school, will he attain a postgraduate degree on completing his course? If another student studies physics at university, will she graduate with a degree in anthropology? If we choose to study medicine, will we emerge after many years of dissection and anatomy classes with a history degree? Different bona fide systems prepare us for particular levels of achievement. Therefore, we have to look closely at some of these systems in order to consider whether we desire to attain the goals they offer.

In the *Bhagavad-gita*, Krishna explains that religious goals are dependent on whom one worships, and how. Can we venerate the impersonal aspect of God and attain His personal aspect? No, that is impossible. Can we follow a system based on teachings about how to reach the heavenly planets, but arrive in Goloka Vrndavana? Of course not, because the goal is different. In one sense, all spiritual mentors are selling a particular *sastra*, amplifying its message with the idea of recruiting people. Just as when we go to the market, we have to be clear about the type of goods we wish to buy, and the quality we require, so too when we seek a spiritual path, we need to know what result we wish to attain, and what constitutes genuineness. Then, from the standpoint of knowledge, we pay the price, or do what is necessary to attain what we desire. Through his unique methods of spreading Krishna consciousness, Srila Prabhupada gave us a wonderful chance to experience sacred teachings in a way that is quite appropriate for modern times. As long as we are connected with its actual essence, we do not necessarily have to be concerned with the many intricate details associated with the Vedic culture of ancient India, details which may be irrelevant to the needs of spreading Vaisnava philosophy worldwide.

The Dangers of Fundamentalism

Srila Bhaktivinoda Thakura's concept of *adhunika-vada* is especially relevant to the application of Krishna consciousness in different situations. *Adhunika-vada* indicates a perspective of looking at the world in terms of the present. It involves an appreciation of what is healthy for modern times, what is practical for devotional service, and a separation from that which is unhealthy and no longer viable. As Vaisnavas, we are interested in neither antiquity nor modernity. Rather, we care about what is spiritual. Sometimes, it seems as if we are in favor of modernity, while at other times it appears as if we are embracing antiquity, while in actuality we are simply concerned about connecting with Krishna's love as it manifests in different ways. Krishna's love has always been coming forth and will continue to come forth with great heterogeneity and great adventure, not just in orthodox ways. We can absorb ourselves in that love by being open to the unconventional manner in which Krishna can display His potency. If not, we risk getting locked into fanaticism. Or we could go to the other extreme, and become totally detached from the *paramartha-prada*, from things that we should hold onto for dear life.

In all religious institutions, there are in-house struggles between those who wish to access multifold ways of connecting with the divine, and the fundamentalists who look at most things in a very literal, and often myopic, way. Fundamentalists can usually connect with God only when they are with people who dress in a special way, sing particular tunes, or speak in a predetermined fashion. If the connection with the Godhead does not come in the exact way in which they think it should come, then they feel that all is lost and that there is no hope. Every group of faith has its fundamentalists who do not realize that religion is alive. They fail to see that the Lord's love is ever-increasing, constantly growing, and approaching us in a multitude of ways.

Often, the self-righteousness of fundamentalists turns into outright arrogance. It is the fundamentalists who often become fanatics and who even become empowered for destruction. It is the fundamentalists who are easily attacked by Kali (the force of modern degradation) to do the opposite of what they preach. They cause many people to become atheistic by wounding those who genuinely try to become spiritual. If we are sincere in keeping a sense of humility, then growth will always occur. There will always be a chance to understand things from a deeper perspective. However, anytime we reach a point in which we think, "I know it all," or "My way is the only way," we are in danger, because an authentic spiritualist is always unfolding. Krishna's nature is also one of expansion. Transcendence itself is an ever-increasing process. But when one feels, "I know it. Now I must simply help everyone else to reach a level at which they know it like I know it," then, of course, we are treading a perilous path. 'Knowing it all' is the quickest way to place incredible limitations on Krishna's potency and His love.

In rare situations, although a spiritualist might be aligned with a particular faith, his or her spiritual greed is so intense that he or she becomes empowered to exceed the teachings of that faith. In other words, there are those who, though following religious systems such as Judaism, Islam, and Christianity, have gone beyond those basic theologies into intimate understandings of the Godhead. And why should they not reach such understandings? The same Krishna is in everyone's heart, and He is able to respond to the desires of all His devotees. When a teacher of first-grade students perceives that she has an enriched student in her class, why should she not allow that student to confront third-grade knowledge, if that student has the capacity? Occasionally, the teacher may even allow the student to skip a grade. This situation is exceptional, but it is definitely possible.

Madhurya-Rasa in Diverse Spiritual Traditions

In the history of this planet, certain spiritual teachers from various traditions have immersed themselves so profoundly within a particular path that their realizations have fallen into alignment with the Vaisnava understanding of the Godhead. St. Francis of Assisi (1181 CE-1226 CE) is such an example. St. Francis was a very austere monk. In his practices, he was similar to a very deep *bhakta*, a dedicated *yogi*, or a *babaji*, a renunciate in the Vedic system who is on the topmost platform of love of God. In St. Francis' writings about his experience of prayer, he discusses being embraced by the Lord and resting his head on the Lord's chest in what is essentially *madhurya-rasa*, the mood of conjugal love. St. Francis speaks in a spirit that goes beyond just knowing God as the supreme autocrat. Although he was following a system which has as its central goal the attainment of Brahmaloka, or the other heavenly planets, because of his deep level of austerity, genuine love of people, and sincere desire to know God, St. Francis surpassed the general standard of his tradition in order to access the more personal aspects of the Lord.

One barometer of sincerity and intensity in spiritual practice is that the topmost follower ultimately becomes more aligned with the personal aspects of God, no matter what bona fide tradition he or she follows. The deeper we plunge into religion, the more we touch on certain universal realities. For example, St. Teresa of Avila (1515 CE-1582 CE) was a simple Christian nun, but at the same time, she was exceptionally austere and enormously dedicated. Always chanting the names of God and praying, her realization of God was also in the mood of *madhurya-rasa*. Other Christian mystics who related to the Lord in the spirit of conjugal love were St. John of the Cross, St. Bernard of Clairvaux, and St. Hildagard of Bingen. Occasionally, some Sufi spiritualists and mystic Jews relate to God with a corresponding intimacy. This similarity of experience across religions, although unusual, demonstrates the power of Krishna in the heart. The Hadith says that the highest experience in paradise is to behold the vision of Allah, while the Bible relates that the pure at heart will see God. The same Supreme Personality of Godhead makes Himself available throughout history by sending numerous teachers to reach certain segments of people based on their degree of surrender. In Krishna consciousness, we are given an exact description of who God is, what He looks like, and what is required from us in order to learn how to see Him. When we perceive the Lord's form through *darsana* with the Deity, we understand that spirituality is not just a vague conception. We find out specifically about the Father to whom Lord Jesus refers, the same God whom Muhammad beheld face to face in his ascension when he went beyond heaven to Allah's abode.

The Experience of Krishna Consciousness

While *sraddha* is very important, ultimately it must produce results. If *sraddha* cannot be measured in experiences of transcendence, then what is the value of that faith? Simply to keep wishing and hoping that maybe tomorrow, maybe next year, or maybe in the next life we will experience a connection with God is not sufficient. If we do not have frequent experiences that sustain and increase our faith, we may start to think that this process may not even work. The goal of spirituality has never been merely to read books and to think of what they describe as history, or simply to reflect on what the great teachers did. We reflect on their experiences, so that we can join them. We read scripture, so we can experience similarly in due course. It is not that we should become *karma-kandis*, and think that we deserve to have distinct reciprocation based on our endeavor. We should feel unworthy, but, at the same time, we should understand that this process is about elevation, and about a greater level of realization. If it is not, how then do we continue year after year, hoping and wishing, but failing to attain strong results? As we persist in Krishna consciousness, we need to experience powerful reciprocation, otherwise we risk losing our faith.

If we take the spiritual medicine, and it does not work, then we must examine whether we really took it according to the prescription. If the doctor, the medicine, and the discharge of the prescription are all in order, then we should experience distinct results. If the doctor has real knowledge of the ailment, if he gave us the correct prescription, and if we took it in the proper way, but we failed to derive any benefit, it means that something has interfered with the process of recovery. In other words, if we are following this process, but we go on year after year without deriving some clearly discernible results in our spiritual lives, then we need to take a close look at how we are following in order to discover the obstacles to our advancement.

We want to make light neither of the instructions of *sadhu*, *sastra*, and *guru*, nor to be in a consciousness in which we limit their potency either by fundamentalism or by a lack of chastity. Because Krishna consciousness is a science, the more we connect with the process, the more we establish transcendental connections. These are more accessible to Vaisnavas, firstly, because the goals are clear and, secondly, because the process is passed on through an unbroken line by the eternal associates of the Lord who come into this universe to wake us up. They call out to us, *"Jiv jago, jiv jago,"* or "Wake up, sleeping souls!" as Srila Bhaktivinoda Thakura envisions Lord Caitanya singing in Part Two of *Arunodaya-kirtana, Kirtana Songs to be Sung at Dawn*, which appears in *Gitavali*.

Fanaticism Leads to Destruction

As we are all individuals, we see the world according to our particular natures, and therefore we engage in devotional service based on our distinct propensities. When Krishna was in a wrestling match with Kamsa, the evil ruler dominating the world at the time of Krishna's manifest presence, everyone saw the Lord differently, depending on their relationship with Him. The *yogis* perceived Krishna as the Supersoul, while those who were devious and immoral imagined Krishna to be cruel death personified. Those who related to Krishna in a paternal mood recognized Him as their lovable child, while those who had intimate conjugal feelings for Him envisioned Krishna as the greatest lover. Even among those who associate directly with the Supreme Personality of Godhead, an immense variation exists in how they relate with Him.

Fundamentalists, however, do not allow for much variegatedness in spiritual expression because they are too attached to ritual. In *The Nectar of Instruction*, Text Two, Srila Rupa Gosvami writes that *niyamagraha*, or fanaticism, may lead to a falldown produced by either an over-attachment to, or minimization of scriptural rules and regulations.

Desiring Heaven

Sri Isopanisad states that those with a poor fund of knowledge worship the demigods. One reason for this statement is that the boons bestowed by the *devas* are temporary. If we worship the *devas*, we may find ourselves joining them. Srila Prabhupada explains that we can go to the higher planets via three basic methods:

- By worship of the demigods
- By space travel
- By mystic power

However, from the highest to the lowest, not one of these different material planets is permanent, so ultimately we will not be fully satisfied. But if one is very attached to going to the heavenly kingdoms, and one follows the prescribed austerities very nicely, then one also derives some spiritual benefit. In the Vaisnava system, we instruct people to be authentic about their present innermost desires. Therefore, Srila Prabhupada told Christians to follow Christianity authentically, because by following a genuine system, they will make spiritual advancement. If one attains to the heavenly planets in a bona fide way, the eternal associates of the Lord will meet one there, and instruct one further. Vaisnavas, however, want to reach the spiritual world, and therefore we engage in *sadhana-bhakti* in order to prepare for the next life. Whatever one's goal or one's level of spiritual advancement, Krishna provides so much help and facilitation.

Running Away from God

Unfortunately, many of us do not always avail ourselves of the spiritual assistance available, because we have a tendency to become stagnated by the external environment. As the majority of entities on the planet are running away from the Lord, the normative scheme of the world is focused on how to avoid Krishna. Most people are captured by that trend, allowing themselves to be swept away by the general wave of deviation. At the same time, a few rare souls will decide that they do not want to be ordinary sense gratifiers, living a mundane life of eating, sleeping, mating, and defending. They will sense that life has a greater meaning than just these mundane activities and they will seek deeper truths. It takes a substantial amount of courage to resist the norm because it is very easy just to fit into the normal patterns of deviation, and to try to be satisfied with the little pleasure obtained from temporary sense stimulation—*for a moment.*

When we are in knowledge and we digress from the spiritual path, then the intelligence will invariably kick in and make us miserable. Very quickly we realize that we have engaged in a ridiculous encounter, and that the misery which follows overrides glimpses of temporary stimulation. This is why Vaisnavas preach that there is no happiness in the material world; *that is, no pure, enduring happiness.* Engaging in sin results in a tiny amount of satisfaction followed by chastisement awaiting us right around the corner. After a while, we realize that what usually gives us the illusion of happiness is simply an invitation for inauspiciousness to enter our lives.

Practice and Perseverance Makes Perfect

Since we have access to higher knowledge, and we know that gratifying the senses leads to suffering, most Vaisnavas are ready to undergo austerity in order to attain a higher goal. In fact, everyone knows intuitively, if not consciously, that to achieve any important goal, one must make a genuine effort. To achieve anything worthwhile, a certain level of perseverance and determination must be expended. For instance, in order to be able to compete in an event like the Olympics, athletes need to practice for hours day after day. The majority of those who win gold and silver medals practice consistently like this for many years. To achieve a level of excellence in any field in this material world takes a tremendous amount of dedicated practice. Good musicians rehearse daily for many hours, while actors sometimes run through a part over a hundred times just to make a little commercial. Why do we think that when it comes to devotional service, we can just chant a few rounds for a few months, and then immediately achieve self-realization? Spiritual life involves intense dedication and resolve.

As we cultivate these qualities, we realize that the goals promised us are attainable, and, indeed, that we can reach them. Every few years, we hear that a new record has been broken in the realm of sports. Generally people are amazed, especially when previously they considered all possible records to already be broken, and that achieving anything greater was not humanly possible. However, when people realize what is possible, they feel inspired by a greater level of determination to aim higher in their own lives. As we become more cognizant of what the goals are, and as we become more aware of what others have accomplished, then the goals become more attainable for us as well. If an athlete trains nicely for a few months, but then becomes slack, will he or she be able to succeed? Similarly, in spiritual life, many people start off, but some lose heart and become weak. Those who attain the goal remain determined and do not become distracted. Over time, they see that although there were many who began practicing with them, and many who joined them at different times, only a few remained focused.

Often, what gives an athlete the winning edge nowadays is not as much physical skill as psychological advantage. Competitive athletes often hire special trainers who are skilled in human potential techniques, and who are able to train them in visualization and positive thinking. Through visualization, athletes are trained to see themselves accomplishing the goal even before they are physically competent to do so. In this way, the subtle body becomes connected with the objective and then the physical body automatically adjusts itself in harmony with the subtle body. The mind is more powerful than the body because it is subtler. In the majority of competitive events, athletes are matched physically; therefore, the one who has the strongest mindset, and the one who is able to harness the subtlest energy, is the one who will be successful. This holds true also for us as devotees. Krishna knows our level of spiritual advancement. Since He knows our abilities, as we connect with Him through a mood of *vandanam*, internal prayer, and through a strong desire to attain His abode, our internal devotional creeper gets watered. Externally, this produces very powerful effects.

Sincere Desire Produces Miracles

As Vaisnavas, we appreciate all bona fide religions, but, at the same time, we are disturbed by hypocrisy wherever we find it. Hypocrites bring confusion. Some are empowered for destruction, and many cause people to become bewildered about God. However, we rejoice when we see those in any bona fide tradition who are trying to be serious, because we know that when they are serious, Krishna will reach out for them. And if they are exceptionally serious, then the same Krishna who is in everyone's heart will guide them in the most amazing ways, and give them the most marvelous realizations. Sometimes, people who live in very isolated places suddenly become devotees. In places in which no temples, no preaching centers, no bookstores, and no *sankirtana* devotees are to be found, Krishna will make some miraculous arrangement in order for those who have a genuine desire to make contact with the movement. Devotees exist who have come into Krishna consciousness through very unusual situations, simply as a result of their intensity of yearning. If we have strong faith that Krishna will do His duty as we do ours, and that He will reach out, then we will want to try and connect with Him not through bribery, not through the demigods, or through His impersonal aspect only, but through His personal aspect. We can ask ourselves, "Where is all this coming from? How can we connect with the *saktiman* rather than with only the *sakti*?"

Sadhu, *sastra*, and *guru* assist us to link with the energetic. While *sastra* provides the guidelines and *sadhus* offer us practical instruction, the *acaryas* coordinate the entire process. If we take shelter in this way, we will be able to come to the *vasudeva* platform of seeing Krishna face to face. Most theologies promise that the pure in heart shall see God; religious worship is not merely concerned with thinking of Him and fearing Him. When we come to the *suddha-bhakti* platform after having abandoned all forms of mixed devotion, then nothing is left but pure vision, pure association, and pure relationship—at which point we can attain the *darsana* of Krishna.

More Humble than a Blade of Grass

In conclusion, we have to be careful to be chaste, but not sectarian. Sometimes, in our efforts to preach, inadvertently we may be offensive to other bona fide scriptures and also to other teachers. Although Lord Caitanya was often insulted by the Mayavadis, He was very humble. He set an example by His humility in order to demonstrate a higher path, as Srila Krsnadasa Kaviraja Gosvami recounts in *Sri Caitanya-caritamrta, Adi-lila,* Chapter Seven. When Mahaprabhu was passing through Varanasi on His way to Vrndavana, He was blasphemed by Mayavadi philosophers for chanting and dancing with the masses, instead of engaging in dry study of *Vedanta* and impersonal meditation. Mahaprabhu merely smiled, and said nothing to them. Later, on His return to Varanasi, He met a group of Mayavadi *sannyasis* from Benares in the home of a *brahmana*. After meekly taking His seat in the unclean washing area, Mahaprabhu was approached by the leader of the *sannyasis*, Prakasananda Sarasvati, who challenged the Lord. After defeating Prakasananda Sarasvati by quoting His spiritual master, as well as from *Bhagavad-gita* and *Srimad-Bhagavatam*, all the Mayavadi *sannyasis* accepted Mahaprabhu as non-different from the Supreme Lord Himself and begged to be excused from their previous offenses.

Another example of Mahaprabhu's humility is recounted in *Madhya-lila,* Chapter Six, concerning the liberation of Sarvabhauma Bhattacarya. After losing His external consciousness in the temple of Lord Jagannatha, Mahaprabhu was carried to the home of Sarvabhauma Bhattacarya, who, at that time, was an impersonalist *guru*. Although Sarvabhauma Bhattacarya was attracted to Mahaprabhu, he considered the Lord to be a second-class *sannyasi* and therefore his inferior. Assuming the position of Mahaprabhu's superior, Sarvabhauma Bhattacarya instructed Him in *Vedanta* philosophy for seven days. After Mahaprabhu patiently revealed the flaws in Sarvabhauma Bhattacarya's philosophical conclusions, he humbly submitted himself to the Lord and begged forgiveness for his offenses due to pride. Sarvabhauma Bhattacarya later became a pure Vaisnava who was then followed by other learned scholars in Jagannatha Puri.

Mahaprabhu was extremely humble not only in his dealings with impersonalist Mayavadis, but also with demigod worshipers. On his tour of South India, Mahaprabhu would go to visit the various temples dedicated to Lord Siva, and offer His obeisances. By seeing everything in relation to Krishna, but by maintaining chastity and utilizing any opportunity to be accessible, Mahaprabhu revealed to the devotees of Lord Siva the royal path of *bhakti*. In *Sri Caitanya-caritamrta, Madhya-lila 9.76*, Srila Krsnadasa Kaviraja Gosvami writes:

> *amrtalinga-siva dekhi vandana karila*
> *saba sivalaye saiva 'vaisnava' ha-ila*
>
> *Seeing the Siva deity named Amrta-linga, Lord Caitanya Mahaprabhu offered His obeisances. Thus He visited all the temples of Lord Siva and converted the devotees of Lord Siva into Vaisnavas.*

By following in the footsteps of Sri Caitanya Mahaprabhu, we can humbly use our knowledge of Lord Krishna's personal aspect to elevate those who worship Him indirectly either through the *devas* or the *brahmajyoti*.

Earlier, we referred to spiritualists who sometimes advance beyond their standard theologies. If these spiritualists had the opportunity to hear about Krishna consciousness, it would seem so natural to them, because the Lord in the heart has facilitated them to such an enormous extent. The philosophy of Krishna consciousness would simply crystallize what they already experienced. If St. Francis of Assisi, or even St. John of the Cross, St. Bernard of Clairvaux, St. Teresa of Avila, or St. Hildagard of Bingen had heard some of the literature of the *gosvamis*, they would have been overwhelmed. They would probably have left their bodies immediately. Each would have thought, "I knew I was not crazy, not just a radical who desired to know God most intimately. How wonderful to know that I am especially blessed to be given the boon to worship the Lord as my lover." To serve God confidentially is a dynamic adventure. We can all cultivate such loving experiences and associations with proper purity, guidance, and blessings.

Questions and Answers
Question: Is it possible that one can exist simultaneously in different *yugas* in various universes?

Answer: Since the *atma* is energetically the same in quality as Krishna, in its natural state of total purity that living entity acquires some of the abilities of Krishna. One of these abilities is to be able to transcend the dimensions of time and space. Therefore, it is feasible for great souls to exist simultaneously in different environments. For example, Dukhi Krsnadasa, a disciple of Srila Hrdoy Caitanya, underwent transcendental experiences both on this planet and in Goloka Vrndavana. One day, when he went to draw water for Srila Jiva Gosvami from Kanaka-kunja, he chanced upon a beautiful bejeweled anklet. Later, he spied a gorgeously effulgent girl searching for the anklet. The girl turned out to be Visakhadevi, while the anklet he had found belonged to Srimati Radharani Herself. Dukhi Krsnadasa managed to obtain the *darsana* of the Queen of Vrndavana, who dipped the anklet into *kunkuma*, and made a permanently effulgent *tilaka* mark on his head. Anything is possible, depending on our level of purity. For instance, sometimes when an entity is a *saktyavesa-avatara*, his or her existence can be the result of a divine connection between particular aspects of different beings.

In one sense, every one of us exists simultaneously in many different realms at any given time. We each have a physical body, a subtle body comprised mainly of the mind, the intelligence and the false ego, and a soul, our real identity. All of these aspects of ourselves are in existence and receive feedback from the environment concurrently. As we become more and more spiritual, the intelligence, the mind, and even the body begin to integrate and to take on the actual qualities of the soul. It is important to bear in mind that the personality with whom we identify, the engagements that are important to us, and our so-called normal tendencies may be completely dissimilar from our real nature in our *siddha-deha*, or perfected spiritual body.

Even in the conditioned state, separate aspects of ourselves function on different levels at the same time: the soul is fully conscious, while the body is in gross ignorance. The whole of this material world, including all the material universes, are actually part of the spiritual world; they are simply covered by the elements of the *mahat-tattva*. We are unaware of the spiritual world to the extent to which we identify with matter. Even though we think we are in the material world, we can still experience being in different places simultaneously. For example, we can be in our rooms, resting, but in our minds we can be in a distant land of the past or in some imaginary future time. When we awaken from our daydream, we may notice that our mind drifted only for a few minutes although it seemed to be a long time to us.

Similarly, in this lifetime, a person may have acquired the physiology of a male, although his soul may be distinctly feminine in its eternal service to Krishna. In the gross conditioned state, we experience almost no contact with our eternal selves. When we become spiritually involved and learn how to diminish our false ego, more of an integration occurs between the different parts of ourselves. In this way, advanced souls become aware of their original identity. Externally, they may continue to act as if they are still in a conditioned state, but internally they are fully cognizant of their real identity, and from time to time they may revisit who they really are. So as not to cause problems, they go on dealing with the material environment, but on the inside they relish an awareness of their original, on-going service to Krishna. They may be quite elderly in the material world, but in the spiritual world they may be of a different gender and of quite a young age. As they relate to Krishna in specific *rasas*, their false covering falls aside and their real essence comes forth.

Since the pure devotee places no restrictions on the love Krishna has for them and the love they have for Krishna, they are able to tune into the spiritual world, practically at will. This is one of the reasons why it is no problem for such high-level, unalloyed devotees to go to either the hellish planets or to the heavenly planets. Their concern is simply that as long as they can serve Krishna, they can be anywhere. For such devotees, there is no such place as hell, because wherever they find themselves, they are always thinking of the Lord. What could be hell for us may even seem like paradise to them. Their only experience of hell is an absence of Krishna. As a mundane example, we may consider that if we feel a strong affection for someone, it does not matter where we are as long as we are together. Even sitting down on a park bench in the rain becomes an enlivening experience when we are with someone we love. Circumstances that normally would disturb us suddenly become pleasant. Conversely, we may be on the most beautiful island on the planet, but if we are with people whom we do not care about, then we will feel miserable. We will simply meditate on escaping the situation. However, pure devotees, who are captivated by simply thinking of Krishna, experience the spiritual world twenty-four hours a day. For them, it does not matter where they are situated physically, because they are always intensely absorbed in the spiritual world.

Question: May we appeal to the demigods for their assistance in advancement in Krishna consciousness? And, if so, how should this be done?

Answer: Yes, we may make all kinds of prayers to attain the lotus feet of the Lord. To help us to become unalloyed devotees, we may pray to every single one of the demigods. Dozens and dozens of times, we may ask, "Please assist us to be unalloyed servants of Krishna. Please help us to get rid of our desires for sense gratification. Please make it easier for us to have great love for the *sadhus*." Yes, this kind of appeal to the *devas* is not problematic. It is not bribery; it is simply an engagement in secondary activities in order to attain the primary goal.

Question: It seems hard for different religions to exist in harmony. For example, Christians have faith that all we have to do is to believe in God in order to be saved. How is this way of relating to God in harmony with Krishna consciousness?

Answer: By understanding the essence of *sastra*, we see that it is possible for different religions to exist in harmoniously. While Romans 10:9 states, "If you confess that Jesus is Lord, and believe that God raised him from death, you will be saved," Romans 10:12 clarifies further that faith is not confined to Christianity: "This includes everyone, because there is no difference between Jews and Gentiles; God is the same Lord of all and richly blesses all who call to him." The essence of this passage is that by the mercy of the sons of God, namely, by the mercy of the *guru* (in this case, Lord Jesus Christ), one is able to meet God, the Father. The Father does not invest only one son with the potency to take the disciple back to Godhead, but He is so merciful that He sends many *acaryas* to save His fallen children. Unfortunately, a literal or fanatical reading of this teaching creates sectarianism. Some people have a tendency to present *sastra* from a sectarian point of view because they do not appreciate others. They do not realize how merciful and grand the Lord is. They think that Krishna can only reach out in one specific way, and when He reaches out in other ways, they reject Him.

Question: Does a person have to resolve all relationships from our past lives in order to be liberated?

Answer: We cannot resolve all *sambandha*, as associations with other living entities will always exist. We are not voidists, and therefore we do not endeavor to run away from relationships. In fact, we should run towards positive relationships, which strengthen our Krishna consciousness. We should not attempt to kill desire, because that is futile. Rather, we aim to transform desire. Transforming desire involves interactions and relationships. However, we must be careful that the nucleus is proper, meaning that our relationships should center around our shared devotion to Krishna.

Question: How can we bring someone who has lost faith back to Krishna consciousness?

Answer: By becoming more faithful ourselves. Let us cultivate our faith so superbly that others who have lost faith will become involuntarily motivated as they see the results of the strongly faithful. If those who have lost faith look around and see others whose faith is similar to or even weaker than their own, they will become even more faithless. They will think to themselves, "At least I am honest; I have lost faith and that is why I am not observing the rules and regulations so strictly. Although you also do not have much faith, you are merely putting on a show. Or perhaps you have faith, but it is not producing any serious transformation. You have faith, but what is the benefit? What are the results? What are the signs that all of this endeavor and austerity is worth the price?"

We strengthen our faith when we see that the goal is practically attainable. Therefore, when we become genuine carriers of faith ourselves, our example and our achievement will entice others. Our love and mercy will stimulate them, too. As our love enables us to reach out and support them, so our purity will encourage them as they undergo their struggles. Everyone has to endure their own individual battle of Kuruksetra. At certain points in all of our devotional lives, we will experience various types of difficulties, which we have to expect. During those times, we will need other devotees to be there for us, to help us, and to understand us. As we offer that kind of help to one another, we will be able to create a balance in our devotional lives and in our communities.

Mantra Thirteen

*anyad evahuh sambhavad
anyad ahur asambhavat
iti susruma dhiranam
ye nas tad vicacaksire*

It is said that one result is obtained by worshiping the supreme cause of all causes and that another result is obtained by worshiping what is not supreme. All this is heard from the undisturbed authorities, who clearly explained it.

Purchasing a Ticket to Goloka Vrndavana

In his purport to this verse, Srila Prabhupada applies the analogy of everyday travel to elucidate how various levels of worship function as roads leading to different destinations at the time of death. Srila Prabhupada explains that when a person purchases a ticket to travel to a certain town, he or she is then scheduled to arrive at that destination. If someone decides to buy an airplane ticket to New York, for instance, he or she will not arrive in London. If somehow they end up in London instead of New York, most people would become extremely disconcerted. To obtain a ticket to New York, they made a request at the airline counter and paid the required price; therefore, they expected to be delivered to the place specified on their boarding pass. If they wanted to travel further than New York, then they would have requested a different ticket and paid more for it. In a metaphysical sense, it follows therefore that those who worship the *devas* will join the *devas* in their next life, while those who venerate the forefathers will go to Pitrloka, or the planet of the forefathers. Others, who desire to merge into the impersonal Brahman, will be able to achieve their goal if they are willing to undertake specific methods of purification and austerity prescribed in the *Vedas*.

Similarly, once we decide to engage in devotional service, in effect we are requesting a ticket to Goloka Vrndavana, the original planet in Krishna's abode. We have opted to travel the greatest distance from the material world, and therefore the price asked will be the most expensive. Usually a ticket to Goloka Vrndavana does not include stopovers in either the middle planets or the higher planets. Mostly, those who are standing in line to purchase tickets to Goloka Vrndavana do not even want to stop off in the Vaikunthalokas, or the other planets in the spiritual sky. We want a direct flight, with no detours or delays. As we are asking for something which is very difficult to attain, we will need to meet certain requirements, make definite commitments, and endure many austerities in order to acquire our heart's desire. Mere wishing is not enough. The further we wish to travel, the higher the price. We must be prepared to meet the cost.

Obtaining a Specialization in Devotion

As devotees, we embrace undergoing the necessary purification because we understand its necessity. Just as a student who wants to obtain a postgraduate degree is required to study for more years than one who simply desires an undergraduate degree, more is required from the devotee of Krishna than from the general religious practitioner. Most students who register for the undergraduate program at universities acquire a broad-spectrum education. Only a few will decide to continue their studies and to specialize in a particular field. Similarly, Krishna consciousness requires specialization. We are not run-of-the-mill religionists. We are fortunate enough to have the opportunity to become specialists in the Divine. Therefore, we must incorporate our basic theistic knowledge (undergraduate study) within our investigation of deeper areas of spirituality (postgraduate study). In this way, we will be equipped to appreciate all genuine religions, and to offer our greatest respect to all *sadhus* who have descended in the various bona fide lineages, while at the same time remaining fixed in our particular area of specialization. Personally, I find it incredibly empowering to be personally strict and focused, yet nevertheless accepting of other bona fide traditions.

Sometimes, due to the demanding lifestyle of the Krishna conscious process, devotees leave and join other faiths or *yoga* organizations. Initially, devotees may feel more comfortable in these groups because they are not expected to undertake such great austerities, yet they are still able to connect with some

Mantra Thirteen

degree of spirituality. We can compare the decision to 'downgrade' one's spiritual path to the practice amongst some highly qualified professionals in the secular world to voluntarily accept a demotion. Although sometimes people obtain training in sought-after professions such as surgery or psychiatry, they may subsequently choose not to practice due to the demanding nature of these occupations. Desiring to work in a more relaxed environment, they take up other jobs which are not considered as serious. Although they may receive less pay, they gain a greater sense of well-being due to the fact that they do not have to work as hard, or undergo as much stress. However, those who decide to remain surgeons or psychiatrists are willing to bear the extra burdens inherent in those professions because they realize that the rewards they stand to receive in terms of status, pay, and job satisfaction are the topmost.

Similarly, in our devotional lives, we should continually remind ourselves why we have decided to undertake so many extra commitments. Because we are spiritual specialists, not only do we avoid intoxication, but we also abstain from drinking tea and coffee; and not only do we shun meat, fish, and eggs, but we accept only pure vegetarian foodstuffs offered to the Lord. Of our own accord, we agree to many restrictions due to our responsibilities and our services. In all *asramas*, we abide by certain rules and regulations, which involve both the avoidance of certain activities, and the positive observance of others. Often, devotees face criticism for being 'over-involved.' Our material associates may exclaim, "Why do you have to bother with God all the time? Is it really necessary to chant all the time and to go to the temple everyday?" Most people feel that a weekly visit to their place of worship is sufficient, and that more is obsessive. However, always keep in mind that we want to become specialist lovers of God. Therefore, when we are absorbed in an occupation that is as wonderful as service to the Supreme Lord, it naturally dominates a large part of our daily thoughts. We cannot help but organize our lives based on such captivating subject matter. Our dedication is a sign that we are trying to become real devotees.

The Ultimate Beneficiary of All Sacrifices

In *Bhagavad-gita* 9.25, Krishna describes various paths of worship:

> *yanti deva-vrata devan*
> *pitrn yanti pitr-vratah*

> *bhutani yanti bhutejya*
> *yanti mad-yajino 'pi mam*
>
> *Those who worship the demigods will take birth among the demigods; those who worship the ancestors go to the ancestors; those who worship ghosts and spirits will take birth among such beings; and those who worship Me will live with Me.*

While Krishna concedes that human beings are engaged in varying types of religious activity, the Lord also reveals that ultimately He is the object of all worship. Although the conditioned souls are largely unaware of His existence, Krishna confirms that He is the sole enjoyer and beneficiary of all sacrifices. Any boon offered by the *devas* is first sanctioned by Krishna, as verified by *Bhagavad-gita* 9.23:

> *ye 'py anya-devata-bhakta*
> *yajante sraddhayanvitah*
> *te 'pi mam eva kaunteya*
> *yajanty avidhi-purvakam*
>
> *Those who are devotees of other gods and who worship them with faith actually worship only Me, O son of Kunti, but they do so in a wrong way.*

According to a person's mode of worship, he or she will achieve a particular status in the next life. In many ancient civilizations, people turned to ancestor-worship, which can only be described as a dangerous practice. Krishna declares that we take our next birth among those to whom we pay homage. The real problem is that no one really knows in what realm of reality the ancestors are situated. Quite possibly, they could be on the hellish planets, where we may join them. By abandoning ancestor-worship, we should not feel that we are being insensitive, or that we are evading our responsibilities to maintain the family heritage. Practicing *bhakti* means that, by engaging in a much higher form of worship, we are making the best possible arrangements for our relatives who have passed on. They will automatically accrue exponential benefit based on the fact that there is a devotee in their family. We must be careful not to give up our spiritual life. If we do, we actually cheat our ancestors of the greatest benediction available.

It is true that most people will not take to Krishna consciousness because they are distracted by the material energy. Most of our materialistic relatives do not have a clue about the real attractions of Krishna consciousness. Sometimes, when we feel overwhelmed and discouraged by the misunderstanding of the people closest to us, we can take solace in the realization that we are not working only for our own well-being. We have a clear choice: either we can react sentimentally, and merely give into our relatives' personalities while we avoid really helping them, or we can consider that *for their ultimate benefit*, it is even more important to be fixed in our devotion, despite the confusion or criticism we might encounter.

Qualifications for Hearing Confidentially

Krishna personally reveals all the transcendental knowledge contained in *Bhagavad-gita* to Arjuna because Arjuna has particular qualifications; namely, he is *anasuya*, or non-envious of Krishna, and Krishna considers him to be His very dear friend. Normally, we would not reveal anything important to a person whom we feel does not really care about us. If we tell an envious person something very intimate about ourselves, most probably he or she will use it to hurt us. But if we consider someone to be a friend, then it is our duty to reveal our minds. Real friendship means genuine communication. Arjuna is the recipient of so many wonderful transcendental truths in the *Bhagavad-gita* and the *Mahabharata* because he does not have any ulterior motives, and he is eager to take advantage of what Krishna is sharing.

Utsaha, or enthusiasm, is also a vital factor for advancing in devotional service. Why do the *gosvamis* emphasize this quality? For the simple reason that if we are not enthused by devotion, we will be stimulated by *maya*. The energy of the mind must always be directed towards an object. Therefore, if we are not full of gratitude because we have come into the process of Krishna consciousness; if we are not feeling animated about the possibilities of communicating our wonderful discovery to others; or if we are not thrilled about our accomplishments in service, then naturally our excitement will emanate towards all sorts of unhealthy practices. These unwholesome obsessions are detrimental to us not only in the present, but also in the future, as the mind draws us towards our next body. If we truly realize that the form of worship we meditate on will determine our next body, then we will focus all our energy on Krishna's service. A sign of real knowledge is manifest when our actions become aligned with this understanding. Knowing means not just to reflect, but also to *engage* in action. A person who has real knowledge engages in devotional service with great *care* and *dedication*. He or she is not distracted by worshiping either the forefathers or the demigods. Such a person is ready to persevere as a spiritual specialist.

Questions and Answers
Question: Is it possible to return to the spiritual world from the higher planetary systems?

Answer: That possibility does exist, but it is not a very strong one. Most living entities on the higher planets do not desire to be with Krishna sufficiently. Usually, a sojourn in the heavenly planets is detrimental to our spiritual lives. The tendency in the higher realms is to minimize the opportunity to delve deeply into devotional life. Therefore, higher entities usually have to come back down to the earthly environment in order to develop a strong enough desire to get out of the prison house.

While overseeing penal reform programs for the state of New Jersey over thirty years ago, I was amazed to discover that some prisoners were actually not interested in being set free. In prison, they had acquired social status, they received free food, and they did not have to pay rent. A number of them viewed the outside world as a frightening place in which they were sure to be excluded from any social support system. I even encountered individuals who would purposefully commit crimes in order to stay in prison. Shortly after they were released, some ex-prisoners would break store windows, and then stand by until the police came to arrest them.

In some ways, the situation of those in the heavenly kingdom can be compared to that of the prisoners at New Jersey State Penitentiary. In the higher planets, sensual enjoyment is of such an elevated kind that those who live there are comfortable enough to consider not ever leaving the prison. Therefore, it is very difficult for them to approach Krishna. It is similarly problematical for those entities who live in the lower planets to concentrate their minds on attaining the lotus feet of the Lord. Because their misery is so great, usually they are simply concerned with escaping pain.

During a talk I gave at the Centre for Conflict Resolution at the University of Cape Town in April 2002, I mentioned to those pious individuals who are concerned with establishing national peace that they had undertaken a very difficult task. Usually, those who can barely find enough money to maintain themselves do not have time to think about deeper issues, while most of those who occupy positions of authority are so absorbed in enjoying the perks of their positions that they ignore problems that affect society at large. Often, those in the elite sector directly profit from the misery of others; therefore, they are seldom interested in adjusting the status quo. Inhabitants of the heavenly kingdom are situated in positions very much like those of the privileged in our society. The levels of sensual intoxication they are able to experience is many times more intense than the greatest pleasure we can obtain in our earthly bodies. They are much less afflicted by the various miseries with which we have to deal. Since the denizens of heaven are situated in cushy positions with lots of 'extras,' they do not fully realize their predicament. They have little conception that eventually their situation must come to an end.

Their position can also be compared to a vacation. When we take paid leave from our jobs, we experience a certain amount of relaxation because we are relieved of our daily responsibilities and simultaneously do not have to worry about paying the bills. After a while, however, we have to go back to work and return to every day life. Dwelling on the heavenly planets is very much like visiting a holiday resort. At some point, the vacation has to end. A few inhabitants of heaven will be elevated directly to the spiritual kingdom as a result of the association of a pure devotee, but the majority will come back down to the earthly kingdom. The human form is quite special because it facilitates the experience of a mixture of pleasure and pain. Our incarceration in these bodies means we have been given a wonderful opportunity to go back to the spiritual kingdom. Are you willing to take advantage of it?

Question: Recently, the world has been subjected to a spate of suicide bombers, who kill others as well as themselves, ostensibly for a religious purpose. Does the Lord approve of this kind of radical sacrifice?

Answer: Although followers of all bona fide religions are usually sincere, it is important to realize that a certain percentage possess ulterior motives. They may have dysfunctional patterns, and are sometimes empowered for destruction. These personalities are present everywhere—in commerce, in politics, and in big business organizations. Generally, they are captured by the material modes of ignorance and passion. They are not really religious people. For them, religion is merely a powerful organization behind which they can hide, a vehicle through which they seek to gain power by exploiting the dedication of their followers. Through harnessing religious paradigms, they seek to dominate and control.

The majority of suicide bombers come from deprived sociological environments, which breed fanaticism and discontent. Anyone who lives in an atmosphere of hopelessness and impoverishment will become captivated by the idea of escape. Some, but not all, Islamic leaders contend that one engaged in *jihad*, or a holy war, will achieve a better life in the next world. Furthermore, they claim that about sixty other family members are able to accompany soldiers who die in the name of Islam. Therefore, one who participates in a *jihad* frequently believes that others will also benefit from his or her actions. They will all enter paradise. The parents and relatives of suicide bombers often feel blessed, thinking, "I know that he will choose me." Therefore, they will often assist one bent on such a mission of destruction.

Kali is very happy when people become confused about religion. The most powerful soldiers in war are those engaged in espionage. They are trained to enter an environment and appear to be a part of it, while constantly attempting to find ways to destroy it. The greatest demons are not criminals, atheists, or even cheating politicians. The greatest demons are duplicitous religionists, so-called spiritualists who actually hate God and who are empowered for evil. They enter spiritual communities only to scatter them and bring about chaos. These kinds of fanatics are found in every religious institution, as when divinity is evoked, aspects of *maya* are also present and subsequently revealed.

When we read about descriptions of heaven in the Koran, the Hadith, and the Muwatta, we can understand that it is a place of massive sense gratification. Men are supposed to possess up to seventy virgins and many slaves. But how can this be? Slavery is not part of a godly paradise! How can the women be exploited? Such descriptions sound to some like hell, not heaven. Therefore, this particular understanding of paradise, as well as the violent way advocated to attain it, is surely problematic.

Question: I am a devotee, but the rest of my family are not interested in Krishna consciousness. In fact, sometimes they laugh at my practices. What can I do to maintain my devotion despite their lack of interest?

Mantra Thirteen

Answer: We can strengthen ourselves by realizing that we are not engaged in devotional service only for ourselves, but for our loved ones as well. When we feel distracted by those close to us, it helps to remember that we are really working on their behalf. Believe it or not, many of your relatives who are presently disturbed by your lifestyle will experience great shame when they leave their bodies, as at that time they will realize the importance of your devotion. In fact, they will feel guilty that they did not take more advantage of your association. When they are dragged before Yamaraja, the lord of the underworld, they will evaluate all the opportunities they missed to connect with Krishna. They will berate themselves, "How many times did my daughter come home and try to give me a book filled with transcendental knowledge, but I brushed her off? How many times did my son call and ask me to come to the temple, but I refused? I was so rude that I did not even take the *prasadam* that was offered to me."

It is imperative for us to ensure that those with whom we are connected do not become hostile towards us, because then they will incur even more suffering when they finally realize their mistakes. Rest assured that your family members will derive great benefit from their relationship with you, regardless of whether they take to Krishna consciousness in this lifetime or not.

In his purport to *Srimad-Bhagavatam* 1.12.17, which describes the birth of Pariksit Maharaja, Srila Prabhupada writes that "due to the birth of a first-grade devotee the members of the family, past, present and future up to one hundred generations, become liberated by the grace of the Lord, out of respect for His beloved devotee." Elsewhere, in Chapter Sixty-four of *Krishna Book*, which describes the story of King Nrga, Srila Prabhupada advises that "if someone becomes a pure Vaisnava, or devotee of the Lord, ten generations of his family before his birth and ten generations after will be liberated." There are a number of different references in our scriptures. Srila Bhaktisiddhanta Gosvami writes that when a pure devotee takes birth, people living for many miles around the birth area will receive the highest blessings. He mentions that an *uttama-adhikari* will liberate one hundred generations, a *madhyama-adhikari* will elevate fourteen generations, and a *kanistha-adhikari* will elevate three generations. However, whether it is three, ten, fourteen, or one hundred generations, it is a fact that if we take to the process cent percent, we will be able to liberate, or at least elevate, a number of souls besides ourselves. Therefore, it is imperative that we guard against becoming stagnant and complacent in our spiritual lives. If we choose to be selfish, we will cause many souls to continue their material bondage, souls who, in most cases, do not have a clue about spiritual life or transcendence. By not doing our part, we are in effect turning our backs on them. We should be ready to make a sacrifice not only for our own liberation, but also for the sake of those connected with us. If we choose to let our own anxieties and problems overwhelm us, and as a result stop being serious in our devotional lives, then we demonstrate not only a tremendous lack of gratitude to Srila Prabhupada and to the *parampara*, but also a lack of caring towards those people with whom we have karmic connections in this lifetime.

Mantra Fourteen

sambhutim ca vinasam ca
yas tad vedobhayam saha
vinasena mrtyum tirtva
sambhutyamrtam asnute

> One should know perfectly the Personality of Godhead Sri Krsna and His transcendental name, form, qualities and pastimes, as well as the temporary material creation with its temporary demigods, men and animals. When one knows these, he surpasses death and the ephemeral cosmic manifestation with it, and in the eternal kingdom of God he enjoys his eternal life of bliss and knowledge.

True Knowledge

Mantra Fourteen elucidates two themes which resonate throughout *Sri Isopanisad*. The first theme is the cultivation of an understanding of transcendence alongside that of nescience. As devotees, we usually strive for realization of knowledge related to the eternal kingdom of God. However, here we are told that if we wish to attain Goloka Vrndavana, we should also cultivate a powerful awareness of the temporary material manifestation. The second theme relates to Krishna's *nama, rupa, guna,* and *lila*. Knowledge of Krishna is directly linked to transcendence. In *Bhagavad-gita* 4.9, Krishna promises Arjuna:

> *janma karma ca me divyam*
> *evam yo vetti tattvatah*
> *tyaktva deham punar janma*
> *naiti mam eti so 'rjuna*

> *One who knows the transcendental nature of My appearance and activities does not, upon leaving the body, take his birth again in this material world, but attains My eternal abode, O Arjuna.*

Krishna tells us unequivocally that whoever knows the pastimes pertaining to His appearance and disappearance does not have to take birth again. However, what does it really mean 'to know'? Knowing, in a deep sense, means to acquire not just a theoretical understanding, but also realization in the heart. True knowledge is demonstrated by a readiness to go one step further than merely imagining. *True knowledge means to act with understanding.* Some of us may have initially heard Krishna's words and mistakenly thought that because once we read about some of the Lord's pastimes, we now have an automatic guarantee to go back to Godhead. While reading or hearing precedes knowing, reading or hearing does not necessarily mean heartfelt acceptance. The important factor is not only to hear, but to accept. Accepting our original identity as spirit souls indicates that we no longer desire to engage in pretend-play; that we are no longer covered by amnesia; and that we are fully prepared to allow ourselves to be transported back to the spiritual world. This level of realization cannot be faked. The Lord in the heart knows to what degree we have accepted and understood—or not.

The material world is described as Martyaloka, or the planets on which death is certain. Our daily environment is one of mortality. In reality, the entire material world is filled with the living dead. People think that they are alive, but in actuality they are simply roving around like sleepwalkers, who act as if they are awake but are largely unconscious of their activities. Similarly, when people are intoxicated, they exhibit comparable sorts of weird behavior, which later they either do not recall, or do so selectively. We all know people who may be timid in temperament, but as soon as they drink a little alcohol, they go wild as their inner desires pour forth uninhibitedly. The majority of the world's population, intoxicated by *maya*, is in this state of spiritual bewilderment.

Bewilderment by the material energy can be compared to the disease of amnesia. People suffering from amnesia do not know *who they are, where they have come from, or where they are headed.* Actually, this mental disease is an accurate reflection of the state of our present civilization. Most people do not know their true selves, because they cannot accept that they are spiritual entities. Neither do they have a comprehension of where they have come from. Generally, people believe that they came into being merely through the biological process of fertilization in their mother's wombs. Clinging to particular ethnic identities, average people cannot conceive of life beyond the material body. Most importantly, however, people do not have a clue about where they are headed in the future. If they actually realized the likelihood of ending up in the lower planets and understood that many of them are already on their way to join the ghosts, hobgoblins, spirits, and disembodied living entities, many would change their ways very quickly. This is true knowledge. Really *knowing* means taking action to ensure that we do not have to undergo such inauspicious experiences again.

Philanthropy: A Distraction?

Sometimes, when people involve themselves in spirituality, they become distracted by philanthropic work. Assisting those in need and giving in charity are constructive activities; however, they become unfortunate when we base our entire existence on them. We do not deny the fact that we have to deal with the material energy. Nevertheless, we should avoid channeling all our energy into making cosmetic adjustments for the satisfaction of the body, while at the same time evading core issues such as spiritual rehabilitation and liberation. The great *acaryas* tend to adopt a condescending view of philanthropy as they see it as a distraction from our attempts to reconnect with Krishna. While humanitarian work may offer some immediate benefit, it does not penetrate into the root of the problem. Philanthropy, therefore, fails to offer a permanent solution. Suffering peacefully is not the highest goal. We want to stop the suffering completely! For example, while painkillers may dull the pain of a rotting tooth, they will not prevent the tooth from falling out. While dentists can assist patients with ways to quell the immediate pain, they will usually inform their patients that mere anaesthetization will not help in the long-term. The pain is an indicator that a serious problem is present, which must be addressed. In some cases, taking painkillers is detrimental, because they mask the real problem.

As devotees, we are not to be in denial about the true benefits that can result from humanitarian activities properly undertaken. We should see these activities for what they are—temporary solutions that can be used to reach out to others, and to facilitate people in their progress towards a higher end. For instance,

ISKCON has opened a successful school in Ghana. Over a hundred children from various ethnic and religious backgrounds attend it daily. As a result of our efforts, people in the surrounding community have become much more favorable towards our ideas, even those who previously harbored some ill will towards us. In India, we have established a free medical program run by trained professionals who are devotees. Because these doctors, medics, and nurses volunteer their time and skills to help those in need, local people accept ISKCON in a very wonderful way. The establishment of a first-class hospital in Mumbai, managed by ISKCON, has had an immensely positive effect on the residents. It goes without saying that our free food distribution programs all around the world have helped thousands of people value ISKCON highly. Although some cannot grasp our philosophy, and those who do may still be reluctant to embrace us, generally most locals have developed a certain degree of receptivity for Krishna consciousness because it is linked to humanitarian aid.

Prasadam Alters Karma

At times, those who cannot relate to the philosophy or lack the desire to investigate beyond the mundane reality nevertheless undergo a karmic shift simply by taking *prasadam*. We may introspect and recall that initially some of us may not have been very favorable towards the process, yet somehow we continued to visit the temple because we were attracted to the free vegetarian food. Gradually, however, we experienced a change in our consciousness and found ourselves looking more closely at the deeper aspects of Krishna consciousness. All over the world, many temples distribute *prasadam* as part of their preaching strategy at various festivals and gatherings. Often, those who take *prasadam* are firmly on their way to assuming animal bodies in their next births. However, merely by taking mercy from the Lord and speaking with His devotees, these souls experience alterations in their destiny whereby it becomes possible for them to take human forms in their next lives.

We should view everyone to whom we preach, give books, or distribute *prasadam* as part of the Lord's personal arrangement for us to assist in going back home, back to Godhead. At the same time, we benefit immensely, as we receive credits that enhance our own spiritual lives. It is amazing to know that if someone we help becomes a pure devotee, then we can be given a free ticket back to Goloka Vrndavana. Nevertheless, we should be careful not to become fruitive.

Mantra Fourteen

If we wish to return to the spiritual world, we simply have to follow the process sincerely and preach. The benefits of the spiritual world far outweigh those of the heavenly planets, or paradise, where pleasures are temporary. As Krishna tells Arjuna in *Bhagavad-gita* 8.16:

> *a-brahma-bhuvanal lokah*
> *punar avartino 'rjuna*
> *mam upetya tu kaunteya*
> *punar janma na vidyate*
>
> From the highest planet in the material world down to the lowest, all are places of misery wherein repeated birth and death take place. But one who attains to My abode, O son of Kunti, never takes birth again.

In our previous births, we have all been demigods as well as inhabitants of the lower planets. Now we are in the fortunate position to understand that this entire material creation is nescience. Therefore, we should not hold on to the temporary, but instead work towards what is actually *sanatana*, or eternal.

For those who still want to go to paradise instead of the spiritual world, the *Vedas* describe how to attain such a destination. Seekers of paradise do not have to become suicide bombers. What kind of God expects us to be destructive to acquire His mercy? What kind of God says, "Love Me and serve Me by giving Me the blood of many animals, or the flesh of non-believers?" Obviously, this understanding does not reflect a high level of spirituality. Sacrifices that involve killing animals for serving the demigods exist; however, undertaking them will not take us to the spiritual world. Ultimately, devotees know that even in the higher planets, we will meet with death and disappointment.

Time Consciousness

An extremely important factor in our devotional service is our use of time. A sign of a serious devotee is that he or she is time conscious. One who is spiritually mature recognizes that time belongs to Krishna; consequently, he or she uses Krishna's time in the most productive way. Has anyone ever heard of a lazy pure devotee? A lot of activity is involved in the service of the Lord. The *gosvamis* were always in an energetic mood, engaged in their *bhajana.* They were always dedicated to working for the welfare of all the conditioned souls, while at the same time they participated in many discourses with other Vaisnava *sadhus.* Srila Haridasa Thakura thought that if he did not finish his one hundred and ninety-two rounds of *japa* daily, he would fall into *maya.* Great devotees are always agitated about how to serve. When our agitation is nicely channeled into spreading Caitanya Mahaprabhu's mission, then we do not experience disturbance in the mind, the belly, and the genitals. Agitation is inevitable. Do we want to be agitated by *maya,* or by Krishna's *sakti?*

The relativity of time is perfectly demonstrated by the story of Lord Brahma and his stealing of the cowherd boys and calves. In one realm of reality (Brahmaloka), the incident lasted for a moment, while in another realm (Martyaloka), it lasted for a whole year. Srila Prabhupada often speaks about the time of the demigods versus human time, and about the difference between a day in the heavenly kingdoms in contrast to a day on earth (six months on earth is equal to one day in heaven). In *Bhagavad-gita* 8.17, Krishna instructs Arjuna about the calculation of time on the different material planets:

> *sahasra-yuga-paryantam*
> *ahar yad brahmano viduh*
> *ratrim yuga-sahasrantam*
> *te 'ho-ratra-vido janah*

> By human calculation, a thousand ages taken together form the duration of Brahma's one day. And such also is the duration of his night.

Sri Krishna explains that the time factor in the material world operates at different speeds on various planets. The higher the planet, the slower the progression of time. Ultimately, however, *time destroys.* This law of nature cannot be avoided, even on the planet of Lord Brahma, who lives for many millions of years. Interestingly, in the spiritual world, the nature of time is completely the opposite. Spiritual time is not only perpetual, but rejuvenates rather than destroys. We should remind ourselves that the amount of time we spend engaged in devotional service is only a moment in eternal time. Therefore, when we feel overburdened by what appears to be a complicated process, and become frustrated at how long it seemingly takes to develop pure God consciousness, we should realize that our perception of difficulty is directly linked to our experience of time. We evaluate time according to our bodies, specifically by how long it takes the body to go a certain distance, and by how long it takes for the body to reach devastation. We can acquire a sense of happiness through the realization that the amount of time we spend engaged in *sadhana-bhakti* constitutes an insignificant interval of spiritual time. *When we wake up, we will be back in the spiritual kingdom.*

The Importance of Setting Personal Goals

It is inevitable that problems will arise in our devotional lives. One of the main reasons for difficulties is that, although we are encouraged to be personalists, the majority of us generally deal impersonally with awkward issues. We know that the ultimate goal is to give up all sense gratification and become unalloyed devotees, but if we do not set short-term objectives, then the ultimate goal may begin to seem abstract and unattainable. To become a pure devotee is no easy feat. Therefore, we need a plan of action consisting of smaller, more reachable goals, which will lead us steadily towards the greater end. When we do not go about our devotional lives in this manner, problems will arise without a doubt.

Often, we set long-term goals, which deep down we think are practically impossible to achieve, and then later on fail to understand why we lack the motivation to put them into motion. While we know that ultimately we are supposed to think of Krishna continuously, this objective may appear to be unattainable at first. We can approach our goals in a much more effective manner if we strategize ahead of time and make firm plans about how we are going to achieve a consistently higher level of *bhakti*. If we do not plan, then Maya-devi makes plans for us. She schemes precisely about how to pry us away from Krishna and the devotees and sometimes she succeeds. As we are individuals, we all have different aspirations, which we want to actualize within the scope of Krishna consciousness. *What is your goal?* One devotee, for instance, may aim to have read three-quarters of the *Srimad-Bhagavatam* by the same time the following year. Another may set a goal that by next Gaura-purnima, she will be chanting extra rounds on a daily basis. Let us look at ways to push ourselves towards a higher level of excellence, impelling ourselves forward so that when we accomplish certain objectives, they become an integral part of us.

Honest with Ourselves

New devotees often expect that they will advance very rapidly within a few months of taking to the process. However, after some time has elapsed, they may find that they now have more problems than ever before! When they came to Krishna consciousness, they had conceptions of themselves as peaceful, kind, loving, and tolerant, only to find that after spending time with devotees, they have become anxious, angry, restless, and agitated. These perceptions arise as a result of a lack of regular introspection into our own state of consciousness, and our relationships with others. When conflicts are not addressed honestly and openly, the purity of individuals is often compromised.

High levels of promiscuity invariably result within New Age settings and other religious organizations if such environments lack effective methods of conflict resolution. Instead of an atmosphere which denies their existence or reinforces their deviation, people need to be encouraged to rise above their lower natures through an environment which encourages open and honest communication. As the mode of goodness facilitates control of sexual passions, we must cultivate this mode. Many alternative communities have fallen apart as the result of misplaced sexual energy. Often, within the New Age community, many people are engaged in different healing modalities and alternate therapies, which simply stimulate *kama*. At New Age fairs, it is very common to be greeted with the sight of someone lying on a bed while receiving a massage from an attractive man or woman beneath a sign which proclaims: 'Get in Touch with Your Spiritual Side.' While these activities may have a metaphysical component, at the same time, they unleash an abundance of sexual energy. Is there any wonder so many difficulties and personality problems arise in the majority of these settings, in which everybody hides their true feelings under the guise of a pseudo-spiritual serenity?

The Value of Enthusiasm

The nature of the mind is restless and flickering. If the energy of the mind is not sufficiently harnessed through the making of plans in devotional service, then how will that energy be directed? Like a wild horse, the mind has to be tricked in order to be tamed. Engaging in special projects, like preparing for a book marathon or for a festival, brings devotees together and increases the enthusiasm of the whole temple. Stop for a moment and evaluate the times when you were most happy in Krishna consciousness. If we are honest with ourselves, most likely we will find that our happiest times were when our minds were fixed in service to *guru* and the devotees. When enthusiasm gushes forth, the mind automatically becomes focused. It is important that we check in with ourselves regularly to see what goals we want to achieve, and what steps are necessary for us to attain them. While we should avoid goals that are merely based on our material self-interest, we should *dynamically pursue spiritual goals*. By surrendering to our spiritual goals, our senses become locked into our offerings to Krishna. In this way, we will experience a high likelihood of avoiding the lower planets.

Let us be under no illusion: in Martyaloka, we are in the camp of Maya. The basic environment is negative and it is engineered to keep us prisoners. Therefore, we have to plan our escape actively. Intelligent prisoners do not merely dream of breaking out, but they actually hatch a getaway plan. They study their situation, make a blueprint of it, and then use their knowledge to escape from it. As suggested by *Mantra Eleven* to *Mantra Fourteen*, we should cultivate an understanding of nescience and transcendental knowledge side by side. Understanding the temporary does not mean that we can hold onto our material attachments and simultaneously cultivate spiritual life. It does not mean that we should engage in serving both energies, or that one day we serve Krishna, while the next we pursue Maya. What understanding the temporary means is that we should acquire a deep comprehension of material dynamics in order to either *avoid* them, or to learn how to *use* them in Krishna's service. It is certainly not essential to undergo all the experiences offered by a sinful culture in order to become convinced that we do not want them. Let us look at ourselves and consider our goals carefully. Ask yourself, "How can I add value to the temple programs? What contribution can I make that would enhance the preaching efforts in my town, in my country, and in the world?"

Stepping Stones to Surrender

By making ourselves more accountable, we automatically strengthen our devotion. It is imperative to revisit our goals from time to time in order to evaluate whether we have made progress, and to what degree. If, for instance, we aim to read the entire *Caitanya-caritamrta* in two years, then we need to create a schedule which will allow us to actualize that goal. A schedule also includes smaller goals. For example, in order to increase our reading time, we could aim to reduce our *prajalpa*, or whimsical conversations unrelated to devotional service. If taking too much *prasadam* is making us sluggish, then restricting the amount we eat will free more energy for us to study. We all possess the ability to make plans, which will enable us to embrace the higher goal. In the secular world, successful people apply a variety of strategies in order to attain long-term goals. They set realistic interim goals as stepping-stones to their ultimate objectives. Devotees are very intelligent people. If we are really serious about attaining Krishna, then we will be prepared to do the in-between work, gradually reaching the highest goal of life. Let us try to worship Krishna with every aspect of our being. In this way, without doubt we will attain a level of deep surrender.

Questions and Answers
Question: How can we help to bring about peace in a world torn by ethnic conflict?

Answer: A lot of negative karmic currents are sweeping the planet at present, which have resulted in global clashes of immense proportions. For example, the conflict between the Arabs and the Jews in the Middle East is due to a build-up of unfavorable *karma* over many lifetimes. Certain souls constantly take birth in the same environments, into which they bring layers of anxiety and pain accumulated over hundreds of years. Relentlessly exposed to violence, they are trained to think disparagingly of others who they believe are their enemies. A further increase of negative energy results from the trauma of losing a dear one. These experiences create a weighty karmic force, which breeds a vicious cycle of anger and revenge. In this heavy atmosphere, sinister beings flourish, and their plans to ignite confusion and fear succeed.

Vibrations of anxiety that arise from these intense conflicts affect the entire planet, lowering the consciousness of the mass of people. When we honor fear, *we push out love*. We become closely guarded. We worry about who may attack us, or whether we should attack them first. When we plan a strategy that is based on fear, our lower passions are fuelled. Ultimately, fear prevents us from giving love to those people whom we really want to cherish.

To deal efficiently with Maya's influence, we must strive to create a balance. Balance is brought about through the efforts of those spiritualists who are willing to share the culture of *bhakti* with others in a serious and an active manner. An increase in *bhakti* will create balance on the planet. Our aim is to become focused in devotion in order to avoid succumbing to the existing atmosphere

Mantra Fourteen

of anxiety and materialism. One of the tenets of our movement is to try to create stability in society. Innumerable imbalances need to be corrected. If we are to properly assume our duty to the international community, we cannot be identified only as monks who live in *mandiras*, or temples, detached from worldly activities. Srila Prabhupada directed us to be part of a movement to respiritualize the planet. We are to be chaste to Vaisnava culture to such an extent that our purity spills over into other communities. Srila Prabhupada wanted us to become such deep carriers of our beautiful Vaisnava heritage that everything we do will have a meaningful impact on people. From our example, others will realize that we hold something significant from which they can benefit. We are not just a religious, philosophical, or esoteric movement. We are intimately connected with ancient wisdom and universal knowledge about the soul and God. We should aim to be like the *gosvamis*, who were kind and helpful to everyone, regardless of whether they were rich or poor, criminal or virtuous. They guided whoever sought their advice, assisting people to move from ignorance to passion, and then from passion to goodness. Those who encounter us should think, "Here are people whom I can trust, and who can give me blessings." We should behave in such a way that other communities cannot help but respect us.

Question: I feel confused about the circumstances surrounding His Holiness Tamal Krishna Gosvami's passing away. How could the Lord allow such a great devotee to die suddenly in a motor vehicle accident?

Answer: Many devotees experienced shock when they heard of His Holiness Tamal Krishna Gosvami's sudden passing on March 15, 2002, while he was traveling from Mayapura to Calcutta. It is very auspicious that Gosvami Maharaja left this world in the holy *dhama* near Phuliyagrama, a place where Srila Haridasa Thakura chanted three hundred thousand names of God daily. When such great personalities leave, it has a tremendous effect on the movement. It causes everyone to examine what is really going on in their lives. Hopefully, many people will maintain that introspective mentality, and will be inspired to reflect on their devotional associations, as well as their relationships with their spiritual masters, in a more serious light. Gosvami Maharaja's passing can be seen as a wake-up call: many of us need to become more serious and to give greater attention to our relationships with our *gurus*. Disciples are asking themselves, "While our spiritual master was on the planet, did I show him how much I truly care for him? Did I try to take some of the responsibility off his shoulders?" One day, our *gurus* will not be with us. None of us wants to end up being one of those disciples who look back at the past with regret in the heart, knowing that they did not really act in the proper way. When a devotee has kept his or her mind focused on the Lord for many years, as had Gosvami Maharaja, Krishna will unquestionably give him or her special mercy.

Recently, many devotees left the planet. In some cases, these devotees had previously succumbed to *maya*, but Krishna was so kind that He slowed them down with some form of illness towards the end. Through experiencing physical sickness, these lapsed devotees became aware that they had a limited amount of time left. As a result, they become very serious and were given the opportunity to leave the planet in a Krishna conscious state. In His Holiness Tamal Krishna Maharaja's case, his disappearance from the physical realm appears to be quite an abrupt experience. At the same time, however, it was very favorable, because when such an important servant of Srila Prabhupada leaves his body, there is no doubt that Srila Prabhupada will reach down and ensure his safe return back home, back to Godhead.

Mantra Fourteen promises that one who knows perfectly the Personality of Godhead, Sri Krishna, and His transcendental name, form, qualities, and pastimes, as well as the temporary creation, surpasses death. In the eternal kingdom of God, he or she enjoys an everlasting life of bliss and knowledge. As His Holiness Tamal Krishna Gosvami undoubtedly fits into this category, we can rejoice in the knowledge that he is enjoying an eternal life of bliss and knowledge in Krishna's spiritual abode. Let us work very hard so that we can also be among those who really 'know,' and thus qualify to enter into the Lord's everlasting kingdom. Gosvami Maharaja has always been a leader. He has gone ahead to arrange for us to come and join him. Beloved, let us not keep him waiting too long.

Mantra Fifteen

*hiranmayena patrena
satyasyapihitam mukham
tat tvam pusann apavrnu
satya-dharmaya drstaye*

O my Lord, sustainer of all that lives, Your real face is covered by Your dazzling effulgence. Kindly remove that covering and exhibit Yourself to Your pure devotee.

Desiring for Krishna

Srila Prabhupada's commentary on *Mantra Fifteen* opens with a discussion concerning different aspects of the Lord's potency:

> Brahman, Paramatma and Bhagavan are three aspects of the same Absolute Truth. Brahman is the aspect most easily perceived by the beginner; Paramatma, the Supersoul, is realized by those who have further progressed; and Bhagavan realization is the ultimate realization of the Absolute Truth. This is confirmed in the *Bhagavad-gita (7.7)*, where Lord Krishna says that He is the ultimate concept of the Absolute Truth: *mattah parataram nanyat.* Therefore Krishna is the source of the brahmajyoti as well as the all-pervading Paramatma.
>
> *Sri Isopanisad, 110*

In this powerful prayer, we ask Krishna to remove His dazzling effulgence so that we may approach His divine form directly. Normally, we are strongly captivated by worldly sumptuousness and flamboyance and captivated by material opulence due to our material consciousness. If we examine our attraction to worldly splendor carefully, we will observe that we constantly try to exploit it. Much of the world order now is structured as a 'take' society. The more commodities we accumulate, the more we are considered successful.

Interestingly, the difference between materialists and spiritualists—and specifically between materialists and devotees—lies in the consciousness behind their actions, rather than in the actions themselves. For example, although both materialists and devotees may accumulate all kinds of belongings, devotees do so in order to offer them to Krishna. Ironically, we want possessions so that we do not have to worry about them. Often, we desire facility, money, and good health in abundance in order to avoid any anxiety, which may interfere with our service to the Lord. We want the material competence and capacity to worship the Lord with devotion. As our desire to attain Krishna increases, we find many ways to glorify Him. Glorifying Krishna is not just a matter of emotion or sentiment. It involves strategy and facility. Therefore, the more facilities that are made available to us by the grace of the Lord, the more we are to use them in the service of the Lord. In this way, we avail ourselves of every opportunity to experience Krishna's love, which is so wonderfully diverse. We honor Krishna by using everything in His service.

Why Krishna Takes Away

Often when our devotion increases, Krishna gives us increased material facility with which to serve Him. However, sometimes Krishna eliminates certain aspects of our lives in order to facilitate our spiritual growth. He takes away from us those things to which we are too attached, which constitute obstacles on our path of devotional service. Elimination is also necessary on a subtle level. Psychologically, we need to empty ourselves of the lower qualities that slow down our spiritual progress. The enemies of the mind are *kama, krodha, lobha, moha, mada*, and *matsarya*. We want to be liberated from every one of them.

We also want to be free of *ahankara*. We must endeavor to stop identifying ourselves with relative and transitory activities. These activities attract us and provide some flickering happiness, together with a heightened anticipation of more pleasure. However, when we do not find the fulfillment we crave, we become even more frustrated than we were previously. If we introspect, we will discover what desires or parts of ourselves we need to release. To the exact degree that we are prepared to shed our conditioning, to that degree we become pure. Our purity is not based on the aggregate of what we collect, but on how much we *understand* how to use what we collect, and how much we can *eliminate* that which is superfluous and unnecessary.

Do We Want Krishna or Maya?

As we rediscover the science of self-realization, we revisit who we truly are. We have forgotten our true identity. This process of rediscovery is not an imposition, but an integral part of our essence. Many of the difficulties we experience in letting go arise from *bhaya*, or fear, triggered by the duality of the *mahat-tattva*, which keeps the living entity imprisoned lifetime after lifetime. A major part of that fear is *fear of Krishna Himself*. Actually, we do not want to fit into His plan. If our trust, faith, and love in Krishna were stronger, we would have less difficulty with His plans for us. Could we try to make His plan primary and everything else secondary? One advantage of trusting Krishna is that we will not become overly disturbed about the secondary issues in our lives. In this way, we can keep delusion by the material energy at bay.

Maya-devi is constantly testing us to see whether or not we really want Krishna. She has so many different strategies to reclaim us at her disposal. "Here," she says, offering us a glittering object of sense gratification. "Take this. It's easier and faster than serving Krishna." Usually, we are tempted to accept her offering, for the tendency of the conditioned soul is to want to get as much as possible while giving as little as possible. If we have a 'take' consciousness, we will constantly fall prey to Maya's allurements. Much of devotional service is based on how little we become distracted from the royal path of *bhakti*. One way of assessing our level of *bhakti* is to observe how much we are able to focus on the goal. While some of us engage in *bhoga-tyaga*, others are distracted most of the time. When we become distracted, we are inattentive and misunderstand reality. This is called *pramada*, or madness.

We live on Martyaloka, which is a material abode. Although we are eternal spirit souls, we inhabit material bodies. This incongruity creates duality. Sometimes, Maya tries to draw us away by tempting us with prestige, wealth, or knowledge. Maya might say, "Why don't you give up Krishna? You don't have to surrender to the Lord to get what you want. Just use your intelligence, and I will help you achieve your heart's desire." If we start to meditate on our own powers, instead of trying to surrender to Krishna, then Maya will find many ways to entice us.

If we remain fixed in our spiritual pursuits, however, we can resist her allurements. We have the choice to respond firmly, saying, "Maya, I have been in so many different situations and I have acted in countless sinful ways—not only in this lifetime but in many other lifetimes. I do not, I repeat, *I DO NOT* have any interest in what you have to offer anymore. I know your tricks." However, Maya does not give up very easily. She will continue to knock on our door. "Remember me?" she says. "Remember what we used to do together? Friends come to see each other every now and then." Maya wants to enter our lives and make herself comfortable. We can tell her that we are busy with devotional service, but she will continue to knock, presenting herself as our friend, until she is completely convinced that we no longer have any attraction for her.

Rarely do we decide, "Today, I will fall into *maya*." We often think the opposite, "I will endeavor not to fall into *maya* today." Our entrapment by the material energy occurs due to a build-up of rationalizations, which allow us to minimize the spiritual process. By minimizing Krishna, we open the door for Maya. "I've missed you," she says. "Now you're doing the *bhakti-yoga* thing and don't have time for old friends anymore." And once Maya is comfortable, we experience enticement in different ways. She will attempt to con us all the time. Therefore, the speaker of *Mantra Fifteen* prays for the ability to remain fixed on the Lord in a mood of personalism, and not to be distracted by the Lord's external energies. If we persist in our devotional service despite the challenges, Maya will finally concede defeat and say, "Okay, I give up! I bless you to become intoxicated with unalloyed love for Krishna."

Krishna says that one who is dear to Him is not affected by happiness or distress. One who is dear to Him is oblivious to material pleasure or pain, and therefore is not controlled by the duality of the material energy. He or she remains unchallenged by unnecessary thoughts. Duality brings complexities, ambiguities, and subsequent disappointments, but Krishna does not disappoint anyone. As we develop genuine faith in Him, we find it easier to focus seriously on the real goal of self-realization. We pay less attention to distractions that can negatively affect our devotional service as our trust in Krishna increases.

Maya's Attacks Are Unavoidable

Although ultimately Maya may concede defeat if we are very determined to surrender to Krishna, initially she aims for everyone to experience *dvesa*, or hate, for the Lord. Maya, or Kali, wants us

Mantra Fifteen

to hate God. If we cannot hate Him, then her next goal is to make us ignore Him. "If I really cannot convince you to join the 'hate campaign,'" Kali says, "then become a downright atheist, and just disregard Him. If somehow you cannot get this Krishna out of your system, then just enjoy His *sakti*. If you want *bhukti*, or material opulence; *mukti*, or liberation from distress; or *siddhi*, or mystic potencies, I will help you to achieve them without acknowledging the Supreme Person from whom all energies emanate."

Sadly, some souls get trapped in Maya's plan, and become enamored of the Lord's potencies while ignoring Him. Maya possesses some amazing tricks, which include distracting devotees by 'in-house' fights, or attacking devotees who are sincerely endeavoring to do everything properly. In these ways, we may become discouraged and start to forget Krishna again. "You almost got it right," Maya says as she welcomes us back, "but then you got depressed and you came back to my camp. I knew it wouldn't be long before you realized how much we need each other."

It is common for those of us who pursue Krishna consciousness to experience different kinds of challenges and attacks although we read, chant, and hear daily. Even when the Lord's eternal associates came into this world, they experienced many difficulties. Actually, they were attacked more than anyone else. When we reflect on the lives of the great *acaryas*, we realize that they underwent more intense opposition than anything we will ever have to experience. These hindrances were so severe that in some cases their lives were at risk, and people tried to assassinate them. Although these personalities are pure souls, sent to help us understand what constitutes the most basic conduct of human life as well as the highest philosophy, the Lord arranges for them to experience great difficulties. This is for our benefit. We learn from their examples how to overcome obstacles and reach the supreme goal of life.

Srila Prabhupada is a typical example. Struggling alone to sell his fortnightly *Back to Godhead* magazine, he was gored by a bull on the streets of New Delhi in 1956 three years before he took *sannyasa*. While sailing abroad the *Jaladuta* from Calcutta to Boston to begin his life-work of spreading Lord Caitanya's mission in the Western world, Srila Prabhupada suffered a heart attack. In 1965, he arrived in a major city, New York, and for one year, nothing happened. He battled to maintain himself by selling his books, but then they were stolen together with his typewriter and his tape recorder. He underwent so many difficulties, but they did not deter him in any way.

Why does Krishna allow us to hear about the struggles of His very special agents? Why is it that even when He descends, many apparent challenges appear in His *lilas*? For instance, Lord Ramacandra underwent much austerity, pain, and loss. There are always trials at every level. At the same time, they do not stop the Lord's *lilas* from happening. Challenges can never stop His love from being available. Until we are able to say *NO* genuinely, Maya will draw our attention, pull us into her schemes, and cause us to stagnate.

Arrive at Gratitude

If we wish, we can immediately come to a place of gratitude in our lives. After evolving through 8,400,000 different species, we have finally acquired 'escape bodies.' In this human form of life, we can become excited about the possibility of entering the spiritual kingdom and residing there eternally, completely free from the miseries and dualities of material life. Naturally, as they reach the end of their sentences, prisoners will feel very excited at the prospect of being released. Despite all the challenges they still need to undergo, they will endure with equanimity, thinking, "Only a few more months in this place, and I'm out of here!" Likewise, we cannot experience ultimate happiness in the prison house of the material world, but we find comfort in the knowledge that soon we will be released. We take pleasure in knowing what awaits us.

Maya can be likened to an equal opportunity employer. She does not discriminate based on age, geographical location, gender, or how long we have been chanting Hare Krishna. Maya will say, "I have a special job for you. You have accrued many credits due to your chanting of the *maha-mantra* and performance of devotional service for some years now. But if you work for me, I will make you a supervisor and pay you a lot quicker than Krishna!" We know that Krishna has no favorites. As we allow ourselves to become distracted by Maya, we show that really we do not trust Krishna enough. Our distraction is a sign that we still want to experience the duality of the material world. In some cases, we will experience it until we finally become so frustrated that we turn to the Lord in desperation.

We can conclude, then, that if we really want Krishna, any situation can act as a catalyst to accelerate our spiritual lives. If we truly see Krishna in every situation, then we can capitalize on each moment. If we realize that everything comes from Krishna, then in our hearts we will know that a good reason exists for whatever He has brought upon us. With such a mindset, we can see these events as ones which can contribute positively to our ultimate growth. However, if we think that events occur based on haphazard, extraneous concerns, we ignore the critical controlling aspect of the Lord. If we ignore the Lord's ongoing involvement in our lives, we might as well be atheists. If we really accept that Krishna is constantly present; that He monitors everything in the form of the Supersoul in the heart; and that He never gives anyone a burden that they cannot bear, then we can make fast progress. Although the Lord never favors anybody, our minds often bewilder us into believing this false conception. Sometimes, when negative events occur, we may even think that He has checked out for the day. No, Krishna is always there. We want to be in the mindset of truly desiring to have those things removed that impede our progress. When we are genuinely grateful for how Krishna has intervened in our lives, we avail ourselves of the chance to focus on the Lord single-pointedly, and thus attain Him.

Going for the Gold

Let us consider for a moment the *quality of endeavor* it takes to become an Olympic gold medallist, or even a participant in events in which the topmost athletes from all over the world vie for excellence. All athletes who participate in the Olympics, which occur once every four years, have undergone rigorous daily practice for an extended period. Their entire lives are centered on the goal of winning a gold medal. They set short-term objectives, from which they systematically progress towards their medium- and long-term goals. From early childhood, many of them were determined to do whatever was necessary to reach the top. This deep fixation on the goal before the result is achieved is an incredibly good motivator. Within a short space of time, many of these athletes actually reach the goals they set for themselves. To attain excellence in any field, whether in business, in the academic world, or in the performing arts, it is essential to follow a set plan on a day-to-day basis.

If this scenario of goal-setting and daily discipline works in the mundane arena, then it will be just as effective in our spiritual lives. As devotees, the onus is on us to lead by example. As Krishna consciousness is a way of life, not only do we have to 'talk the talk,' but also we must 'walk the talk.' By behaving in a way that is consistent with our philosophy, we reach a level of excellence, which then becomes part of our identity. At the same time, we must be careful not to fall into the trap of thinking that spiritual life is finite, or of making our short- or medium-term goals ends in themselves. For instance, we may have achieved our medium-term goal of chanting the *maha-mantra* for fifteen years, but we also may have been lackadaisical in our *japa*. Some days, we may not have chanted the prescribed number of rounds on our beads. Simultaneously, we may have caused *aparadhas*, or offenses to others. Nevertheless, we have attained our goal. Therefore, we may feel that we have the right to make demands from Krishna. "Krishna," we may say, "I've done my part, so what are You going to do for me now? Although You have placed billions and billions of people on this planet, only a few of us are trying to come to You. I read in *Bhagavad-gita* that You want us to come to You even more than we desire to attain You. Therefore, it's up to You to amplify my efforts. After all, I have given up so much for You."

Of course, this is not the proper mood. We know that the ongoing journey towards our ultimate goal requires a serious commitment. We are always faced with choices. The nature of the living entity is to be mad, one way or another. Do we want to be controlled by our maddened senses, which keep us in perpetual anxiety or do we want to allow Krishna to enter into our lives completely, and to be maddened by His mercy? What is absolutely certain is that any one of us can reach perfection in this lifetime. Sportsmen and women know that the possibility exists to break records in their fields. They set distinct goals, and often succeed in reaching them. Similarly, we know it is possible to attain Krishna at the end of this life. We can ask ourselves, *"Why not me? If the goal is reachable, why should I not achieve it?"*

Be Prepared to Pay the Price

We find many wonderful examples throughout the *sastras* of devotees who intensely desire that Krishna remove all unnecessary obstacles from their lives. They are ready to pay any price to see the Lord. Think for a moment about a personality in our tradition who inspires you. By remembering their challenges, we can allow ourselves to feel energized by their examples. Their life histories serve to remind us what we are to do and be within Krishna consciousness. Below, I will share the histories of some great personalities who felt that any sacrifice was insignificant compared to the eternal satisfaction of acquiring self-realization or being in the Lord's association. From them we can learn that any price we have to pay in this lifetime is nothing in comparison to what we will ultimately achieve eternally. Even if we have to struggle for the rest of our lives (which are not very long, after all), it will be worthwhile to finally end the cycle of *samsara*. Just a little bit longer, and we can close our current chapter in the material world and enter into the highest level of animated happiness and sublime realization in the spiritual world. Is it not worth persevering?

Lord Buddha Attains Realization after Many Tests

The Buddha is an example of one personality who underwent extreme austerities in order to achieve a higher purpose. We can learn from his unflinching determination to discover truth before he became 'Buddha,' or 'The Awakened One.' Born as Siddhartha Gautama, the son of King Suddhodana in the Kingdom of the Sakyas, the Buddha's early experience of life was sublime; he had no exposure to old age, sickness, suffering, and death. On leaving the shelter of the kingdom as a young man, Gautama experienced the suffering of others and longed to find a way to end it. Exchanging the riches of life at the palace for the simple life of a holy man, Gautama exposed his body to great hardship and torment in order to appreciate the anguish of the world. After performing intense austerities, Gautama still did not receive the answer to his questions regarding why suffering exists in the world, and how to end it. He sat under a great *Bo*, or fig tree, at a place now called *Bodh Gaya*, and decided he would stay there until he found the answers, or if need be he would die trying. One evening, Gautama went into a deeply meditative state and gained the knowledge that he sought. He attained a state of *nirvana*, the negation of all material desires, which is the first part of transcendence. Through his intense endeavor, the Buddha achieved a high level of wisdom, compassion, and freedom from suffering.

The Trials of Queen Kunti

Queen Kunti is another sublime personality from whose story we can derive great benefit. Whatever difficulties she experienced always helped her to intensify her absorption in Krishna. As the wife of King Pandu, the emperor of the world approximately 5,000 years ago, and the mother of the Pandavas, Kunti's lifetime was marked by tragedy and loss. As Dhrtarastra, Pandu's older brother, was born blind, Pandu, although younger than his brother, became the successor to the throne. After Kunti married Pandu, her husband was placed under a curse which prevented him from begetting children. Forced to abdicate his throne, Pandu retired to the forest with Kunti and her co-wife, Madri. With Pandu's permission, Kunti invoked the benediction given her by the great mystic Durvasa Muni to conceive three sons, namely Yudhisthira, Bhima, and Arjuna from the demigods Dharma, Vayu, and Indra respectively. After Pandu's untimely death, Kunti and her sons returned to the kingdom. Her eldest son, Yudhistira, was meant to assume the throne, but was cheated out of this position by his power-hungry cousin Duryodhana. Duryodhana also made numerous unsuccessful assassination attempts on the lives of the Pandavas and Kunti. To Kunti's great sorrow, the Pandavas were exiled to the forest for thirteen years after tolerating the abuse of their wife, Draupadi, by Duryodhana's relatives, the Kauravas.

After the thirteen years of exile had ended, the Pandavas set about trying to reclaim their kingdom in a peaceful fashion. Yudhisthira sent Lord Krishna to negotiate with Duryodhana, who obstinately refused to relinquish the throne. A devastating war ensued leaving millions of warriors dead. Only Lord Krishna, the Pandavas, and a few others survived the massacre. In a last attempt at revenge, one of the surviving Kauravas, Asvatthama, murdered Draupadi's five sons while they were sleeping. As a final blow, Kunti suffered the death of her grandchildren.

Queen Kunti's sufferings were far greater than any ordinary person could endure. However, her prayers are not self-serving because she does not beg for relief. An ordinary person might say, "Krishna, You are simply making my life difficult. Please, be fair to me. Enough is enough." On the contrary, Queen Kunti requested more suffering. After the Lord saved Maharaja Pariksit, the only surviving descendent of the Pandavas, from the *brahmastra* weapon thrown by Asvatthama, Queen Kunti prayed to the Lord as follows:

vipadah santu tah sasvat
tatra tatra jagad-guro
bhavato darsanam yat syad
apunar bhava-darsanam

I wish that all those calamities would happen again and again so that we could see You again and again, for seeing You means that we will no longer see repeated births and deaths.
Srimad-Bhagavatam, 1.8.25

Is Krishna Consciousness Too Difficult?

How often do we think that the worship of Lord Krishna is too difficult? Occasionally, some of us may consider it easier to worship demigods like Lord Siva, for by worshiping the demigods we can receive instant reciprocation, although it is fleeting and material. We fail to perceive that we are often our own worst enemies. We evaluate our experiences based on our perceptions. How we perceive and codify what happens to us determines how we respond to it. We have much more power within ourselves to make a difference at every moment than we actually realize. Usually, we cannot change our environment, but we always have the ability to adjust how we respond to it. We have the power to accept situations, *sankalpa*, and the ability to reject them, *vikalpa*, based on what is most favorable for our advancement in Krishna consciousness. In this way, we can make choices and decisions that are aligned with our ultimate spiritual goals.

Perhaps one of the worst experiences we can undergo is the death of a loved one, or the falldown of our spiritual mentors. When some *gurus* left our movement, many lost faith in the devotional process of Krishna consciousness and in Krishna Himself. Some decided to revert to old habits like drinking alcohol and taking drugs. Lamenting terribly, these devotees failed to capitalize on the positive elements offered by such an intense experience. The negative way they chose to perceive it hurts them not only in the present, but also slows down their future growth. Others, faced with a similar situation, chose instead to focus on scrutinizing the devotional process and consequently deepened their commitment to it. We always have the choice to take responsibility by searching out good *sadhu-sanga* or by studying *sastra* scrutinizingly. These activities will accelerate our advancement towards the Supreme Lord as they increase our understanding of how to avoid the gross and subtle attacks of *maya*. Difficulties can increase our dedication and enrich us as devotees. A tough situation might expose our blind faith or the way in which we rationalize our sense gratification. In the midst of calamity, we can become more careful and dedicated while simultaneously intensifying our cry for the mercy of the *parampara*.

Maharaja Pariksit Welcomes Death

The life of Maharaja Pariksit, the grandson of Arjuna and Subhadra-devi, is a prime example of how to accept unjust circumstances with equanimity. Hunting in the forest one day with his bow and arrow, Maharaja Pariksit was overcome by tiredness and thirst. In search of water and a place to rest, Maharaja Pariksit entered the hermitage of Samika Rsi, a great sage residing in that forest, and encountered the sage in deep meditation. Thinking that Samika Rsi was feigning trance in order to avoid receiving a member of the lower *ksatriya*, or warrior caste, Maharaja Pariksit became angry and garlanded the sage with a dead snake. When Srngi, the sage's son, observed what Maharaja Pariksit had done, he retaliated by cursing the king to die after seven days had passed.

In the meantime, Maharaja Pariksit felt remorseful and repented for his actions. As a result of the insulting manner in which he had dealt with the sage, he prayed for a calamity, the due reaction he saw fit to match his offensive act, to befall him as soon as possible. On learning that he was cursed to die within seven days, Maharaja Pariksit rejoiced, as death would enable him to let go of all material attachments and attain perfection. In our age, people who know that their lives are nearing the end sometimes throw huge parties, draw all their money out of stocks and bonds, and travel around the world to eke out the last bit of enjoyment from their final few months. However, in previous ages, many people used their last days on earth for gaining insight into the genuine, important aspects of life. Instead of desiring to maximize his sense gratification, Maharaja Pariksit decided to become more focused on his real purpose as a spiritual being, as part and parcel of the Supreme Lord. He renounced all fruitive activities, including religious rituals and economic dealings, and firmly fixed himself on cultivating his natural love for Krishna. Sitting down on the banks of the Ganges to fast until death, Maharaja Pariksit inquired from Sukadeva Gosvami how one who is about to die could attain perfection and return to Krishna.

The Austerities of Dhruva Maharaja

The story of Dhruva Maharaja, recounted in the Fourth Canto of the *Srimad-Bhagavatam*, instructs us further to value setbacks as part of the process of spiritual advancement. When he was a five-year-old child, Dhruva Maharaja's stepmother Suruci prevented him from sitting on the lap of his father, King Uttanapada. Enraged, Dhruva Maharaja vowed to attain a kingdom larger than that of his grandfather. Following the advice of his mother, Suniti, Dhruva Maharaja went to the Madhuvana forest to worship the Supreme Personality of Godhead by the performance of severe austerities. Steadfast in his determination, he was able to control the *prana*, or life air, within his body to such a degree that it affected the *prana* throughout the planet. Lord Visnu appeared before him in

Mantra Fifteen

person and fulfilled Dhruva Maharaja's desire for his own kingdom by creating Dhruvaloka, or the polestar, which is never destroyed even when the rest of the material world is annihilated. However, now that Dhruva Maharaja had developed his love for the Lord, he viewed the prestige and opulence he had previously hankered for as pieces of broken glass in comparison to the diamond-like brilliance of the Lord's direct association.

Without doubt, fixed determination and austerities evoke increased potency in both material and spiritual endeavors. It is up to us how we direct our energy. Nothing can happen without power, whether it is the *bahiranga*, *tatastha*, or *antaranga-sakti* of the Lord. If we think that we can break through the material modes of nature without great focus and without a strong alignment with *sadhu-sanga* and *sastra*, then we are sorely mistaken. Taking proper shelter of *sadhu-sanga* and *sastra* results in the removal of unwanted desires, enabling us to access the real powerhouse of Krishna in the heart. If we do not have sufficient fear of failure and disappointment, or of Yamaraja, then we will not be able to generate enough power to end our entanglement in the cycle of repeated birth and death.

Simply the fact that we chant Hare Krishna does not preclude us from meeting Yamaraja. Sometimes, we are so fallen that Yamaraja appears before us as a facilitator. To whom much is given, much is expected. When a *bhakta* or *bhaktin* falls down, the consequences are serious; when an initiated devotee decides to stop practicing, it is even more serious; when a *brahmana* fails to uphold his or her vows, the situation is grave; and when a *sannyasi* falls, the result is disastrous. Each of these phases of devotional service offer increased opportunities for us to advance in our spiritual lives. When we refuse to take advantage of them, we become sabotaging agents. Therefore, we may have to appear before Yamaraja after death. In such a case, he will end up telling us, "You again! You were chanting the *maha-mantra*, you wore *tulsi-mala*, or sacred neck beads, and you had *darsana* with the Lord in His *arca-vigraha*. What are you doing back here? You were so close to attaining love for Krishna. You will have to undergo severe reactions for such neglect."

How We Sabotage Ourselves

In *Mantra Three*, we read about *atma-hanah*, the killers of the soul. In *Mantra Ten*, we read about *vidya* and *avidya*. Knowledge that is misused is even worse than nescience, or ignorance. Krishna consciousness is a highly dangerous process, because there is a price to be paid for hearing, for learning, and for associating. When we do not apply our knowledge correctly, the consequences are most serious. For instance, in almost every society, premeditated murder is considered far more severe than murder motivated by passion, or by self-defense. A murder is still a crime, regardless of the motive. Nevertheless, a difference exists. When murder is planned, it shows that knowledge was deliberately used in an inappropriate way; therefore, serious consequences must follow. One of the reasons devotees may suffer so much in devotional service is that they either neglect or misuse their opportunities for transcendence. It is risky to come so close to devotional practice, but simultaneously to refuse to optimize our chances for advancement.

It is as if we are standing on the front line, wearing the uniform of Lord Caitanya's army, but we find ourselves unprepared for battle. The enemy says, "What are you doing here? You have forgotten to bring all of your weapons." We hurry away to fetch the remainder of our weapons and return to the front line once more. The enemy notices that although we now have all the appropriate weapons, we forgot to bring the ammunition. The enemy then says, "You have come to fight, but you are still inadequately prepared. We will deal with you quickly and expediently." Similarly, Maya says, "Oh, you are a Hare Krishna devotee. You are connected with the most internal aspect of the Lord in all the universes. You are connected with Krishna who comes in the *bhava*, or mood, of Radharani. You are connected with the blessings of the Divine Mother Herself. You are connected with the Godhead, who has entered the material realm to directly convey His message to you, and who is the most munificent incarnation. Yet, you still choose to deny the Lord's love."

Srila Rupa Gosvami and his younger brother, Sri Vallabha, praised the Lord at the home of the Deccan *brahmana* at Prayaga as follows:

> namo maha-vadanyaya
> krsna-prema-pradaya te
> krsnaya krsna-caitanya-
> namne gaura-tvise namah

> *O most munificent incarnation! You are Krishna Himself appearing as Sri Krishna Caitanya Mahaprabhu. You have assumed the golden color of Srimati Radharani, and You are*

widely distributing pure love of Krishna. We offer our respectful obeisances unto You.
Caitanya-caritamrita, Madhya-lila, 19.53

If we choose to deny Krishna even in His most magnanimous form as Sri Caitanya Mahaprabhu, Maya will find many ways to assist us. She will continue to entice us to make absolutely sure that all we desire is the Lord Himself.

Maya: Krishna's Secret Agent

The *Brahma-samhita*, written by Lord Brahma in glorification of the Supreme Personality of Godhead, and translated by Srila Bhaktisiddhanta Sarasvati Gosvami, explains that the very same Maya-devi, who pushes us down, is simultaneously a maidservant of the Lord:

*srsti-sthiti-pralaya-sadhana-saktir eka
chayeva yasya bhuvanani bibharti durga
icchanurupam api yasya ca cestate sa
govindam adi-purusam tam aham bhajami*

The external potency Maya who is of the nature of the shadow of the cit potency, is worshiped by all people as Durga, the creating, preserving and destroying agency of this mundane world. I adore the primeval Lord Govinda in accordance with whose will Durga conducts herself.
Brahma-samhita, 5.44

Every time we say *NO* to Maya, and *YES* to Krishna, and every time we have gratitude for Krishna regardless of whatever Maya offers, we accelerate our growth towards the Lord. In essence, Krishna consciousness is a process whereby we are meant to remove anything that blocks us from reaching Krishna. Eventually, all we want is Krishna. Anything that takes on more priority means another birth. Desiring separately from Krishna means that a part of us still wants to experience certain material situations before we are entirely ready to receive the total force of Krishna's love, or to give our complete love to Him. Krishna wants to give Himself in full, but we cannot receive Him in full when we are too preoccupied with secondary activities, and attracted to His lower energies. Whatever happens to any of us is nobody's fault. Events occur based on our own life space, *karma*, and growth experiences. They are not accidental. The question remains: How do we respond to them?

No example exists in Vaisnava history of a personality who did not have to contend with tremendous obstacles in the realm of illusion before he or she was able to return to the spiritual sky. Difficulties are ever-present even in Krishna's pastimes; the significant factor is how we address them. Often, we fall under the delusion that life is meant to be unproblematic. This mentality is due to our cheating propensity, enhanced perhaps by our former religious backgrounds. In Judeo-Christianity, the goal of spiritual life is often seen to be heaven, which means that most practitioners think, "I want peace, I want my enjoyment and my kingdom. I don't want anything to bother me." Demigod worship is connected with similar types of territorial sovereign interests. The demigods know Krishna and His supreme position; nevertheless, they desire their own areas of control. Unalloyed devotional service to Krishna is not of the utmost importance to them. Therefore, they cannot enter Vrndavana, although they acknowledge and respect the Lord. Many denizens of the heavenly kingdoms have to return to the earth planet, to be shaken up by the material energy.

The Sorrows of Devaki and Vasudeva

As we know, Devaki and Vasudeva are confidential servants of Lord Krishna, who act as the Lord's parents in His manifest pastimes here on earth. On her wedding day, Devaki's brother, Kamsa, heard a voice from the sky informing him that his sister's eighth child would bring about his demise. Desiring to kill Devaki instantly, Kamsa was pacified by her husband Vasudeva's promise that the couple would surrender each child to him once it was born. Before the birth of the Lord, Devaki and Vasudeva experienced the traumatic death of their seven children at the hand of Kamsa. They knew that when Devaki gave birth to Krishna, Kamsa would want to kill Him too. Nevertheless, they were willing to undergo intense agony in order to have the Lord as their child. Imagine the pain inherent in this pastime. Those who have experienced the grief of a miscarriage, or the passing of a child, say that it is like death. Many parents never fully recover from such a tragedy. However, Devaki and Vasudeva knew that their suffering was not in vain, and that it was worth enduring for the higher goal. They were not ordinary spiritualists, but pure devotees of Krishna. The more devotees evolve and purify themselves, the more intense the challenges they have to face. Often, the severity of the challenge reveals their pinpointed devotion. They are all for Krishna, and Krishna is all for them. And ultimately, victory will triumph over nescience.

Haridasa Thakura's Beatings

Srila Haridasa Thakura, an intimate associate of Lord Caitanya, was beaten in twenty-two market places for chanting the holy names of the Lord. Normally, this kind of punishment would bring death to an ordinary man, but Haridasa Thakura did not feel any pain. On another occasion, Haridasa Thakura overcame Maya-devi's tricks when she arrived at his cave in the dead of night in the form of a beautiful prostitute. Instead of succumbing to her or chasing her away in anger, Haridasa Thakura asked Maya to stay while he chanted the *maha-mantra*. Although she exhibited feminine postures that would bewilder the mind of even Lord Brahma, Haridasa Thakura remained unperturbed. At the end of three days of chanting, Maya-devi surrendered to him, and begged to be initiated into the chanting of Hare Krishna. A neophyte devotee, presented with a similar situation, might not be so fixed in his determination. He may think to himself, "I have been pretty good for quite a while. Krishna is too busy to notice my little deviation. A little bit of *maya* from time to time increases my enthusiasm for His service. Besides, I am better than most devotees." Haridasa Thakura did not rationalize his behavior by thinking that any act of sense gratification would go unnoticed. He remained fixed in his determination to chant three hundred thousand names of God daily, and therefore he was undeterred by distractions.

In some countries, devotees risk their lives to preach. In some cases, the challenges are overwhelming and some lose faith. "Why," they ask, "if we are serving very nicely, do we still get smashed over and over again?" Krishna never gives us more than what is necessary for our maturation. If we feel that Krishna is giving us too much—to the point that we cannot take it anymore—we can be happy in the knowledge that even if we leave our bodies, we will derive immense benefit from the purification we were forced to undergo. It is important to introspect and assess experiences internally. There is really only *prema*. It is just a matter of directing some of the intensity of our *kama* towards Krishna. Uncomfortable experiences then become catalysts to hasten our journey towards our eternal residence in Krishnaloka.

Srila Prabhupada's Sacrifice

It is important to remember that Srila Prabhupada came to America with neither money, nor disciples, nor established temples. Due to his revolutionary efforts, today thousands of disciples in ISKCON compete to wash their spiritual master's clothes, to drive him around, to cook for him, to attend to his health, and to offer funds for his projects. Nowadays, we may become complacent, not realizing that a few pioneering devotees struggled intensely to establish every one of our temples. They distributed books on the street to collect funds, and sometimes did not have anything to eat. Many simply existed from day to day. In the beginning years, the public did not understand the importance of our movement. Currently, large congregations are flourishing in many places, whereas formerly just a tiny group of temple devotees existed. Generally, simplicity and austerity help the devotional creeper immensely. It can be dangerous to become content, and to expect much without being ready to do our part.

Accustomed to have everything readily available, we quickly lose our determination when a resource is suddenly lacking. Over time, ISKCON has acquired more facilities, but simultaneously it has become more complex, with more controversial issues, and at times, more *maya*. Whether in periods of abundance or in times of scarcity, we want to say, "Thank You, Krishna." At present, we can express our gratitude to Krishna for the wonderful family of devotees He has given us. Most of us are surrounded by many personalities—godbrothers, godsisters, uncles, aunts, nieces, and nephews—all of whom allow us to work on ourselves as we interact with and purify one another.

Jayananda Thakura's Battle with Leukemia

While Sriman Jayananda Thakura was on the planet, he worked tirelessly to spread the Ratha-yatra, or the Festival of Chariots, throughout the world. A disciple of Srila Prabhupada, he was renowned for his service attitude, humility, and good humor in the face of difficult circumstances. Although Jayananda was diagnosed with leukemia, he continued to build the carts for Lord Jagannatha, Lord Balarama, and Lady Subhadra with his own hands. Right until he left his body, Jayananda worked tirelessly, in spite of intense physical pain, to fulfill the instructions of his Guru Maharaja. In May 1977, shortly after Jayananda left his body, Srila Prabhupada ordered that a picture of Sriman Jayananda Thakura be placed in front of Lord Jagannatha's cart at future Ratha-yatras, and that his disappearance day be honored at all temples throughout the world.

Eliminating Distractions

The *Mahabharata* provides us with many stories, which illustrate how fixity of purpose and one-pointed focus can help us attain any goal. Dronacarya's mastery in teaching the military arts, as narrated in the *Adi-parva* section of the *Mahabharata*, is particularly instructive. Engaged in training the Pandavas in various methods of combat, Dronacarya assembled all of his students to test their comparative proficiency. He placed an artificial bird at the top of a tall tree, and then ordered his students, one after the other, to shoot it down. In reply to Dronacarya's question regarding what they saw when they looked at the tree, all of his students, except Arjuna, replied that they saw either the tree or the leaves or the bird itself. Arjuna's response was that he could see only the bird's eye. Very pleased, Dronacarya instructed Arjuna to aim and shoot. Arjuna saw only the goal. When he released his arrow, it shot directly into the bird's eye and the bird fell to the ground. Although many obstacles obstructed Arjuna's view of the bird, he systematically eliminated them through his single-pointed focus. Similarly, we should imbibe Arjuna's determination, and approach the ultimate goal with confidence.

We have discussed many remarkable cases of devotees who, despite tremendous challenges, have not only maintained but have deepened their level of Krishna consciousness. If they can do it, then so can we. Look around you, and you will notice someone whose own troubles make yours seem insignificant. Whatever issues each one of us has to face, know that there is always someone else who must deal with even greater challenges, yet who remains faithful and fixed in his or her devotional service. It will help us greatly to develop our own devotion if we actively seek out and honor devotees within our own communities who are currently confronting extraordinary problems, yet who are triumphing despite them.

Let us assist one another to shed our lifetimes of acculturation to the material energy. When Maya comes knocking, we must try to warn those around us. "*Prabhu!*" we can say, "Don't open the door; it's the same Maya with all her tricks." And we should definitely not help another devotee open the door for Maya. Yes, we know what we want, but Krishna knows what we need. We attain maximum benefit when we want Krishna to give us what we need. A number of wonderful personalities in our history have shown the goals to be achievable. Let us peel off the coverings that stand in the way of

Krishna-prema. We can either take lifetimes to return to Krishna, or we can go back instantly. We can take the simple road or the convoluted one. We should strive to attain the mood of the pure devotees, such as the Buddha, Queen Kunti, Draupadi, Maharaja Pariksit, Dhruva Maharaja, Devaki and Vasudeva, Haridasa Thakura, Srila Prabhupada, Jayananda Thakura, and Arjuna, who ultimately derived great bliss from completely surrendering to Krishna.

Questions and Answers

Question: Secular associates of mine are often shocked when they discover that I am a member of ISKCON, as they tend to place devotees in the same category as other religious fanatics. What can I do to allay their fears?

Answer: While Krishna consciousness offers direct benefits to everyone in society, at times our movement is not perceived in a positive light. In the current climate of the planet, it is extremely important to present our philosophy and our lifestyle in a way that is not fanatical. The whole world is studying fanaticism closely. Religions that show any sign of extremism are destined to meet with heavy opposition. As all religions are under scrutiny, it is vital for us as devotees to clarify any misconceptions that may arise. It is also imperative that we execute our Krishna conscious activities responsibly and are sensitive to the perceptions of others. We do not have to alter our lives, or to compromise on fundamentals, but we can package the philosophy in such a way to ensure that genuine communication and enlightenment occur. If we are not receptive to the perceptions of the communities in which we live, then we may face strong opposition from them. In some countries, the government attacks devotees, takes away their registration, and generally makes preaching difficult. It is vital to show others that we are definitely concerned about the well-being of all people on this planet. While we are proud of our own culture and spiritual identity, at the same time we must contribute to the common good.

We preach because we want others to take advantage of the spiritual benefits our movement has to offer. One way to examine the activities of an institution, especially an international institution like ours, is to spend time among its practitioners. Therefore, we may find that spies will infiltrate our movement to verify the value of our process. We must be careful that everything is done legally, and that we organize our different projects in a professional manner.

Mantra Fifteen

Question: ISKCON has received some bad press over the years. What action can we take to counter this?

Answer: Even those who find our way of life too difficult and cannot join us should be able to consider us trustworthy and reliable people. Be aware that if pious people do not appreciate our movement, then it is our fault. Some pious people may not have esoteric knowledge of God, but because they are looking for God, they honor integrity and ethics in others. Too many places exist on the planet where pious people have questions and doubts about us. While we may be lacking in integrity or maturity at times, they also may not understand us due to false perceptions. In order to correct this situation, we must be effective, genuine, and compassionate in our dealings with others. If we are able to shift in a positive direction, we will enable many pious people to come forth and connect with our movement in different ways. Conversely, impious people who hate God will become distracted by our success. This is to be expected. Our goal should be to demonstrate that we are caretakers of the knowledge of God and that we have access to the technologies to connect with God.

As we practice what Srila Prabhupada has given us more genuinely, not only will devotees become stronger, but also we will be able to facilitate the mass of people towards understanding our philosophy more effectively. An increased understanding about the practical potency of Vaisnavism will encourage many more people to participate in our movement. Humanitarians exist all over the world who are capable of facilitating projects and helping our movement grow. People often come to our society, read a book or two, and are impressed. Some may not be able to dedicate themselves completely due to their lifestyles, or because they do not have sufficient *ajnata-sukrti*, but they will still want to assist. Many people are amazed to meet someone who is following the regulative principles, living an austere life of dedication, and who is also well-versed in *sastra*. People who are exposed to a sincere devotee will naturally feel a strong motivation in their hearts to assist him or her.

Question: Frankly, I'm worried that in the coming years we will not have enough people power or financial resources to manage our current projects, let alone expand the movement. How can we solve this problem?

Answer: Money should not be a significant problem for us, as our movement started with no money at all. Amazing miracles have spread our movement throughout the world. Intelligent people will naturally want to give to us. They will continue to give of their time and resources if they see that what they have given is appreciated and is being used effectively. When people donate their money, they see it as part of themselves. Therefore, they want to see it grow and develop. If they feel that it is going to be misused or bear no fruit, then they will not be eager to give in the future.

We often judge the potential success of a project on the finite amount of people power, finances, and management that we have available. This is not really a spiritual perception. When there is a high level of spirituality, the results we achieve can be far beyond our practical means. Krishna can empower a sincere devotee to do extraordinary and exceptional work. Although that devotee may exert only a little effort, the results manifest, nevertheless. However, when the spiritual potency is weak, a huge effort has to be put in to achieve an insignificant result. Throughout the world, our major projects have often been completed by a small core of devotees. These devotees were serious, engaged in austerities, and determined to try and serve Krishna. Therefore, Krishna reciprocated. Unfortunately, once the pioneering spirit dissipates, then personality issues and other conflicts arise, bred by an atmosphere of complacency.

Combining maintenance and growth in correct proportions is vital to our success. When Krishna sees that we are using what He has given us wisely, then He will be inclined to bless us with new facilities. When the facilities, which Krishna has provided, are abused in any way, then they will be reduced or taken away. In certain circumstances, our facilities have been removed by legal cases. Litigation is often a sign of inauspicious *karma*, and a sign that we have not been employing Krishna's facilities in a proper manner. We can combat this inauspiciousness by renewing our pioneering spirit and focusing on our purity. When we achieve this, Krishna will fulfill His promise to carry what we lack and maintain what we have. We must be careful of Maya at all times, as she is actively trying to take away what we have. We cannot stop Maya from enticing us, but we can decline her offers in the knowledge that *as we say NO to Maya, we are saying YES to Krishna.*

Every time that Maya knocks, wanting to come in, we should emphatically refuse her entry. The more we remember how so many great personalities underwent serious difficulties and challenges, the more it should strengthen our resolve to face our own issues.

Just as these remarkable personalities emerged from their difficulties as even greater devotees, so should we become more eager than ever to have all our coverings removed, so that we can behold the Lord's smiling face.

Mantra Sixteen

pusann ekarse yama surya prajapatya
vyuha rasmin samuha
tejo yat te rupam kalyana-tamam
tat te pasyami yo 'sav asau purusah so 'ham asmi

O my Lord, O primeval philosopher, maintainer of the universe, O regulating principle, destination of the pure devotees, well-wisher of the progenitors of mankind, please remove the effulgence of Your transcendental rays so that I can see Your form of bliss. You are the eternal Supreme Personality of Godhead, like unto the sun, as am I.

Approach Krishna through Humility

Mantra Sixteen encapsulates a central theme of *Sri Isopanisad*; that is, the desire to uproot any remaining desires and impurities which separate us from Krishna. Let us briefly cast our minds back to *Mantra Fourteen* and *Mantra Fifteen*, in which related themes are broached. In *Mantra Fourteen*, Srila Vyasadeva emphasizes that a complete knowledge of the material world is necessary in order to transcend it, while *Mantra Fifteen* is a plea to the Lord to take away His dazzling effulgence so that His devotee may meet Him face to face. *Mantra Sixteen* reiterates a similar desperation for seeing the transcendental form of the Lord. In order to attain such a benediction, it is necessary for us to remove all that is unnecessary from our lives. In such a way, we can purify our existence, and engage with Krishna as the Supreme Person.

Devotees think and live in fundamentally different ways from how people ordinarily conduct themselves on this planet. Devotees try to be humble and submissive always, although not to the degree that they lose their self-esteem and become foolish. Bear in mind that the right humility will bring us progressively closer to Krishna. We naturally feel humbled by experiencing Krishna's genuine grace, and by appreciating that He is doing far more for us than we deserve. While materialists endeavor to acquire as many possessions as possible in one lifetime, devotees strive to replace, transform, or eradicate anything that is not related to the service of Krishna. As we engage in serving the Supreme Lord with a sincere heart, we will notice that even though many universal laws act under His direction, His mercy, love, compassion, and reciprocation far surpass them.

In actuality, we can never do anything to repay *guru* or Krishna for the mercy they bestow upon us. Since it is impossible to fully reciprocate with the Lord, we can simply try to do our very best to our limited capacity. Even though we can do comparatively little, however, we should remember that we have a duty to make an effort. In return for our slightest endeavor, the Lord gives so much. Imagine what would happen if we really gave of ourselves. Imagine if *ALL* we truly wanted was to see Krishna's form, and have His loving protection, service, and association.

This *mantra* expresses the deep humility of those rare devotees who desire complete surrender to and intimate knowledge of Krishna. These devotees fervently pray to the Lord to remove His effulgence, which they see as secondary. The humble spirit of this request is conveyed by the devotee's rejection of anything in his or her environment or body that distracts him or her from being able to serve the Lord. As we try to remove distractions, we realize that our greatest and most stubborn encumbrance is *ahankara*. It is ten times thicker than all the previous material layers that encase the conditioned soul, which are respectively *bhumi* (earth), *apa* (water), *anala* (fire), *vayu* (air), *kha* (ether), *mana* (mind), and *buddhi* (intelligence).

The Dangers of Distractions

The Vedic literatures are overflowing with warnings against the dangers of entertaining distractions. For instance, the story of Bharata Maharaja vividly demonstrates the perils of maintaining material attachments, which keep us bound to the cycle of birth and death. As a wealthy king who renounced all connections to his kingdom, Bharata Maharaja was a very exalted devotee. Nevertheless, while meditating in the forest, he became attached to an orphaned deer. Even though he had given up so much opulence and security, a seed of material attachment remained in his heart.

Mantra Sixteen

This seed, fructified by his meditation upon the deer, caused him to think of the animal instead of Krishna at the time of death. Thus Bharata Maharaja was forced to return to this world. We should take a careful look at ourselves and uncover whatever is stopping us from rendering unalloyed service to the Lord. To achieve purity, we require both good association and proper desires.

The danger of material distractions is also one of the messages underlying the tale of Bilvamangala Thakura, a *brahmana* who was shamelessly attracted to a prostitute called Cintamani. Fortunately for him, however, Cintamani was a sincere devotee of the Lord, although engaged in an unsavory profession. One night, Cintamani instructed Bilvamangala Thakura that if he had the same insatiable greed to attain Krishna as he did for her body, then he would become a great devotee. Dumbstruck, Bilvamangala Thakura looked upon Cintamani as his *guru* and decided to change his life. On his way to Vrndavana, the wife of a rich merchant caught the eyes of Bilvamangala Thakura, who began to lust after her. Since Bilvamangala Thakura was considered to be a saintly person, the merchant instructed his wife to serve him in any way he wished. As the merchant's wife approached him, Bilvamangala Thakura instructed her to loosen her hair. Requesting her hairpins, Bilvamangala Thakura plucked out his eyes in order to eradicate any further diversions from attaining the Lord's lotus feet.

Dealing with Tricks of the Mind

Of course, we should not harm our physical bodies in any way. When our *acaryas* say that we should beat the mind a hundred times with a shoe in the morning, and then another hundred times with a broomstick in the evening, they are speaking metaphorically in order to emphasize the need to remove all distractions which cloud our consciousness. If a devotee hits himself with a shoe when he gets up for *mangala-arati* in the morning, his behavior is to be regarded as dysfunctional. Instructions about damaging the body are not to be taken literally; they merely communicate, in a very graphic way, the vital requirement of monitoring distracting thoughts with sharp attention. Because our senses continually disturb our minds, we must be prepared to eliminate unwanted diversions.

The story of Bilvamangala Thakura demonstrates that if we allow our senses to remain unchecked, they will go wild and literally take us down to hell. It is natural to be particularly careful of danger. Therefore, if we regard the mind as a major threat to our spiritual lives, then we will be sufficiently wary of it. Bilvamangala Thakura's decision to pluck out his lusty eyes shows that he was prepared to undergo much suffering in order to remove the thick covering that causes us to take repeated births in this world, and that prevent us from returning to Krishna and our original home. Continuing attachment to material situations—including our jobs, our husbands or wives, our homes, and the trappings of success—means further separation from Krishna. If we devote a higher proportion of our time, energy, and consciousness to worldly affairs than to our spiritual lives, then our commitment to Krishna will become less and less of a priority.

Instead, let us focus on removing unnecessary distractions until nothing comes between Krishna's service and us. Sometimes, we place our yearnings for material accomplishment above our desire to attain Krishna; and sometimes, we emphasize our anxieties more than our longing to achieve Him. These are just different ways of playing God. We can pray to Krishna in an ostentatious mood while we meditate on our achievements, or we can pray to the Supreme Lord in a mood of self-pity, filled with bitterness about our inadequacies. Both moods reflect selfishness. In *Mantra Fifteen*, the speaker pleads with the Lord to remove His divine effulgence because it is a distraction from the ultimate experience of the Lord's personal form. Likewise, we need to examine our consciousness closely and evaluate any latent desires within it. We should ask ourselves, "How many things are more important to me than my spiritual life? When I do not carry out my spiritual commitments, do I try to rationalize and justify my actions?" Neglecting our spiritual duties in favor of karmic duties is a tremendous enemy to our ultimate acceleration.

Developing Intense Spiritual Greed

The meditations found in the books in my *Beggar* series are compatible in spirit with *Mantra Sixteen*. When I composed these meditations, I endeavored to capture the mood of a devotee who is powerfully hankering to obtain Krishna's lotus feet. Such a devotee is confronted by an apparent paradox: while he or she thinks that it is impossible to continue to live for another day without becoming an authentic devotee, he or she also feels completely unworthy of Krishna. Central to these prayers is the desire to become Krishna's slave. The English word 'slave' has very negative connotations, as it evokes the mastery of one person over another. Human masters are lusty and will exploit slaves to satisfy their own desires. Slaves are therefore usually pitied and considered very unhappy. However, this

Mantra Sixteen

understanding of slavery is applicable only in the material sense. The devotee wishes to have Krishna as his or her master and to be used in His service to the maximum. In the spiritual sense, being a slave means being fully captured by Govinda, the ultimate giver of pleasure to the senses.

In *Sri Brahma-samhita*, Lord Brahma recites beautiful verses praising such a captor of the heart. In his commentary on Text 31 of this scripture, Srila Bhaktisiddhanta Sarasvati Gosvami Thakura writes that Lord Brahma is captivated not only by "the transcendental region and the spiritual names of Govinda," but also by his "eternal beautiful form" and "amorous pastimes" (*Sri Brahma-samhita*, 51). Enslavement to any of these variegated aspects of the Lord brings unlimited bliss. We can voluntarily choose to become Krishna's slave, and so too experience ever-increasing ecstasy.

Begging for Captivity

Ironically, it is the constant misuse of our free will and intelligence which causes us to return to this world. We have been given free will because this quality exists in Krishna, and it is therefore an integral part of our identity. Ultimately, we should develop faith in Krishna to the degree that we yearn to turn ourselves over to Him completely. In the *Beggar* meditations, I beg Krishna to take away my free will, as misuse of it has put me into this predicament lifetime after lifetime. I wrote these prayers in a mood of extreme destitution and desperation.

It will be immensely beneficial to our spiritual lives if we attempt to pray in a mood similar to that of the pure devotee who utters the verses of *Sri Isopanisad*. Let us beg the Lord, "Please take away everything—all my *anarthas* and all my *aparadhas*. Please uproot any longings I may have for *bhukti*, *mukti*, or *siddhi*. My dear Lord, please remove even Your magnificent effulgence, which may bewilder me. Eliminate everything that obstructs my true relationship with You." With such an intensity of faith, we will eagerly surrender our own motivations, secure in the conviction that Krishna knows exactly what we need and will take good care of us. We do not have to endeavor separately from His desire.

Draupadi, the exalted wife of the five Pandavas, perfectly exhibited this type of intense, concentrated faith in the Lord. Draupadi found herself in a difficult predicament when the sons of King Dhrtarastra, headed by Duhsasana, tried to insult her by stripping her naked in the royal assembly. At first she tried to hold onto her sari, but soon realized that it was futile. What power could she have against the strength of those mighty warriors? Praying to the Lord in the mood of exclusive dependence exemplified by Uttara, the wife of Abhimanyu, Draupadi threw her hands in the air and said, "My dear Lord, you are the supreme mystic. Only you can save me." When Uttara was under attack by the *brahmastra* weapon of Asvatthama, the son of Dronacarya, she beseeched the Lord as follows:

> *pahi pahi maha-yogin*
> *deva-deva jagat-pate*
> *nanyam tvad abhayam pasye*
> *yatra mrtyuh parasparam*

> *O Lord of lords, Lord of the universe! You are the greatest of mystics. Please protect me, for there is no one else who can save me from the clutches of death in this world of duality.*
> *Srimad-Bhagavatam, 1.8.9*

In the case of Draupadi, Krishna responded by making the length of her sari endless. The warriors pulled and pulled until they were exhausted. Although engulfed by reams of cloth, they were never able to disrobe her.

This story, recounted in the Vedic literatures, illustrates that nothing should be more important to us than our service to Krishna. Understand that ultimately it is only Krishna who can protect us. Thus, again and again, the *Vedas* instruct us to cultivate a mood of surrendering to Krishna. Why should we surrender? Because Krishna truly knows what is best for us.

"Take Away My Will, Krishna!"

The following prayer from *The Beggar One: Meditations and Prayers on the Supreme Lord* expresses a desire to be captured by the spirit of submission demonstrated by Draupadi:

> *Take away my will Krishna, I am Yours. Force me to do what is right and best. Use me as You like. You be my intelligence. You be my mind. You act as my will. I don't know what is best for me. In this lifetime I am trying so hard and nothing is working. I ask You to put me in the right place at the right time for the right thing. Whatever is best, whether it is auspicious*

Mantra Sixteen

> *or inauspicious, bring upon me what I need. My desire, my intelligence, even my will—they are all contaminated. I offer them all to You, my dear Lord Syamasundara. I am Yours. You do with me what is best. Help me to be eager to accept, not in a grudging mood, but with real zeal and enthusiasm, as I submit myself and ask You what can I do?*
>
> Special Daily Meditation, back cover

Often, it is best to pray to Krishna *not* to satisfy some of our desires, especially those that are inappropriate, as the fulfillment of unhealthy wishes will bring negative reactions in this life and the next. Another way of dealing with our improper desires is to pray to Krishna not to allow us to *act* on them. The more we genuinely mean what we say, the more Krishna will step forward to guide us and to arrange what is best. As we draw closer to the Supreme Lord, however, sometimes our faith wavers. A voice at the back of our minds whispers, "Krishna, I know I should surrender. Yes, I will surrender—but in my own way and on my own terms." However, we can choose to override our doubts, and dare to approach Krishna by pleading, "My Lord, I want to come back to You. Please let whatever is necessary happen in order for me to return to You." Meditating on the spirit of inner submission that emanates from great devotees like Draupadi, Uttara, and Maharaja Pariksit will help to strengthen our resolve.

Although cursed to die in seven days by a foolish *brahmana* boy, Maharaja Pariksit was eager to receive any experience, good or bad, that would allow him to return to the supreme abode. Our present lives are of such short duration that even if we have to undergo some inconvenience or suffering for the rest of this lifetime, we should not think it a problem. Rather, we should be eager to face it, while meditating upon the transcendental loving experiences that await us.

Faith and Trust in God

If we let the Lord use us exactly how He chooses, then He will save us from any situation. We should never think that any kind of *maya* is bigger than Krishna. The Supreme Lord Himself defeated huge, ferocious demons like Ravana and Hiranyakasipu. No demons in this universe are as powerful as they were. Similarly, no demoniac impression in our minds is greater than Ravana and Hiranyakasipu. Krishna has already shown us what He will do when He is confronted. The Lord demonstrates practically time and time again that He will not hesitate to eliminate any distraction to aid His genuine devotee. Whatever our addiction, attachment, or *anartha* may be, and however monumental our greed or fear, they are infinitesimal from Krishna's perspective. All we need to do is to ask Krishna sincerely to remove them.

We must cultivate the totally irrational *laulyam* exemplified by the great devotees. At many points in their lives, occasions arose when they could just have given up, reacted negatively, held grudges, or taken revenge. They may even have felt insecure when Krishna did not deliver them in time, or in a way in which they felt He should have. However, the intensity of their greed was such that it did not allow them to be distracted by such doubts.

While we are in prison, we can never be completely happy. Instead, our happiness lies in knowing that soon we will be set free. The accumulation of wealth, with the aim of merely increasing one's possessions, is futile. If we do not use our possessions in Krishna's service, they become a disturbance. What is the value of sleep? Most people slumber one third or more of their lives away. Even while in the dream state, we should think of Krishna, prepare for our service to Him, or develop some realizations. The cultivation of fame, friendship, and any other material goal of life that does not enhance our ultimate service to Krishna actually increases our term of incarceration in the world of duality. Therefore, material aspirations, which cannot be dovetailed in Krishna's service, must be rooted out. Our waking and sleeping should always be spent in searching to connect with Krishna's powerful love, and in looking for ways by which we can return to Him.

While the devotee tries to pray to Krishna to remove any distractions, people in general usually approach the Supreme Lord to provide them with their heart's desires. A mood of asking for our senses to be satisfied will never elevate us to Vrndavana. It is contradictory to the nature of Krishna's devotees, who long to be His slaves, and to experience untold happiness by allowing Krishna to use them in whatever way He wishes. To be truly content with whatever Krishna arranges for us means to be situated on the ultimate platform of *bhakti*.

Hoping against Hope

According to Srila Rupa Gosvami, a characteristic of one who has developed ecstatic love for Krishna is the "strong conviction that one will certainly receive the favor of the Supreme Personality

Mantra Sixteen

of Godhead" (*The Nectar of Devotion*, 137). Hoping against hope that the Lord will accept him or her, the advanced devotee remains convinced that simply by following *sadhana-bhakti*, he or she will go back to the spiritual world. Maintaining spiritual hopefulness in the face of one's own lack of spiritual qualification is a state of consciousness called *asa-bandha*. In his summary study of Srila Rupa Gosvami's *Bhakti-rasamrta-sindhu*, Srila Prabhupada explains that the following prayer by the leader of the six *gosvamis* exemplifies *asa-bandha*:

> *I have no love for Krishna, nor for the causes of developing love of Krishna —namely, hearing and chanting. And the process of bhakti-yoga, by which one is always thinking of Krishna and fixing His lotus feet in the heart, is also lacking in me. As far as philosophical knowledge or pious works are concerned, I don't see any opportunity for me to execute such activities. But above all, I am not even born of a nice family. Therefore I must simply pray to You, Gopijana-vallabha [Krishna, maintainer and beloved of the gopis]. I simply wish and hope that some way or other I may be able to approach Your lotus feet, and this hope is giving me pain, because I think myself quite incompetent to approach that transcendental goal of life.*
>
> The Nectar of Devotion, 137

Srila Rupa Gosvami clearly conveys the understanding that Krishna's mercy is even greater than His love. Once we are genuinely ready to hand ourselves over to Krishna, all kinds of seemingly improbable and impossible things will occur. In the following meditation from *The Beggar One* entitled "I must be Ready to Make Any Sacrifice," I endeavor to approximate Srila Rupa Gosvami's mood of *asa-bandha*.

> *Dear Lord Syama, there is nothing too difficult to tolerate when it comes to getting Your direct association. The more You hide Yourself, the more ecstasy there will be when we finally meet.*

Dear Lord, being away from You and Your servants is unbearable. The only way I am able to sustain my life is in anticipation of that glorious reunion. I know that once I meet You and Your servants, I will immediately forget the suffering and confusion I have experienced for millions of lifetimes.

Dear Lord Syama, I become a madman thinking about Your spiritual associates and their selfless love. When I reflect on how long lust has kept me imprisoned, I want to immediately give up this body. It is my desire for these bodies that has kept me away from You. Knowing this, how can I remain in one for another day?

Dear Lord, now that I am being reminded about You, I see how irrelevant mundane scholarship is.

Dear Lord Syama, when I think about wealth, I think of the chore of monitoring one's assets. When I am sleeping, unless I can dream of You, I might as well be dead. Any action that doesn't center itself around You is a waste of time.

Of friendship? Anyone who cannot direct me to You is not a true friend. When I think of fame, I think how burdensome it is to attract any attention that doesn't focus itself on Your glories.

Conversation that does not deal with the exchanges between You and Your servants is like a loud noise ringing in my ears. Reading anything that cannot be used for Your service is a waste of time.

My dear Lord Syama, afraid of facing another night void of Your association, I try to stretch each day, thinking: "Before this day is over, I will see the lotus feet of the Lord." Now waking and sleeping are the same, as I am never at rest, for I must search You out, wherever You may be.

My dear Lord Syama, I will be so persistent in looking for You that Lord Brahma will say:

"This soul is more bewildered than I was before I heard the order of 'tapah.' Please Lord, give him Your mercy."

My dear Lord Syama, I will work so hard to see You that Hanuman will shed tears, and coming to You he will beg You, saying: "Please have mercy on this soul."

My dear Lord Syama, I will study so intensely to understand Your workings that Goddess Saraswati will have difficulty supplying the necessary knowledge. As she tries, she will call out, "Lord, have mercy on this poor soul."

My dear Lord Syama, I will pass so many tests, pushing maya's challenges far away one after another and screaming out for You, that Indra will personally intervene, asking that I be given no more tests. He will plead: "Lord have mercy on this soul."

My dear Lord, my fixed determination in getting Your association will cause Kapila to discuss such pastimes with His mother. It will cause Sukadeva to pause for a moment in his conversation with Maharaja Pariksit, and say: "Lord, have mercy on this poor wretched soul."

My dear Lord Syama, Rupa Gosvami himself will be so embarrassed to see a fool such as I, devoid of all qualifications, trying to be a renunciate in this hellish age of Kali. Seeing that impossible situation, he will plead my case, saying: "Lord, have mercy on this poor soul."

My dear Lord Syama, I will even attract the attention of Prahlada. He will say: "This man has such a low birth, is extremely crude, and has no attraction for the process. He is offensive to the devotees, envious of the sadhus, and does not relish bhajana or kirtana. He has no attraction for the Holy Name, is full of doubt and lust, and is even thinking that he will get direct mercy from the Lord. Oh! Lord! Have pity on this poor soul, for without Your causeless mercy, there is no hope for such a worthless case."

> *My dear Lord Syama, without aid from Your servants, without a glance of concern from Your devotees, Your sweet association is impossible. There is nothing that can fully qualify us for Your direct attention. Therefore, I stand ready to do whatever is necessary, although I cannot do anything.*
>
> *I am so pitiful that only if such glorious personalities petition You on my behalf can all my great sins be forgiven. I have no qualifications of my own. All I can do is pray to somehow or other attract one of Your pure servants to plead for me.*
>
> *I am the beggar that has no hope for Your association, but cannot live another day without it.*

Diunital Realities

All the highest aspects of devotion seem paradoxical initially. For instance, advanced devotees feel that they cannot live another moment without Krishna's *darsana*, while simultaneously they consider themselves totally unworthy of that benediction. Many aspects of Krishna's nature may appear contradictory at first. In *Sri Brahma-samhita*, Lord Brahma calls Krishna the *adi-purusa*, the original enjoyer. He is also *yogesvara*, or the master of all mystic power. Krishna is *nava-yauvana*, the youngest person, and simultaneously *purana-purusa*, the oldest. In His Bhagavan feature, He is the greatest person, but as Paramatma, He is contained within the atom. Although Krishna is never preoccupied by His creation, not a blade of grass moves without His sanction. Krishna is the greatest lover as well as the greatest warrior!

However, all these variegated features of the Lord are not as contradictory as they may seem initially. They are all simply parts of the *summum bonum*, God as the Absolute Truth. In the realm of high-level spirituality, apparent inconsistencies are reconciled. A contradiction is only a contradiction when we look at it from a myopic perspective. With vision corrected by the spiritual master, seeming oppositions merge together, resulting in a greater understanding of the whole. Our attempts to attain Krishna are similarly marked by two seemingly paradoxical endeavors. On the one hand, we need to be extremely humble for Krishna to bestow His mercy on us, but on the other hand, we must be extremely bold. This understanding of spirituality may seem to be inconsistent in human terms. How can one be both humble *and* fearless at the same time? Hence, Rupa Gosvami's seemingly impossible state of *asa-bandha*. Despite being bound by so many chains, the imprisoned soul remains convinced that eventually he or she will be liberated.

Why Think Small?
Since no obstacle is ever too big for the Lord, it is almost a sin for us to think small. How can we think small when our supreme father, friend, child, or lover is controlling *everything*? Krishna has said that *all* things are under His care. When we think small, we act small, achieve small results, and get beaten by Maya-devi. Always remember that Krishna, *sastra*, and *sadhus* are beckoning us forth. If we do not listen to their call, Krishna hands us over to Maya-devi. Krishna calls us directly, but if we ignore Him, Maya has to help us indirectly by thrashing us with the material energy. The choice is ours: do we return gracefully or do we return after countless knocks, wounds, and beatings lifetime after lifetime? After millennia in this condition, the living entity may acquire some real intelligence and inquire why he or she is suffering so much. Most of us turned to Krishna consciousness after thinking to ourselves, "I cannot carry on like this anymore. There must be an alternative and I have got to find it."

The great devotees are constantly helping us to realize that all we need to do is simply to hone in on Krishna's call. We need not undergo Maya's beatings. We should allow nothing to distract us from Krishna's sweet call, which permeates the entire creation. By using our free will incorrectly, we have become distracted from our true interest. Therefore, we can beg earnestly, "Lord, please do not allow me to operate based upon my harmful desires." To the degree that we are sincere, Krishna will respond. We can plead with Krishna: "My Lord, You want me back more than I want to come back. I am my own greatest enemy. There is always something that I hunger for! I may not even be aware of all my desires. Therefore, by surrendering to You, I trust that You will remove even obstacles of which I am ignorant."

"Lord, this is Kali-yuga and anything that can go wrong, will go wrong. Maya has more tricks than we can imagine. Please take control of my free will, so that I can experience my natural, blissful state once again." We should never be under the illusion that we can dominate material nature. No living entity, alone or with others, will ever defeat Maya! Even great souls fall under her spell. Although

Bharata Maharaja renounced his entire kingdom, Maya still defeated him by evoking his natural compassion for an abandoned fawn. Compassion developed into affection and attachment, which ultimately resulted in his return to the material world in the body of a deer. Maya will even use our good qualities to entrap us in the cycle of birth and death, if we are not situated transcendentally.

The fate of Ajamila conveys a similar lesson. Even though Ajamila had been a highly qualified devotee in the early part of his life, Maya found a weakness on which she could capitalize. When he saw a drunken man engaged in promiscuous activities with a prostitute, his mind became very agitated. Constantly reflecting upon this sight in his consciousness, Ajamila subsequently sought to experience his mental whims.

We should constantly ask ourselves, "How shall I become one of those empowered servants who allows the Lord to use them as He sees fit?" It is merely a matter of being available for Krishna's service, and being eager to do whatever is required. The Krishna consciousness movement is a direct expression of Lord Caitanya's mercy and part of a transcendental continuum consisting of the teachings of Srila Madhavendra Puri, Srila Rupa Gosvami, Srila Jiva Gosvami, Srila Prabhupada, and many other great personalities. The success of ISKCON hinges upon our attainment of their personal blessings. If somehow we are able to sufficiently empty ourselves of personal aspirations, then we may be of service to them.

One of the principles advocated by Srila Prabhupada is that of balance. ISKCON was established to help alleviate the imbalance of values in society and to bring about a major transformation in the world. ISKCON was not established to improve society in a haphazard way, or on a small scale in temples here and there. Rather it was established to bring about wide-reaching and long-lasting transformation. Srila Prabhupada's desire can only be achieved if we shrug off our worldly consciousness. Once this has occurred, Krishna will use us as major catalysts to bring about a global mind shift. *Devotees give up everything in order to gain everything by attaching themselves to Krishna.*

An Honest Broker

The prayers of the *acaryas* often highlight the power of association. Obtaining the mercy of the spiritual master is an integral part of attracting the attention of the Lord. The spiritual master acts like a broker for us. We are obliged to carry out our services and do the necessary, but that on its own is never enough. When a householder who has a small amount of funds wishes to start a business, he or she usually needs to find a partner with a much larger amount of capital in order to make his or her venture succeed. Similarly, when the *guru* adds his greater spiritual weight to our insignificant offerings, then we become empowered to attract the attention of the Lord. When we leave these bodies, many of us may not qualify to go back to the spiritual world merely based on our *adhikari*. However, if the *guru* compliments our small efforts by bargaining with Krishna on our behalf, then we have a greater chance of success.

It is incorrect to think that we are so small that the great saints and personalities will not notice us. If we have an intense desire to further the mission of Srila Prabhupada, then they will pay attention to us. Without a doubt, they are very concerned about the ultimate outcome of Lord Caitanya's mission. It is a misconception to think that Bhakta Prahlada, for instance, has come to this universe and is now gone. Although his physical presence is not manifest, his potency and blessings are here in full. Whenever we act under the protection of the *parampara*, we receive blessings from the entire chain of spiritual masters. The converse is also true. Whenever we are deviant, our individual actions sabotage the efforts of the *parampara*, and therefore we will find ourselves bereft of benedictions. If our desires and actions are improper, the community at large will also become confused as to who Krishna is, what His message is, and who His representatives are. Such a state of affairs stagnates the conditioned souls in their journey back to the Lord. This is very unproductive. Rather, through proper desire and action, we should help people to revitalize their connection with Krishna. The Supreme Lord will notice this and bring us back even faster.

Conclusion

In this *mantra*, the speaker begs the Lord to remove His glaring effulgence so that he may experience the *saktiman*, rather than the *sakti* alone. The allure of the Lord's *sakti* relates to the last snare the devotee must face, his or her false ego. We cannot know all the tricks that Maya has in store for us; therefore, it would be delusional to go head-to-head with her! Rather, we must take shelter of the Lord's devotees. Krishna's blessings and protection come through *sadhu-sanga*. We also want to pray to Krishna to prevent us from functioning based only on our desires. A step beyond even this request is to beg the Lord, "Dear Krishna, You take over. Take back my free will as I have misused it. Ultimately, it is Yours anyway." Thus, we should place ourselves fully under Krishna's care and protection. As we discussed earlier, sincere devotees think that they must have the Supreme Lord at any cost, but simultaneously consider themselves unworthy. Once we think we are worthy of the Lord, then we will make the mistake of imagining that Krishna is not really so compassionate, or that He is too slow in reciprocating. Therefore, although we desire the Lord's association intensely, we should always deem ourselves undeserving.

Never allow obstacles to become more important than service to Krishna. This is *maya*. If we are not ready to put Krishna in the center of our lives, we will not be able to interact intimately with the Lord. Increasingly, we should try to honor the Lord's *arca-vigraha* and the Paramatma. When we revere the Lord sufficiently, then it becomes our rightful claim to enter into the realm in which Krishna is all for everyone and everyone is all for Him. This possibility exists even while we are still in the material world. Beloved, let us desire to become the dear slave of Krishna.

Questions and Answers
Question: How can I realize in my heart that it is essential to let go of material attachments at all costs?

Answer: Just ask yourself a simple question: "How much longer do I want to keep suffering?" The more our lives are filled with sense gratification, the more we will suffer. *Be ready to admit defeat.* At some point, we may realize that we are burning inside, yet we tolerate the situation in the hope that it will improve. However, we suffer precisely because we hold tightly onto a situation which can only bring us more pain. We have to relinquish our addiction to the material energy. We must *do* something about our detestable situation! We should pray to the Lord very earnestly and then bow out of the struggle for sense gratification. Even though we are responsible for our distress (which is never as intense as we think it is), we still cry to Krishna, "I am in agony, I am hurting! I need a *guru* who can help me! Help me, help me—don't You hear me? I am in pain." But then we neglect to do our part by *refusing to let go*.

Question: How can I possibly remember that the material world is illusory while I am forced to function within it?

Answer: A distinct paradox exists in the world. As we study the scriptures, which deal exclusively with the spiritual world, we are aware that just around the corner, nearly everyone is absorbed in

Mantra Sixteen

the illusion of thinking that he or she is God. Wherever we look, we see people working overtime in an attempt to deny simple realities. We have all seen a homeless person dragging a few cans around in a cart, thinking that she possesses something extremely valuable. While most of us can immediately understand that she is crazy, we do not realize that we are exactly like her on a more subtle level, clinging to rubbish instead of searching for what is most precious. Generally, we fail to see the insanity of the entire human population, who are always rushing here and there, out to work or into stores, convinced that they are obtaining prized commodities. It is very hard to penetrate the consciousness of such people. They are so wrapped up in their illusions that when we try to explain the madness of their lives to them, they become angry, even though all we want is to help them. The *nitya-siddhas* are sent again and again by Krishna to help the poor conditioned souls, who sometimes turn against them and try to assassinate them.

When I was at school, I wanted to be a psychiatrist until we visited a mental institution as part of an outing. I rapidly changed my mind! Just by associating with people, we pick up some of their *karma*; therefore, by working so closely with the mentally disturbed, one is bound to become a little mad oneself. Just as we can instantly notice the craziness of mental patients, so too can the advanced devotee perceive the insanity of the illusioned living entities. Patients in mental hospitals are so wrapped up in their own worlds that they become dislocated from the rest of society. If we visit such an institution, we may observe one patient sitting in the corner, knocking his head against a wall. Next to him, someone else will be screaming for no apparent reason, while a third patient will be laughing continually. Similarly, everyone in this material world is suffering from their own individual psychoses as a result of their particular conditioning. Only when they become cured of their mental illnesses will they be allowed back into the spiritual world.

In order to assist their clients, doctors sometimes act as if they have entered into their patients' worlds. To those patients who think they are God, the doctors could say, "You are not God! Neither are you Buddha or Allah! Just stop it." However, it is usually more effective to form friendships with these deluded people and say to them, "So, how is God doing today? Let me hear a little bit about what is going on in your kingdom." When doctors pretend to go along with the illusions of their patients, then the patients are usually more receptive to treatment. In such a way, a relationship is established through which the doctor may convince his or her patient to leave the delusional world.

Srila Prabhupada was the *topmost spiritual doctor.* He was expert at rescuing people from their illusions. When he started the movement in New York, many young people were considered crazy. Hippies used to come to *kirtana* while they were high on LSD or other drugs. During that era, the youth were running away from the constriction of social rules, commitments, and responsibilities. They wanted to be free and thought that spirituality meant to experience as much as possible, while pretending to 'honor' whatever sensation they felt at the moment. Out of his causeless compassion, Srila Prabhupada reached out to them and transformed them into gentle people who could observe a disciplined daily routine, far more stringent than anything they had experienced before. Srila Prabhupada's movement continues to expand further than ever before, because *he is still reaching out.*

Question: How do I deal with opposition from my family regarding being a devotee?

Answer: We must have a strong strategy to protect ourselves from *maya*. The weapon of chanting is especially powerful in this regard. Sometimes, the greatest attacks come from those closest to us. For example, suicide bombers blend into the general population and then attack surreptitiously, killing many innocent people. These kind of degraded actions make us realize how pervasive sin has become in Kali-yuga. Parents may naturally feel very disappointed when a daughter or a son takes to Krishna consciousness, as they think they have lost their child. Often, it is more difficult to deal with the disapproval of people close to us than that of strangers. New devotees may find that relationships with friends become strained, too. Feeling pushed beyond their comfort zone by the choices of their once like-minded buddy, these friends may attempt to disrupt our faith in Krishna and the devotees. Resentment often surfaces when people close to us misunderstand our dedication to Krishna or to *guru*. Although friends may not understand why we do not want to go to the disco, club, or bar anymore, it is our duty to remain devotees, because in this way we can best assist them to return to the spiritual kingdom. Ultimately, our *sadacara* will exert a very auspicious influence on them.

Question: What can devotees do to help their families become more God conscious?

Mantra Sixteen

Answer: Family members benefit greatly from their blood ties with a devotee on any level. Even if that devotee is a neophyte, his or her family will become greatly elevated. Once we realize the extent to which our activities affect so many generations of people, we will naturally make it our duty to avoid being selfish by falling prey both to the comforts of home life and to unhealthy desires. Some of our dearest relatives may be on a fast ride to Yamaraja. Therefore, we owe it to them to assist with our special mercy and knowledge. When these relatives leave their bodies, they will be tremendously embarrassed, because at a certain time during the transition, they will become aware of the true nature of their past life. Knowing that they were previously connected with a devotee of Krishna will also be a great source of relief to them. Thinking about the real welfare of those related to us will help us to stay fixed on our path back to Godhead. This holds true even if they have trouble relating to our devotion to Krishna, and ask such infamous questions as "How long will this 'Hare Krishna phase' last?"

Question: Is there a system of spiritual credit and debit, and if so, how does it work?

Answer: Every time we take part in a spiritual activity, such as watering Tulasi-devi, seeing the Deities, observing an Ekadasi fast, or taking *caranamrta*, or water that has bathed the Lord's feet, we gain spiritual credits. Conversely, every time we make offenses, we lose credits and our balance diminishes. Offenses include *nama-aparadha*, offenses against the holy name; *seva-aparadha*, offenses committed while undertaking service; *dhama-aparadha*, offenses to the holy places of pilgrimage; and *vaisnava-aparadha*, or transgressions against other Vaisnavas. The most serious form of *vaisnava-aparadha* is *guru-aparadha*, which are offenses directed at the lotus feet of the spiritual master. The system of spiritual credit and debit is similar to depositing and withdrawing from a bank. Just observing the four regulations and participating in the morning program means that we automatically become spiritual millionaires—*if we are sincere and take care to avoid offenses*. Depending on the extent of our devotional credits, we may be elevated to the heavenly kingdom or to Vaikuntha at the end of this life.

We can also accrue an amazing amount of spiritual credit through preaching. A major service for all of us involves taking advantage of the opportunities we are given to impart Krishna consciousness to all the living entities we come into contact with everyday. Even if they do not show immediate benefits, they may become devotees in their next lives just because they were kind and favorable towards us.

Question: What does it mean when devotees say, "Maya is testing me?"

Answer: Maya-devi's tests are similar to those we took in school. Many of us will recall that at school, after learning a section of work, the teacher would give us a test in order to see whether or not we applied ourselves sufficiently in class. *When Maya sets a test for a devotee, it is really an opportunity for him or her to graduate to a higher level of spiritual awareness.* If the devotee fails and falls down, the test becomes a missed opportunity. Unfortunately, when a challenging situation appears, we often 'flip out' rather than using it as an opportunity to grow in our service. For example, we may resolve to move towards a more serious attitude in devotional life by working extra hard at temple services, but find that we have taken on more than we bargained for initially and become rude and resentful. Difficult circumstances offer us a wonderful chance to pass the test and to add to our credits, but sometimes we take the test in a negative way and debit our account instead.

Association, especially, is of paramount importance, because it is a distinct barometer of our progress in Krishna consciousness. If our association is poor, our spiritual lives are affected. Our association with one another functions as a metaphysical mirror. Through interacting with others, we begin to see some of our good qualities as well as our own sins and *anarthas*. We should pray to the Lord to remove these bad qualities from within our hearts. However, we must be genuinely prepared to accept the tests that we will be given in order to remove our *anarthas*. If we ask for purification on the one hand, but resent it on the other hand, we will become crazy and start to doubt. This is our madness. A few rare devotees are really mad after the Lord. They think only of Him, and are ready to go to hell if necessary in order to please Him. As they are always thinking of the Lord, hell becomes divine. Even the most heavenly place appears hellish to such elevated devotees if they cannot think of Krishna, serve Him, and associate with His devotees.

Question: Why is devotee association sometimes so difficult?

Answer: It is important to introspect at times and imagine how difficult it would be for us to have to associate with someone exactly like ourselves! If we are honest about our unhealthy qualities, it becomes easy for us to appreciate how awkward it is for others to have to deal with us on a daily basis. We are often unaware of our impact on other people. A useful tool to help us gauge our behavior from other people's perspectives is requesting honest feedback from our different associates. I often hold seminars involving the principle of feedback, because it is a key to advancement in spiritual life. Each member of the group has a turn to be seated in the middle of the room while the other participants share how he or she inspires them in their service to *guru* and Krishna. Once the person in the 'hotseat' has received positive feedback, I ask every group member to also share what discourages or disturbs them about that person in their service to the Vaisnavas. Each person leaves the seminar having gained valuable feedback, encouraged by positive comments and also empowered to work on his or her bad qualities in order to become a better devotee. This exercise is done in the mood of love and open, honest concern for the well-being and advancement of each individual. Participants are asked to write down specific areas in which they need to improve. These lists should be revisited at a later stage to monitor improvement.

In our Vaisnava communities, we should become closely connected to each member. We should appreciate and protect each devotee so that we can offer ever-increasing, excellent service to Srila Prabhupada. Often, however, we find this difficult to do so because many of us have been brought up with a 'survivalist' mentality, whereby we perceive those around us as either friends or foes. We should strive to be more connected with everyone, no matter how they relate to us. We should not slyly try to remove people who do not fit into our plans. As Vaisnavas, we have all been brought together by Sri Caitanya Mahaprabhu. Therefore, the greatest expression of our kinship is to remind one another of Krishna. Reminding one another of the Lord means reminding one another of what we really need to hold on to, and what we must let go of. An integral part of our identity as Vaisnavas is discerning what we should avoid and what is proper. We want to remind each other, Beloved, that it is most proper to beg Krishna to remove all obstacles, distractions, and improper desires so that we can associate with Him in magnificent, rapturous love!

Reflections on Sacred Teachings, Volume Four

Mantra Seventeen

*vayur anilam amrtam
athedam bhasmantam sariram
om krato smara krtam smara
krato smara krtam smara*

Let this temporary body be burnt to ashes, and let the air of life be merged with the totality of air. Now, O my Lord, please remember all my sacrifices, and because You are the ultimate beneficiary, please remember all that I have done for You.

A Temporary Dwelling Place

Mantra Seventeen communicates a fundamental understanding common to all bona fide spiritual systems; that is, the body is temporary, while the soul is eternal. Both the life force and consciousness are functions of the soul. The life force represents the principle of vitality, while consciousness corresponds to the principle of awareness. When the soul departs from the body, no traces of life force or consciousness remain in the body, which immediately begins to deteriorate rapidly. While reciting this *mantra*, the speaker of *Sri Isopanisad* beseeches Sri Krishna, "Dear Lord, while I, the spirit soul, was in this body, I did my best to follow spiritual laws. Please remember me for doing so." While reminding the Lord of his endeavors to be righteous, pious, and devotional, the speaker simultaneously conveys the message that we will be held accountable for all our actions. In fact, *we do not have to petition the Lord* in such a way. Everything that each of us has done is already accounted for by the laws of *karma*. Similarly, everything we experience in the present is the fruit of our past deeds.

The speaker acknowledges the reality of material life, "Dear Lord, I know that this body is temporary, and that I and everyone else will have to depart from this physical place of dwelling." We can compare the body to an apartment. Usually when tenants rent an apartment, they take a lease for a fixed period of time. They then proceed to live in the apartment until the lease expires. Sometimes tenants are alarmed when the lease expires, especially if they have not made arrangements to move to another dwelling. In both material and spiritual life, it is essential to plan ahead. We should organize our lives in such a way that when we need to depart from our present residence in the material body, we will be able to relocate with ease. In order to maintain equanimity when we face death, we need to be assured of our next existence or environment.

Evaluation After Death

When a death occurs, different communities hold various ceremonies in order to dispose of the body properly and to assist the soul in reaching its next destination. In some traditions, the body is buried, while in others, it is cremated. In some parts of the world, the body is thrown into the water, while other traditions call for the corpse to be placed on top of a mountain. Ultimately, however, the result is the same; the body is discarded because the soul has departed. At the moment of transition, most people recognize that what was inside the body—the soul—is more important than the body. By reading the Vedic scriptures, we can gain a good understanding of how the soul moves from one body to the next. Every time the soul leaves the body, an evaluation takes place regarding the type of experience that particular soul will undergo next. The individual soul must endure judgment beyond the realm of the body.

In some ways, spiritual judgment is similar to what occurs in any mundane court of law. All countries have laws. Courts exist as part of a mechanism to enforce those laws. If the citizens do not honor the decrees of the state, they are suitably chastised through the arrangements of the courts. Similarly, there are spiritual laws with accompanying punishments for breaking them. Spiritual commandments are accessible via the great scriptures such as the Vedas, the Bible, the Koran, the Hadith, the Torah, and the Kabbala. Saints of various traditions advise us on how to interpret and apply these particular laws in our lives.

The Story of King Citraketu

The story of King Citraketu, recounted in the Sixth Canto of *Srimad-Bhagavatam*, is highly instructive regarding the

Mantra Seventeen

transmigration of the soul according to spiritual laws. King Citraketu was a great Vedic king who possessed almost everything a ruler could desire. All he was lacking was a son who could take over his kingdom after his death. While the king was lamenting his fate, a great sage named Angira Rsi happened to be visiting the palace. It is relatively well-known in various traditions that sages often hold unusual abilities. As Angira Rsi possessed mystic powers, he could read the minds of others. Therefore, he was aware that the king was disturbed. Even before King Citraketu explained his problem, Angira Rsi understood that the king felt his life to be incomplete without a son. King Citraketu requested the help of the sage, who performed a special *yajna* to produce auspiciousness. At this sacrifice, Angira Rsi offered specially prepared sweet rice to the demigod Visvakarma. The remnants of the sacrifice were then given to the king's first wife, Krtadyuti.

The blessed food was imbued with the potency to enable Krtadyuti to bear a son. She immediately became pregnant, and in due course of time, a son was born. Brimming over with joy because his greatest desire had been fulfilled, the king began to devote all of his attention to Krtadyuti and the newborn child. King Citraketu's other wives became increasingly jealous of their co-wife. Contemplating their situation, the envious wives considered that their lives were far better before this boy had come into their midst. Fighting among themselves, they eventually concluded that in order to attract the king's attention, the best course of action would be to get rid of the child. Plotting together, they decided to poison the baby. As soon as Krtadyuti discovered her son was dead, she became distraught and fell to the ground unconscious. The king was even more distressed. Overwhelmed with grief, his weeping was echoed in all the hearts of the inhabitants of the palace, except in those of the co-wives, who cried pretentiously while secretly rejoicing in the child's death.

Soon after the poisoning of the baby prince, Angira Rsi visited the palace once again, accompanied by Narada Muni. On seeing Angira Rsi, the king recalled that shortly after the *yajna*, the sage had told him that his future son would bring him both the greatest happiness and the greatest distress. At the time, King Citraketu interpreted Angira Rsi's statement to mean that perhaps his son would become proud after he took over the throne, thus displeasing his father. Never did the king think that the grief caused by his son would be so severe. Placing the sage's statement at the back of their minds, the king and the queen had simply immersed themselves in happiness by contemplating the birth of their son; by being with him after he was born; and by meditating about his future as the heir to the throne. However, that so-called happiness was the seed of their unlimited grief. If we reflect on our own lives, we may notice that sometimes, when we are given a wonderful gift and thereafter, it is taken away, we feel worse than if we had not received it in the first place.

Angira Rsi explained the concept of the eternality of the soul to the king. The sage helped him to realize that his initial distress, his subsequent happiness, as well as the intense lamentation which followed, were caused by his attachment to the manifestations of the illusory material energy. Angira Rsi revealed that the body is merely a costume, to be discarded at death for another. In spite of Angira Rsi's explanation, the king still felt distressed. Consequently, Narada Muni summoned the departed soul back into the body of the child. This type of occurrence is unusual, but not impossible. From the Christian scriptures, we learn that Lord Jesus had the ability to bring the dead back to life. Some of the *devas* also possess the *siddhi* to bring the soul back into the body.

At the bidding of Narada Muni, the king's son awakened. The king and queen were overwhelmed with joy. When their son began to speak, he spoke not as the child they had known, but from the viewpoint of the eternal soul. While outside of his body, his soul had experienced other realms and gathered much realization. The soul of their son related how the living entity transmigrates from one body to another, and from one planet to another, lifetime after lifetime. Throughout this journey, the soul experiences many different relationships. In previous lifetimes, the king and queen had been the parents of various other children, and similarly, in their future lifetimes, they would continue to play the role of parents to different souls, according to their *karma*. The boy revealed that he himself had also been the child of many different sets of parents. Therefore, the boy explained, it is foolish to lament for the body. Rather, we should strive to become more astute in our practice of spiritual life. All our material possessions are temporary. At any time, we can lose our wealth, fame, houses, cars, and investments. We come into this world with nothing and we leave this world with nothing, except our consciousness and the results of our actions, which determine our next life.

In this way, King Citraketu's son helped his parents to realize that it is a complete waste of effort to be attached to material relationships. He also challenged them to reassess their conception of time. In the broader scheme of things, our lives are like moments, fleeting and temporary, yet we are greatly affected by our experiences of family life. Initially, King Citraketu and Queen Krtadyuti were unhappy because they did not have a son. When they got a son, they became extremely delighted. When fate took him away, again they became very distressed. When he was brought back to life, they once more became happy. Through the boy's words and Narada Muni's potency, they were blessed with the deep realization that they should pursue neither material opulence nor material relationships, because these arrangements are flimsy and subject to constant change. It is only a matter of time before they were dissolved by the tide of providence. Hereafter, King Citraketu and his queens delved deeper into spirituality and ultimately prepared themselves to return to the abode of the Lord, our real home.

The Story of Ajamila

Another pastime which delineates the science of transmigration acutely is that of Ajamila, which is recounted in the Sixth Canto of *Srimad-Bhagavatam*. Born into a very religious *brahmana* family, initially Ajamila was very astute and focused in his worship of the Lord. He was married to a beautiful, chaste lady, who also came from a *brahmana* family. One day, however, Ajamila had an encounter which would change his life. He witnessed a lusty, low-class man and a prostitute embracing each other in the street. Both of them were intoxicated, and the prostitute's dress had become undone. Although he was a simple *sadhu* with pure thoughts, the sight of the embrace agitated his mind. This impression was so powerful that he could not extract it from his mind. Thinking incessantly about the sight of the prostitute and the low-class man, he desired to engage with her in illicit affairs. Deserting his family and virtuous young wife, he employed the prostitute in his house as a maidservant.

Before long, Ajamila married the prostitute and had many children with her. In order to raise money to satisfy her demands, he engaged in numerous criminal activities. As he grew older, he became very sick. Lying on his deathbed, with his youngest son called Narayana playing nearby, Ajamila was suddenly confronted by the Yamadutas, the gruesome agents of Yamaraja, the universal superintendent of death.

When we are ready to leave our bodies, the type of assistance we will receive depends upon the moral quality of our lives. When a person has led a life centered on love and devotion to God, the

Visnudutas, or personal messengers of Lord Visnu, appear to take him or her back to the spiritual world. When a person has led a sinful life, however, he or she is met by Yamadutas, who look and behave like little devils. They drag the soul out of the body with mystical ropes and take it to the hellish planets. When the Visnudutas appear before those who are dying, these souls have very peaceful looks on their faces. Often, before they leave the body, they smile as they contemplate the wonderful destination for which they will soon depart. In other cases, people cry and scream as they are dying, passing urine and stool as their souls are snatched from their bodies and taken for punishment.

Since Ajamila had led a sinful life, he was met by the Yamadutas. Viciously, they began to drag his soul from the region of his heart. Before they could do so, however, the angelic Visnudutas appeared and stopped them. Challenging the Yamadutas, they asked, "Do you not understand the science of transmigration?" Bewildered, because no one had ever stopped them from executing their duty before, the Yamadutas replied that everyone is accountable for his or her actions, and that the destination of the soul at death is based on the deeds committed during its past lifetime. They were surprised that the Visnudutas had stopped them, especially in light of the fact that Ajamila had been so sinful. He had been a drunkard, a criminal, and had associated with a prostitute. Therefore, no doubt remained in their minds that he must come with them for punishment. However, the Visnudutas countered their arguments by replying that Ajamila called on the name of God, Narayana, with tearful desperation as he was leaving his body. Even though Ajamila thought of his son when he called out the name of God, merely the act of uttering one of God's names offenselessly was sufficient to save him from punishment. Furthermore, earlier in Ajamila's lifetime, he had engaged in devotional service to the Lord. His calling on the Lord's name connected him with his previous worship and piety. His earlier devotional service outweighed much of his sinful activities. The Visnudutas informed the Yamadutas, therefore, that they could not take Ajamila for punishment. Prevented from claiming the soul of Ajamila, the Yamadutas departed.

Near-Death Experiences

Sometimes, people who are very ill or those who have undergone an accident enter into a comatose state in which they are neither dead nor aware of their immediate surroundings. While the conscious mind of the comatose person is at rest, the soul is still present in the body. This state signifies that the outcome of the sum total of that particular soul's life work is under deliberation, and that his or her next body is being prepared. When a decision is made, either the soul enters another dimension immediately, or it is allowed to return to its previous environment. In Ajamila's case, he was allowed to return to his current life. When the soul comes back into the body, the revived patient often recalls various aspects of his or her near-death experience. Occasionally, some people experience such bliss that they do not want to come back. In Ajamila's case, due to the vivid memory of his encounter with the Yamadutas, he realized that his sinful life was wretched and that, on leaving his body, he would have to suffer the results of his past misdeeds. As a result, once he recovered his health, he resumed his initial pious lifestyle.

The story of Ajamila is not a myth, but a hard reality. Many people who have been in comas at some point testify to similar experiences of hovering between this world and the next, while their bodies lay inert below. Often, these people institute drastic positive change in their lives as a result of such amazing realizations.

The science of transmigration of the soul can be deduced merely by observing our own bodies. As a person grows from a baby to a child to an adult, everyone can see that he or she is still the same person, despite the continuous changes which the body undergoes. The personality also alters based on acculturation, maturation, and socialization. Death is merely a continuation of this process, throughout which the soul continues to exist.

The pastimes of King Citraketu and Ajamila are recounted in the Vedic scriptures in order to provide us with knowledge about the soul and life after death. These scriptures provide the answers to many questions, such as: What happens when we return to our ultimate home, the spiritual kingdom? Why do we come into the material world in the first place? What causes the soul to reincarnate in a man's body or a woman's body? Why do we sometimes go to the heavenly kingdoms and sometimes to the lower planets?

Death Indicates a Change of Body

These bodies and our current destinations are based on the quality of life we led previously. All types of material bodies, however, are prison suits, symptomatic of our original envy of the Lord. Life is an amazing transition, but somewhat incredibly, people in general perceive their consciousness as functioning only within a fixed time span—the here and now. In reality, however, the body is nothing more than a garment. Normally, we wear different clothes for different occasions. Similarly, we take on various types of bodies to correspond with the various types of experiences we desire to undergo. As we wear out our clothes, we throw them away and purchase new attire. Similarly, when we die, this body is discarded and we acquire a new one.

There is really no such thing as death. Rather, death is just a transition. The body is alive due to the presence of the soul. When the soul leaves the body, we see the body for what it actually is: matter, a mere combination of the five elements of material nature. The Koran, the Bible, and the Vedic scriptures all explain that the body is the temple in which the soul resides. In the Koran 2.28, it is stated, "How can you deny Allah? Did He not give you life when you were dead, and will He not cause you to die and then restore you to life? Will you not return to Him at last?"

Similarly, in 1 Corinthians 3:16, St. Paul writes, "Surely you know that you are God's temple and that God's Spirit lives in you!" Later, in 1 Corinthians 6:19, St. Paul elaborates further on the distinction between the body and the soul, "Don't you know that your body is the temple of the Holy Spirit, who lives in you and who was given to you by God?" Likewise, in the *Bhagavad-gita* 18.61, Krishna tells Arjuna that the body is like a machine in which the soul is seated as a passenger:

> *isvarah sarva-bhutanam*
> *hrd-dese 'rjuna tisthati*
> *bhramayan sarva-bhutani*
> *yantrarudhani mayaya*

> *The Supreme Lord is situated in everyone's heart, O Arjuna, and is directing the wanderings of all living entities, who are seated as on a machine, made of the material energy.*

Most of us are aware that motor vehicles are propelled by fuel and navigated by a driver. However, if we did not have any knowledge about cars, we might assume that the vehicle moved without either the driver or the fuel. Similarly, the body moves due to the presence of the soul within the heart. Without the soul, the body is inanimate. In the verse quoted above from *Bhagavad-gita*, the individual soul is compared to the passenger, while the Supersoul is compared to the driver of the vehicle. Another example, which further clarifies the relationship of the body to the soul, is that of a bird in a cage. If we take care of a pet bird solely by cleaning its cage, then it will die. The bird itself needs nurturing in the form of food, water, and affection. In the same way, when we do not nourish the soul but merely take care of our physical body, in due course of time, we will dry up internally. Although nothing can kill the soul, it will be starved for nourishment, even though the body in which it dwells may be taken care of nicely.

If we refuse to nurture the soul, we will join the living dead, whose lives are centered on reacting to the material environment. Basically, we will eat, sleep, mate, and defend. Ultimately, we know that life is much more than these four crude activities. Life is about attempting to understand our real purpose on this planet, and about uncovering our true selves. It is about appreciating the ultimate goal of existence, rather than being fixated on our immediate environment, which is temporary and miserable. All of us will soon leave this world. Our situation is similar to that of tenants who stand to receive an eviction notice. If the tenants choose to deny the instruction to vacate the property, at some point they will have to leave their home by force, rather than voluntarily. Similarly, each of us has an appointment to leave the body. Since we know we have to leave, we could focus more on the quality of our life experiences while we still have a lease. Let us consider how to properly align ourselves with the Lord, the creator of all material and spiritual worlds.

Understand the Science of the Soul

Every time we observe a death, especially of someone who is close to us, the experience serves to remind us that life is mysterious. Death makes us think more profoundly about our own existence. Each of us knows someone dear to us who has died or is dying. Our loved ones are with us for a while, but at some point, we will face separation from them. When someone we love dies, usually the experience jolts us into the reality that *death is inevitable*. We start to think about ourselves on a deeper level. For a while, we attempt to be less mechanical in our approach to the world. Hopefully, we can use our experience of death to fix our priorities properly and focus more on our relationships. We should try to give as much love as possible to those around us, for they can leave at any moment.

It is an undeniable fact that we must endure separation from loved ones at various intervals throughout our lives, and that ultimately we will be forced to experience death ourselves. Therefore, it is imperative for us to be well-versed in the science of the soul. In St. Paul's First Letter to the Corinthians, he explains that we have a celestial existence and a terrestrial existence (1 Corinthians 15:35-42). While we are in the terrestrial existence, the physical, we are away from God. St. Paul explains that it is not flesh and blood that enters the kingdom of God (1 Corinthians 15:50). It is not the physical covering, but rather the *atma*, our true self, that enters the realm in which God resides.

Life is consciousness, and consciousness is a function of the spirit soul. In *Mantra Seventeen*, the speaker refers to *vayuh*, the air of life that contains the life force. The *prana*, or the breath in the body, is intimately connected with the soul. The movement of subtle airs within the body, which determines our health and our consciousness, is known as *prana-vayu*. One way of assessing mental illness is to observe the imbalance of the airs in the body. Together with the soul in the heart of all living entities lives the Supersoul. In the Judeo-Christian tradition, the Supersoul is known as the Holy Ghost. It bears silent witness to all our activities, including our deviations, while waiting for us to reform. Through entering very deeply into prayer and meditation, some mystics have been able to be in touch with the Supersoul from time to time. The goal of many systems of *yoga*, such as *dhyana-yoga*, which is also known as the eightfold *yoga* system, is to concentrate the mind and senses on the Supersoul in order to attain *samadhi*, complete absorption in this localized aspect of the Lord. By following this process of meditation sincerely, the devotee receives instructions from the Lord within the heart.

God's Many Representatives

All bona fide religions are based on authorized scriptures and a system of spiritual mentorship, which insures the proper dissemination of scriptural knowledge. Prophets, *gurus*, and *acaryas* constitute different kinds of spiritual mentors. In effect, they are ambassadors from God, sent with the assignment to bring people back from their lives of deviation. Also, they assist in the creation of a favorable environment for spiritual practices on earth. In the New Testament, the story of the prodigal son demonstrates the need for the intervention of a spiritual guide or teacher. The father in this story was dismayed when his younger son left home to become a profligate debauchee. The prodigal son suffered horribly after leaving his family. His father sent a messenger to find him. The son realized, "What am I doing? I am eating scraps from the table, while I could be at my father's house, a place where proper shelter, food, and love are my natural birthright." The prodigal son returned home, and was welcomed by his father with open arms. The story of the prodigal son serves as an analogy for our situation in the material world. Because we rejected our original, blissful state of servitorship to Krishna, our eternal father, we became entangled in an unhealthy lifestyle and made it our reality. By the grace of the Lord, He sends His messengers to rescue us. Angels and archangels, too, come down to the world from their heavenly abodes. There is only one God, who is addressed in different cultures by various names, such as Allah, Yahweh, Jehovah, and Krishna. According to time, place, and circumstance, the same God sends His various representatives to different nations around the globe.

When the Lord's greatly empowered sons and daughters come, their mission is to inspire us to change positively. For example, the prophet Muhammad spoke about the possibility of going to paradise as a result of a genuine adjustment in consciousness. Similarly, Lord Jesus consistently encouraged the Israelites to give up sinful life. The Vedas explain that this material world is like a reformatory. As inmates of the reformatory, we have to learn various lessons in order to graduate from it. If we do not learn, then we must return again and again. So often people ask the question, "Why do disease, old age, death, war, crime, and other such miseries continually manifest, despite all attempts to eradicate them?" The answer is simple: it is the innate nature of the material world. The Lord's agents help us to realize that we do not have to remain indefinitely in an environment of incarceration, but as long as we continue to break the laws of God, we must revisit the prison house. From the viewpoint of the soul, however, it is a temporary stopover. Lord Jesus lets us know that life is far greater and varied than we can perceive with our senses. In John 14:2, he explains, "There are many rooms in my Father's house," meaning that many aspects of spiritual variegatedness exist in the spiritual kingdom.

Prophets and *acaryas* from all traditions remind us that this material world is not our natural environment. Our real home is the spiritual kingdom. Therefore, material life will naturally lead to various types of disappointments. When we are away from home, we cannot experience the complete love and protection that is intrinsic to a place personally designed for us. We will always feel some level of incompleteness, no matter in which situation we find ourselves. We might be very happy within our family, but then if our husband, wife, mother, father, daughter, or son has to leave suddenly, we will experience intense sadness immediately.

Antimaterial Desires

When we speak of life and death, most of us realize intuitively that matter is antithetical to spirit. We may find that we possess antimaterial desires, which are in fact intimately connected with our antimaterial selves, our spirit souls. *Any sane person does not want to die.* Most of us would agree that most coherent, rational people want to be perpetually happy, eternally satisfied, and loved forever. However, we recognize that these desires for eternality can never be attained in a material realm that is temporary. Everyone is looking for love and higher pleasures. These are universal aspirations. If we engage with physicality only, we are limited in terms of what we will be able to experience.

Often, we spend our entire lives acquiring material things, which is a boring occupation because ultimately we will never have enough of whatever we wish to attain. However, if we are able to create and maintain quality relationships, and if we succeed in adding real value to society, then our lives become significant. Conversely, if we choose to lead an unthinking life, trying to experience only material things and refusing nourishment to our inner selves, then we merely cheat ourselves. As we get older, the body deteriorates. Everything shifts, including our sleep patterns, respiration, digestion, and defecation. The body sends a message to us by its changes. It is as if it is telling us, "Realize that time is moving on and this machine is becoming obsolete. Soon, you will be ready for a new model." If we invest our selfhood solely in this mechanical body, then we suffer from spiritual myopia. The majority of people on this planet live solely for physical arrangements and commodities. Therefore, interpersonal relationships have become less meaningful and more opportunistic. People neither feel love nor do they give love.

Questions and Answers
Question: I recently lost a close family member. As far as I'm concerned, he led a good life as an ambassador of God. This was a man whom I had envisaged dying peacefully of old age, but all of a sudden, he was shot in the back. You explained that the type of life we lead currently determines how we will pass over the cut-off line, the death experience. I am very confused. How could this man, who had been a pillar of piety, suddenly have his life terminated without warning in such a violent way?

Answer: Let us recount the story of Ajamila. Initially, he led a very pious life, but he later became attracted by illicit affairs and his life changed. Often, current events in our lives are not due to our present situation, but to reactions from the past. Just as we are all products of heredity, environmental, and social influences, so too are we products of experiences from our previous lives.

Let us examine a simple case in point. Two businessmen from a similar background, with the same resources, work very hard in their respective trades. One of them goes bankrupt despite all efforts, while the other puts in the same amount of energy and time, but is enormously successful. How do we account for the vastly different results despite equivalent circumstances? The Vedas attribute it to previous *karma*. In St. Paul's Letter to the Galatians, he writes, "Do not deceive yourselves; no one makes a fool of God. A person will reap exactly what he sows" (Galatians 6: 7). St. Paul goes on to describe that material actions result in "the harvest of death," while spiritual actions result in "the harvest of eternal life" (Galatians 6:8). *Mantra Seventeen* indicates, too, that when we make a certain action in the world, we are responsible for its result. Generally, we are not very aware of what kinds of seeds we plant. As a result, when they start to germinate, the type of crop that those seeds produce may surprise us.

The way in which we leave our bodies, whether it is through a long chronic illness, an abrupt accident, a robbery, or in our sleep, is not as important as our consciousness at the time of our passing. In the Vedic worldview, we do not evaluate the way a person dies as much as his or her mindset in dying. This gentleman, as you explain, was consistently pious, although he left in an abrupt way. Therefore, he may not have undergone much distress, even though to us, the experience seems horrifying. While his body was destroyed suddenly, the suffering of his soul may have been minimal; it may have been escorted blissfully to higher realms. Consider what occurs when you take off your jacket. Whether you throw it on the ground, whether you hang it up, or whether you fold it, the bottom line is that you have removed a piece of clothing. In the same way, how the physical body is removed from the soul is not as significant as that soul's state of consciousness.

It is important to realize how temporary everything is. Even though we can see our loved one today, by tomorrow he or she can be gone from our lives. Death is like that. The same experience will happen to us. At some point, people who know us now will not see us again in this particular lifetime. We both observe and experience transition everyday. Living entities die all the time, but somehow we try not to think about it. It is an amazing fact that we see death all around us, but imagine that we will live forever. While acknowledging that life on this planet is a temporary experience, we should live without being dismal or morbid, but in the spirit of wanting to invest energy into projects of eternal importance. We should live our lives in such a way that if we have to leave the body immediately, we are prepared and have no regrets. We should aim to die knowing that we gave our best to our loved ones, and that we lived a principle-centered existence with integrity. Most people are not given any warning that they are going to leave. Therefore, we should not place ourselves in a position of anxiety over what we did not accomplish, or of desiring to rectify past actions that we now regret. *Simply put, we are to do whatever possible to the best of our ability each day.*

Question: I've heard that Caitanya Mahaprabhu is the most merciful incarnation of God for this age. Is it true that He delivers even those who are very sinful without them having to make any special effort?

Answer: Grace is concomitant with endeavor. For example, parents of a small child will be pleased when their child endeavors to learn new skills, despite the fact that she is very young and dependent. She may draw a picture of something which they cannot even recognize, but because the child offers it to them with affection, they will accept it lovingly, as if it were a masterpiece. When effort is made from both sides, grace and appreciation are naturally present. The Lord reaches out to us to the extent that we are sincere. We must remember always that we have to act, and not merely expect to gain something without making any attempt. Our effort is never really sufficient to attain the Lord's lotus feet, as our level of spiritual maturation is usually not very high. The degree of effort and the consciousness with which we undertake our offerings to the Lord are the most important factors. We are to try to engage genuinely in devotional service. We are not to be whimsical. If we do our best, we will receive reciprocation.

Question: Can past-life *karma* be undone?

Answer: Yes, that is the ultimate goal of life. Many great philosophers, religionists, and scientists maintain that the fundamental objective of existence is to become free, which essentially means not to have to take another physical form. Physical existence is like a reformatory, and the physical body is like a prison suit. According to the nature of our transgression of God's laws, we have to endure certain penalties. In this lifetime, as we advance towards the uncovering of our authentic selves, we realize that we are spiritual entities undergoing material experiences. We are not material beings trying to connect with something that is spiritual. *Our essence is that we are spiritual.* Our spirituality is lying dormant most of the time because our senses are enslaved by the bombardment of immediate stimulation in our environment. Most people function based on their passions and instincts. They go along with the normative patterns of society. Remember that history has shown that those who have made significant contributions to the world are not afraid of thinking deeply and being different. Because these people possess a certain amount of insight, which they then act upon, they produce a certain level of greatness. Those who just go along with the flow seldom become great achievers. Vision and conscientious risk bring refreshing advances to our society. However, because we are inundated with so much propaganda, frequently we do not take sufficient time to think carefully; we just react. In general, people are so highly strung. Due to their unhealthy lifestyles, people suffer from an enormous amount of hypertension and stress, which cuts their lives short.

Let us always remember that life is much more than a series of material experiences. Life is mysterious because death is always present. Death really means a transition, when the soul moves on to another destination. We have the power to monitor our actions, and therefore, to a large extent, we can determine the experiences we will undergo in our next lives. We all desire to receive the most auspicious situations in this life as well as in the next. Let us therefore become more attuned to living a life of integrity, genuine high character, piety, and humility. Let us pray to the Lord in the following mood, "Dear Lord, Thy will be done. Please facilitate me so I can do whatever is necessary to return to You. Help me to graduate successfully, so that I can be with You eternally in Your abode. Please forgive me for any shortcomings and remember me as one who has persevered in serving You, and who appreciates Your justice, but who is begging for Your causeless mercy."

Reflections on Sacred Teachings, Volume Four

Mantra Eighteen

*agne naya supatha raye asman
visvani deva vayunani vidvan
yuyodhy asmaj juhuranam eno
bhuyistham te nama-uktim vidhema*

O my Lord, as powerful as fire, O omnipotent one, now I offer You all obeisances, falling on the ground at Your feet. O my Lord, please lead me on the right path to reach You, and since You know all that I have done in the past, please free me from the reactions to my past sins so that there will be no hindrance to my progress.

The Principle of Saranagati

Full surrender is the most natural act, because innately we are unalloyed lovers of the Lord. In fact, we are profound lovers of all that is connected with the spiritual paradigm. However, we are temporarily experiencing a certain degree of bewilderment and amnesia, which causes us to minimize who we really are. Gross attachment to matter is the chief symptom of our forgetfulness. Bewilderment manifests in the mindset that ultimately there is no Supreme Personality of Godhead, but only Supreme Energy, Supreme Sound, or even Supreme Knowledge. These forces exist, but only in connection with the Supreme Person. By describing His qualities, *Sri Isopanisad* clarifies the actual status of the Supreme Lord and our eternal relationship with Him. The last few *mantras* of *Sri Isopanisad* emphasize the removal of all things that interfere with the ultimate stage of *suddha-bhakti*. This final verse, which addresses *saranagati*, is the summation of this principle.

Often, we experience a lot of confusion in our attempts to obtain relief from problems. For many people, spiritual life is basically an endeavor to remove any obstacles that interfere with their material goals. Previously, they may have tried to achieve their desires through orthodox means. When orthodox means fail, they often turn to spirituality as just another way of satisfying their mundane desires. They think, "Conventional solutions have not worked. Let me try to do this 'God-thing,' to see if I will get what I want. If I have to undertake some *tapasya*, if I have to execute some *yajnas*, or if I have to follow certain rules and regulations to get what I most desire, then let me do what is required. Perhaps it will help me satisfy my inner longings." However, by manipulating the material energy, we can receive only temporary enjoyment. We cannot receive full freedom from either amnesia or attachment.

We can compare the person who attempts the 'God-thing' as a method of obtaining relief from suffering to a patient who wants to recover from a disease. If the patient constantly places himself or herself in an environment of germs, then more than likely he or she will continue to be in an unhealthy state. Similarly, we cannot become totally unalloyed servants of Krishna while nurturing material hankerings. We cannot really associate with the Godhead without becoming profoundly godly. We are not God but His eternal parts and parcel. Although we are similar in quality to the Lord, we cannot go back to our eternal home without functioning as proper residents of the spiritual world. Fortunately, so much of what is given to us by the great *acaryas* is meant to help us to become qualified for spiritual citizenship. Just as we must fulfill certain criteria to enter particular environments in the material world, so too in order to enter the spiritual world, we must attain a pure state of consciousness. In the material world, we find that the more affluent the neighborhood, the more the stipulations are enforced. In a wealthy neighborhood such as Beverly Hills in the U.S.A, for example, each family has to live by stringent rules in order to remain residents. Such people usually agree because they understand that adherence to regulations is required in exchange for the benefits they receive.

A Dangerous Prayer

This last *mantra* contains a dangerous prayer. The prayer conveys the following state of mind: "My dear Lord, previously I tried so many things, but now I have acquired a greater understanding. Yet, so much still remains to be understood. I do not know to what degree I have made unconscious errors, and to what extent I have unwanted things in the heart that I still need to transcend. But I

Mantra Eighteen

do know that it is possible to overcome them if I sincerely offer myself to You. I ask You to somehow overlook any areas in which I am weak, in which I procrastinate. Anything that interferes with surrender, which holds me back, or which keeps me in amnesia, please take it away." Much of what we do as devotees conveys an unconscious prayer to the Lord to take away all impediments to pure devotional service. As we chant *japa* on our *mala*, calling on the names of Radha, Krishna, and Balarama, we address the Lord's internal energies. As we chant the *maha-mantra*, Hare Krishna, Hare Krishna, Krishna Krishna, Hare Hare/ Hare Rama, Hare Rama, Rama Rama, Hare Hare, we are really praying, "Dear Lord, please pick me up. Forgive me, and bring me back in Your service." We are asking, "Dear Srimati Radharani, dear Krishna, dear Divine Couple, please take away any attachments that help me to maintain the illusion. Take away whatever I am holding onto that brings lifetimes of confusion, and whatever I am doing that is causing me to take these material bodies." On the other hand, we are also saying, "Whatever I need to experience, whatever will assist me to return back home to serve You purely, let those things enter my life." It is not a prayer for the faint-hearted. We beg, "Dear Lord, if I need poverty to come back to You, let it be. If I need opulences to come to You, and that is best for my devotional life, let it come about. If I need chronic illness that is practically debilitating, but which will speed up my return to You, bring it on. Alternatively, if it is great health which will accelerate my devotion to You, then let that be mine. If either loneliness or intense activity in the association of many people is the best remedy for my fallen state, then let whichever happen according to Your will."

Asking for Pure Love

Krishna consciousness is not just a religion, nor is it a method of finding ways to refine our material situation. If we just focus on our material situation, and search for ways to be peaceful, moral, ethical, or comfortable, this is noble, *but deep love goes far beyond comfort.* Deep love consists of intense agitation as we consider how to give love and how to receive it in meditation on the status of our Beloved. When we experience deep love, we are in anxiety due to not giving as much as we are receiving from our Beloved. We anticipate opportunities to try to show our love. Ultimately, spiritual life is about the highest expression of selflessness and compassion. It is the highest romance, void of any obstacles of material greed, lust, egocentricity, or selfishness. Real love can never be sectarian, limited to one's self, or even to one's friends and relatives. Love is not shortsighted. Real love is profoundly pervasive, because it flows from the source. Krishna is the reservoir of love. Therefore, a devotee feels that he or she must have the Lord's association at any price and must connect with the reservoir of all love. As we chant in this mood, even though sometimes we are not fully conscious of it, we are asking Krishna to take away all obstacles that interfere with the attainment of pure love.

This prayer explains why some people, who have never been ill in their lives, find that they are constantly sick after coming to Krishna consciousness. Some people who are very wealthy find that, after becoming devotees, they cannot attract money like they used to in the past. Others find that while money was scarce before, after they started chanting Hare Krishna, they have so much they do not know what to do with it. There is always a way to use money in Krishna's service; perhaps they could build three or four temples, or assist the preaching efforts in war-torn countries.

Taking the Proper Prescription

As we genuinely engage in the process, Krishna brings about what is best for each individual. However, we usually have our own idea of exactly what we think is best. Dictating to Krishna what we need is similar to telling a medical doctor how to treat a serious illness we have contracted. If, on consulting a doctor, we tell him what our ailment is; what specific medicine we require; for what period of time we need to take the prescription; and what our prognosis will be for the coming weeks or months, a cheating doctor will say, "No problem, just put your money down. See you when you come back next time." But a bona fide doctor will tactfully explain that he or she needs to make an analysis based on the symptoms, and then prescribe what the patient needs.

Another type of non-compliant patient apparently accepts the doctor's prognosis, but keeps coming back with the same ailment. When the doctor asks the patient if he or she took the prescription, the patient answers, "Well, I bought it and put it on my shelf, but two weeks have passed, and I'm still sick!" The doctor inquires again, "But did you take the medicine?" Some devotees practice devotional service is this way. They receive the spiritual prescription, but either they do not use it, or they use it incorrectly, just like the patient who buys the medicine and puts it away on a shelf. Simply because we have received the medicine does not mean that the illness will be healed. If we take only some of the medicine, and throw the rest of it away, then we receive only piecemeal benefit. Similarly, if we chant and engage in service, but our consciousness is not one of surrender, then we will receive a certain amount of restoration, but some sickness will still be present. Listening to the prayers of *Sri Isopanisad* will assist us in acquiring a better understanding of how to weed out all obstacles.

Claiming Our Rightful Inheritance

The speaker of this *mantra* makes a powerful submission to the Lord, begging to be freed from all past reactions, and to be brought back to His lotus feet. Although there are times when we experience some sinful reactions due to inauspicious activities from the past, we should continue to offer our obeisances to the Lord with full devotion. In *The Nectar of Devotion*, Srila Rupa Gosvami and Srila Prabhupada discuss that an effective way to overcome difficulties is to tolerate the reactions that are still coming from the past with the knowledge that eventually they will stop. If the devotee maintains great determination and dedication to continue in spite of austerities, the *acaryas* explain that "it is certain that he is going to be promoted to the abode of the Lord" (*The Nectar of Devotion*, 91). They refer to *Srimad-Bhagavatam* 10.14.8:

> *tat te 'nukampam su-samiksamano*
> *bhunjana evatma-krtam vipakam*
> *hrd-vag-vapurbhir vidadhan namas te*
> *jiveta yo mukti-pade sa daya-bhak*

> *My dear Lord, one who earnestly waits for You to bestow Your causeless mercy upon him, all the while patiently suffering the reactions of his past misdeeds and offering You respectful obeisances with his heart, words and body, is surely eligible for liberation, for it has become his rightful claim.*

One who perseveres in spite of some suffering inherits the kingdom of God. In his commentary to this verse, Srila Sridhara Swami, one of the great acaryas in our line, draws attention to the phrase *daya-bhak*, the rightful heir. He asks how a son inherits his father's property. When we ask devotees these questions, they usually arrive at a variety of answers, which include:

- Serving the father
- Being loyal to him
- Employing a lawyer (in Kali-yuga, it is recommended that everyone has a good lawyer!

However, Sridhara Swami points out that all the son needs to do to attain his inheritance is simply to stay alive. If he has been loyal and he has served the father well, but he dies before the father, then he misses his opportunity, and everything has been in vain. However, if he just stays alive, then he will automatically inherit the estate once the father is gone. Similarly, our success in devotional service is based on proper alignments, dedication, and perseverance. By persevering, we stay alive. By cultivating the proper attitude, our devotional creeper stays fresh and vibrant.

Srimad-Bhagavatam gives us everything; we just have to be careful not to become distracted, lose faith, or get disturbed by all kinds of deterrents. Once we come to the human form of life, after passing through the 8,400,000 different kinds of prison suits that the soul can inhabit, we finally have a chance to come in touch with the message of *bhakti-rasa*, the taste one derives from performance of devotional service. Once we take shelter of the great *acaryas*, then so much of what the soul has been yearning for lifetime after lifetime becomes achievable. However, with attainability come the real tests. Once we have made the connection, we are constantly tested to determine to what degree we are able to stay fixed. In the material world, this principle also holds true. For example, medical and law students, who previously may have endeavored very hard to obtain entry into medical or law school, still need to pass many subsequent tests before they qualify. It is simply a matter of continuation, after which, at some future point, the student will graduate, acquire certification, and be able to practice.

Rights versus Responsibility

Lawyers generally are very concerned about defending the so-called rights of their clients. In fact, most people are very interested in their rights; we hear about animal rights, women's rights, minority rights, civil rights, the right to life, and gay rights. Feeling denied one's rights, and wanting to make it clear to others that one is not sufficiently valued is a key theme in world culture. In some cases, it is true that the conditions of certain groups have been minimized. However, frequently we emphasize what we are not given, while we fail to honor our own responsibilities. We all have certain rights, such as the right to act on our free will. We also have certain responsibilities, as we are accountable entities.

The cultural weight we place on 'rights' is directly connected with the desire for justice. Unfortunately, so often people search for a kind of justice, which may be translated as "just us": justice for *my* political party, justice for *my* peer group, or justice for *my* ethnic group. People have different conceptions of justice, which are often relevant only to their particular communities. However, the devotee of the Lord honors the rights of all living entities, as well as the responsibilities that accompany them. While devotees respect justice for all, they are actually not very excited with justice when it comes to themselves. When it comes to the Lord, the devotee wants *more* than justice.

We do not want only justice. We want *mercy*! Mercy is even higher than justice. Mercy says, "Justice is important, but if you beg for the Lord's benevolence, you will be given greater reciprocation than what you deserve." Justice demands rights, declaring, "I'm not getting what I deserve. Give it to me!" Responsibility adds, "I am going to do what is necessary to get what I deserve." Justice insists, "I must be appreciated, so give me what is due to me." But Mercy murmurs, "I need more. I need more than my rights. I need more than my responsibilities, because in truth I am not very good at fulfilling my responsibilities. I need more than justice, because if you give me justice, I will lose. I will miss out. Therefore, I want more than what is due to me. I want clemency: I'm asking for forgiveness and compassion."

This is the platform of *saranagati*. We are not motivated by a desire for Krishna to remember us, to recognize us, and to reward us. We do not approach the Lord because we want something that we feel is rightfully ours. We definitely try to observe our responsibilities, but at the same time we realize that even if we do fulfill them in the most meticulous way, ultimately our effort alone still will not be enough. Certainly, in Kali-yuga, we realize that our standard is actually not sufficient, even when we do our best. However, despite this knowledge, we are not intimidated because we know that the Lord's mercy is always available!

Krishna's Greatest Opulence

Krishna's greatest opulence is His mercy on the conditioned souls. His most magnificent quality is intimately connected with His periodic appearance into the prison houses of the material world, and the manifold ways in which He reaches out to help individuals.

His matchless potency lies in how He keeps trying to reclaim us, even though we find so many ways to run away.

It is possible to draw an analogy between the necessity to beg for Krishna's mercy and the mercy plea, which is sometimes presented by the defense attorney during the sentencing of a criminal in a court of law. Occasionally, when a criminal has been caught, tried, and is awaiting sentencing by a court, the lawyers realize that even though they applied so many different techniques to defend the culprit, it is obvious that he is really at fault and that he will be found guilty. In such a situation, the lawyers may throw everything down and present a mercy plea to the judge and the jury. The lawyers may explain as follows, "Yes, we admit that the crime occurred and my client is guilty. But there were mitigating circumstances, so please have mercy on him. Even though he is responsible, and normally he should be punished excruciatingly, do not allow the full impact of justice to fall upon him. Give him mercy!"

This is the power of Mercy: it goes beyond rights and responsibilities, it goes beyond justice, and it says, "I need additional reciprocation. Actually, I require special understanding. I did wrong, and I need to be forgiven. Please have compassion upon me, and give me the opportunity to endeavor never to do that again." In our deepest aspect of surrender as devotees, we are not hungry just for the Lord's laws, for our rights, for our responsibilities, or even for justice. We are starving for mercy, and as we cry for the Lord with destitution and desperation, the *laulyam* necessary to attain Krishna blossoms in our hearts.

Intense Concentrated Desire

The attainment of Krishna's lotus feet, although very difficult, is actually within our reach. In our own lives, we all experience times when we want something so badly that all we can think about is the object of our desire. We speak about it, we dream about it, and we imagine ourselves having it until finally we have got it. We organize our lives in such a way that we can definitely attain it. Consider that everyday we desire things that are technically beyond our means. We may want a car, we may desire a computer, or perhaps a special sari or beautiful bangles which we do not have the money for right now, but nevertheless we want what we want and realize that we must have it. We may think, "That sari would look perfect on me. Actually, only time is separating me and the object of my desire. It is mine." Often we plan and sacrifice in some other areas in order to attain what we intensely want.

When something is very important to us, we allow ourselves to become deeply focused as we undergo many austerities to achieve our dreams. For example, some people study for a long time simply to get a degree, while others work very hard for many years to obtain a car, or a little three-roomed house. Once they obtain their goal, however, often they become enslaved to it. To maintain a house, for instance, takes hard work. The owner has to pay a mortgage, clean the rooms, and acquire furniture. Some people work so hard to keep their house looking grand that they become slaves to it. They are slaves who live in a beautiful prison. Basically, if we want something, without a doubt we possess the ability to concentrate our energies in order to obtain it. Therefore, we should cultivate such an intense desire for Krishna and for our real palace—our truly beautiful home in the spiritual world.

The Selfless Devotion of Advanced Devotees

Advanced devotees are personifications of mercy. Holy scriptures from all bona fide traditions are full of examples of their acts of compassion and forgiveness. For instance, Haridasa Thakura was whipped in twenty-two marketplaces, but nevertheless he begged Krishna, "Please have mercy on these wretched souls, who were intent on beating me to death." Lord Jesus Christ, too, prayed for those who had nailed him to the cross, saying, "Father, forgive them, for they know not what they do. Have mercy on them."

In the Vedic scriptures, a narration about Ramanujacarya perfectly conveys this mood of divine mercy. The king at the time, Koluttunga I, was very disturbed by the *sankirtana* movement. He wanted to convince Ramanujacarya to give up the mission of spreading the message of Krishna, and worship Lord Siva instead. If he could convince Ramanujacarya to worship Lord Siva, then all the Vaisnavas in his kingdom would follow suit. His initial plan of action was to defeat Ramanujacarya by hiring some bogus *panditas*. If these so-called *panditas* did not succeed in defeating Ramanujacarya, the king's second plan of action was to take the *acarya's* life.

Apprised of the his plan, Ramanujacarya's *guru*, Mahapurna, and one of Ramanujacarya's very special disciples, Kuresa, went before the king. Kuresa fooled the king into thinking that he was Ramanujacarya himself. As Koluttunga I had calculated, 'Ramanujacarya' and his *guru* were not defeated. He then proceeded to severely torture Mahapurna and Kuresa by plucking out their eyes. Mahapurna, who was quite elderly, died from the torture, while Kuresa suffered greatly. Internally, however, Kuresa felt joyful that he was able to receive the torture instead of his spiritual master.

The Power of Forgiveness

Kuresa, blind and wounded, returned to the place in the forest where his *guru* was hiding. Ramanujacarya instructed him to worship a very special Deity named Sri Varadaraja at Kancipurnam in the knowledge that powerful reciprocation would occur. He wanted his disciple, who had given everything for his care, to regain his vision. So elevated was Kuresa's level of devotion that the Deity spoke to him, asking him how he could facilitate his desires. Kuresa was so much situated in the forgiving mood that he simply asked the Deity to please liberate the terrible personalities who had tortured him, and who had killed his *parama-guru* in an attempt to kill his own *guru*. He did not say, "Make these men suffer like they have never suffered before. Make their families undergo pain and calamity, make their whole village endure intense misery, and let this happen for generation after generation. Let them know what it means to bother the devotees of the Lord."

Miraculously, Kuresa simply requested the Lord to liberate his torturers. He was neither angry nor desiring revenge, but instead he prayed for their highest well-being. The Lord could not help but respond to the request of his dear devotee. When Ramanujacarya heard what his disciple had done, he sent Kuresa back to continue with the *puja*, with the plea that the next time he had the opportunity to request something from the Deity, he should ask for his sight back. Only because his *guru* had issued him a distinct instruction to appeal in this way did Kuresa then regain his sight, based on another high-level reciprocation which took place. What occurred went far beyond justice, because justice would have meant that these sinister personalities, who were actually *asuras*, should have been dealt with very viciously. However, as a result of Kuresa's compassion, they received the mercy of the Lord.

Who Returns to the Spiritual World?

We want to forgive so we can be forgiven. We are to be very compassionate in order to receive compassion. We do not want to allow ourselves to keep suffering by not forgiving others. And if some do not want to forgive us, then at least we should forgive them, because they will hurt themselves by not forgiving. In the light of this understanding, let us examine the three types of devotees who qualify to go back to the spiritual world:

- *nitya-siddhas*: pure devotees who are always thinking of the Lord and who have never been separate from Him. Although they have never been conditioned, these transcendental, special agents come into this world to engage in the Lord's pastimes, and then return to Him.

- *sadhana-siddhas*: conditioned souls who engage in executing devotional practices very nicely and so elevate their consciousness from the *sadhana* platform of following rules and regulations to *prema*. In Kali-yuga, however, the position of the *sadhana-siddha* is very difficult to achieve without the mercy of the Lord.

- *krpa-siddhas*: conditioned souls who engage in devotional service with loyalty and dedication, despite their lack of ability to attain high-level *bhakti*. However, because of their perseverance, Lord Nityananda bestows special mercy on such souls. In this way, many of us will be brought back to the spiritual world. The *krpa-siddha* is in a position of beseeching the Lord, "Dear Lord, I need more than my rights. Yes, my responsibilities are there, and I will do what is necessary, but it is not going to be enough. I am a fallen soul. It is never enough to sufficiently glorify You. Therefore, I must connect with Your Department of Mercy."

A *jiva* can become so sinful that the soul cannot attain a human body in its next birth, or even an animal body, but instead it ends up in a germ body. In fact, simply the amount of cow-killing by itself is enough to bring down the whole of civilization on this planet. It is only due to the mercy of those who are carrying the mercy, and who are begging Krishna to be merciful that the full force of the *karma* on the planet is not manifest.

The Svarupa-Laksana

In the *Harinama Cintamani*, Haridasa Thakura explains that taking complete shelter at Krishna's lotus feet is the *svarupa-laksana*, or the primary, constitutional symptom of *bhakti*. While Rupa Gosvami writes in *The Nectar of Instruction* that we are to accept everything favorable, and reject everything unfavorable to devotional service, Haridasa Thakura elaborates further that full dependence on the Supreme Personality of Godhead is essential for the development of *bhakti*. Nothing else can really satisfy us fully. Complete faith in Krishna is the *svarupa-laksana*, while all other aspects of our devotion are ornaments which enhance what is already there. A mood of working towards and looking for the mercy falls within the category of Haridasa Thakura's *svarupa-laksana*. It is indispensable. All other activities we do simply support this primary concern.

We must run very quickly towards Krishna's shelter. In order to approach Krishna effectively, we need to fear *maya* more intensely. Such a consciousness inspires us to flee from that which is inauspicious, while simultaneously giving us a deeper appreciation of the *siddhanta* of all the scriptures. The more appreciation we cultivate for Krishna, the greater the speed with which we will hasten towards Him. Haridasa Thakura concludes his text by discussing doubts. Once we realize the potency of Krishna's *nama, rupa, guna,* and *lila,* Haridasa Thakura writes that we will not allow ourselves to be stopped by any kind of boon. We will even reject associating with Krishna's effulgence in order to connect with the *summum bonum* Himself.

Petition the Lord for Mercy

Once we see how glorious the ultimate outcome can be, we can position ourselves properly by making a petition to the Lord. We may plead, "Dear Krishna, I am Yours. Thy will be done. You know what is best for me. I put myself at Your lotus feet. I surrender myself to You even though I have some reluctance and fear. I implore You to take away unhealthy desires. I entreat You to even operate on my free will, so that I will not do something immature, even with good intentions. I have no idea how much baggage that I am bringing with me from previous lives. In fact, it is incalculable. However, I want to remind You of Your promise of *daya-bhak,* that one who suffers the reactions of his past activities while waiting for Your mercy rightfully inherits a place in the spiritual world. You have also made that promise in *Bhagavad-gita* 4.11:

> *ye yatha mam prapadyante*
> *tams tathaiva bhajamy aham*
> *mama vartmanuvartante*
> *manusyah partha sarvasah*

> As all surrender unto Me, I reward them accordingly. Everyone follows My path in all respects. O son of Prtha.

Now I am ready to allow You to honor Your contract, and in return I will do all that is necessary to stop interfering with Your plans for me. You are my doctor. You are always helping me by giving me the medicine I need, and by arranging specific prescriptions through *sadhu, sastra,* and *guru.* Even though Your prescriptions are always available, for so many lifetimes I have very tactfully found ways not to utilize them in full. Finally, *I have had enough.* I am eager to do whatever is necessary to return to You. Therefore, as I chant Hare Krishna, I truly mean, 'Dear Radha, dear Krishna, take it away.' "

Asking for More than We Deserve
Chanting the Lord's name is a very powerful process. We are really asking Krishna, "Bring to us whatever will help us return to You. Please take away any parts of our personalities that constitute an interference to this goal. We understand that as You remove all these obstacles, and as You bring in all facility to speed up our advancement, right around the corner awaits our rightful claim—magical, animated, and divine experiences which, until now, we have either denied or avoided."

Sincere devotees possess the mood of this final *mantra* of *Sri Isopanisad.* They do not only request their rights, or cite their responsibilities, and they do not even want justice (although they are ready to honor it for others), but they feel that more is needed. So they ask the Lord, "Allow Your mercy to come upon us. Please take care of us in the spirit of not just what we deserve, and not just what we should inherit, but allow us to experience situations that are higher than the quality of devotion we can offer. We are most desperate beggars, but as You love us more than we love ourselves, we know that Your mercy can descend upon us at any time." We have no qualifications, but we know the power of the Lord's love for the fallen living entities. Therefore, although we are hopeless, we should cultivate maximum faith in the possibilities of acquiring the Lord's full mercy.

Questions and Answers
Question: Did the Supreme Lord have any children during the course of His pastimes in Vrndavana?

Answer: When Krishna enters into different universes to execute His amazing *lilas,* they include many human-like activities. *Human-like,* that is, not human. Some of His eternal associates from the spiritual kingdom came before Him, some came with Him, and some come after Him. He engaged in different pastimes with His eternal associates, who return with Him again and again. They were on a mission to annihilate the miscreants and to eradicate the nescience, while giving protection, facilitation, and love to His servants. The Lord does whatever is necessary to make things as simple as possible for the souls who are ready to come back. Krishna's close family members like His father and mother are His eternal associates, *nitya-siddhas* who have never suffered from amnesia by having separated interests.

When Krishna appeared on earth five thousand years ago, He was born into a specific royal lineage named the Yadu dynasty. He married 16,108 wives, and with each of His queens, Krishna begot ten sons. His chief wives are Rukmini, Satyabhama, Jambavati, Kalindi, Mitravinda, Nagnajiti, Bhadra, and Laksmana, many of whom He won as the result of His superior military skill. After killing Bhaumasura, Krishna freed 16,000 princesses who had been held captive by the demon. The princesses fell in love with Krishna and asked Him to marry them, which He did. Krishna lived with all His queens in His capital city, Dvaraka, as their sole husband. When Krishna spent time with one of His queens, it was not as if the other 16,107 wives were left alone. Since the Lord could expand Himself unlimitedly, Krishna would return each evening to each of His 16,108 wives in each of His 16,108 palaces in order to execute His pastimes with every one of them personally.

Krishna's Dvaraka pastimes, in which He plays the role of a stately king, are different in mood to His Vrndavana pastimes, in which Krishna is a simple cowherd boy. In Dvaraka, Krishna's queens associate with Krishna as their husband in opulent, sophisticated settings, while the *gopis* enter into secretive relationships of socially forbidden love with Krishna in the beautiful forests and lakes of Vraja. Krishna's children are therefore part of His pastimes in Dvaraka, and not Vrndavana. In *Krishna Book*, Volume Two, Srila Prabhupada writes that among "Krishna's greatly powerful sons, eighteen sons were *maha-rathas*. The *maha-rathas* could fight alone against many thousands of foot soldiers, charioteers, cavalry and elephants" (470). Pradyumna, the eldest son of Rukmini and Krishna, was the chief of the eighteen *maha-ratha* sons.

Question: I am told that we were initially envious of Krishna, and therefore we were sent to the material world. But how can envy exist in the spiritual world in the first place?

Answer: Everything that exists in this realm is found in the spiritual world, but in a pure sense. Envy is present here only because it is real, just as lust and fear, untainted by material contamination, also exist in the spiritual world. In this realm, however, these emotions are expressed via the modes of material nature as perverted reflections of genuine, pure emotions that have nothing to do with enmity or sabotaging.

As we are parts and parcels of the Lord, we possess similar qualities and attributes to Him. Therefore, we also have freedom. Like Him, we have the tendency for exploration. We have the urge for mastery, too. Coming to this world has a lot to do with an entity's desire to engage in pastimes of exploration and dominion. Therefore, we try to master the material energies. When we tire of striving to control material nature, we can go back and be real masters of unadulterated love, devotion, and selflessness. In the meantime, Krishna has given us this environment where we can pretend to be the Supreme Lord. As soon as we are no longer satisfied with pursuing this kind of mastery, then we will be given the opportunity to make an immediate transition.

Srila Prabhupada explains that one can become Krishna conscious in many, many lifetimes, or one can do it at once. It is a matter of accepting the basic medicine. It is a matter of saying, "Krishna, take it away," and really meaning it. It is a matter of genuinely asking, "Krishna, bring it to me," and truly desiring it. Once we really mean what we say one hundred percent, there will be no *karma* to slow us down or to stop us anymore. Nothing will impede us from honoring our original existence.

Question: How do we know that we sincerely want to make spiritual advancement, when in actuality we may just be pursuing it in order to subtly boost our egos?

Answer: Actually, our very conception of sincerity is not sufficient, because in order to be genuinely sincere, we must be fully aware of who we are and of what we are to be sincere about. As long as we are conditioned, obstacles to sincerity and some lack in realization will always be present. Therefore, while effort is important, it must be connected with mercy. At the same time, we have to make sufficient effort to connect with sufficient mercy. We should neither simply wait for the mercy to come, nor think that everything will happen by our own effort. We need focused, dedicated effort in order to draw to us the mercy that corresponds with that endeavor.

Reflections on Sacred Teachings, Volume Four

The more sincerity and energy we invest, the more the mercy will compensate for the areas in which we are weak. In *Bhagavad-gita* 9.22, Krishna promises Arjuna:

> *ananyas cintayanto mam*
> *ye janah paryupasate*
> *tesam nityabhiyuktanam*
> *yoga-ksemam vahamy aham*
>
> *But those who always worship Me with exclusive devotion, meditating on My transcendental form—to them I carry what they lack, and I preserve what they have.*

Question: When I chant Hare Krishna, I get cold shivers in my body. What is that?

Answer: Firstly, on a practical level, we can recommend that perhaps you should put on some more clothes before you chant. A warm sweater may help you to stop shivering. On a more esoteric level, however, if while chanting Hare Krishna, you get cold shivers and when you finish chanting you have little or no desire for sense gratification, then this is fantastic and you are most fortunate. Krishna is reciprocating in a very powerful and interesting way. But if while chanting Hare Krishna, you experience cold shivers and as you finish chanting you warm up by taking some intoxication, then you have a problem. What is significant is not what we experience at the moment of chanting, but the impact it exerts upon us later. The quality of the experience is shown in its lasting effects.

From time to time, it is to be expected that a devotee will have different kinds of experiences in Krishna consciousness. Sometimes while seeing the Deity, participating in *kirtana*, or chanting the holy name, devotees undergo what is called shadow ecstasy, a little glimpse of possibilities that are waiting and available. Sometimes, the Lord intervenes in our lives by allowing us to have unusual experiences that are quite highly evolved. By coming forth to give us a little taste of mercy, He encourages us to make more of an effort to attain more of the mercy that is available.

Question: Srila Bhaktisiddhanta mentions that if anyone makes offenses to one's *guru*, then we should not even look at such a person's face. How do we remain forgiving to such offenders?

Answer: Do not look at them. Think about them as a spiritual entity and connect with their soul. Do not look at their crazy personality. Put it to the side, and realize that this person is not the offensive behavior that he or she may exhibit. While we do not want to connect with that craziness, at the same time we must realize that this is also an eternal servant of Krishna who is just highly confused. We should search for ways to help that person. The very best way we can assist them is to become very good devotees ourselves. In such a way, those persons who are hypocrites will be able to compare themselves with more genuine *sadhus*, and they will see for themselves how far off the mark they are. We should definitely forgive them, while feeling sad in our hearts for what they are doing to themselves. We have great pity for such persons, realizing that they are like the sick patient who needs a doctor, but who is surely not taking the medicine.

Forgiveness is always there. However, forgiveness does not mean that we deny what happened. In Vaisnava alignment, when an offense is committed, then chastisement follows in the form of punishment congruent to the crime. After chastisement, forgiveness is granted. We must address evil. If we do not punish evil, then rewarding good becomes meaningless, and people in general become confused about what is proper. Therefore, we need to draw attention to the nescience in order to distinguish healthy practice from deviation. Clearly demonstrating the difference between them will act as a deterrent for potential digressions by others within the Vaisnava community. The effects of deviation on everyone must be addressed properly: that is also mercy.

One of the most difficult things for people to understand is how we, as devotees, can honor capital punishment. Of course, in today's world, it is dangerous to be in favor of capital punishment, because often people are convicted who are not actually guilty, or there are all kinds of mitigating circumstances around the situation. But in a situation where justice is properly meted out, when someone commits a very great crime, they are to be chastised proportionately. In the Vedic system, if somebody takes a life, then his or her life will be taken. This act of justice is actually mercy, not only because it sends a message that this behavior is unacceptable, and that consequences exist for indulging in it, but also because it allows the offender to be forgiven immediately. If offenders face the karmic reaction for their crime right then and there, then they are freed from having to carry the karmic burden for their transgression into their next life.

Question: Muslims and Christians believe that Satan exists. Does the Hare Krishna movement consider the existence of Satan to be real, or the Anti-Christ to be a person, or are these perceptions just illusions?

Answer: Satan exists. Yes, it is true that the Muslims and the Christians have a certain understanding of Satan as the personification of evil. In our Vedic tradition, we also recognize that personifications of evil are present on this planet. However, while Islam and Christianity often believe in only one Satan, which would be analogous to our Maya or Kali, we recognize that there are different radiations of evil. Some entities called *asuras* are empowered for evil, while other entities fall under their spell, and become induced to do evil.

Living beings who are quite powerful demons, like Ravana, Hiranyakasipu, and Putana, fall into the same category as Satan. Normally, whenever a very powerful presence of spiritualists and divine teachings exists, the other polarity is also manifest. The more highly potent ambassadors of Krishna enact their pastimes on this planet, the more empowered agents of Maya will appear. Their ambassadorship is to cause chaos and bring down the consciousness of people, while the agents of Krishna attempt to elevate the entire world.

Question: How do we forgive those who repeatedly abuse us?

Answer: Repeatedly get out of their way if possible. We are not saying that we are to be fools, and that if somebody keeps abusing us, we should say, "Oh, thank you, hit me on the other side. And now you have hurt me on both sides, hit me over here next time." Forgiveness means transformation. Since we care for others, we understand that if somebody abuses us, they are hurting themselves. We do not want to allow ourselves to be used for anybody to hurt themselves in the process of hurting us. If a situation is abusive and it continues in that way, then if one cannot help to transform the abuser, it is best to remove oneself from that situation. But, in our hearts, we should still think good of that person and wish them well.

Sometimes devotees think, "I wish you well because I have faith that Krishna will crush you. I wish Krishna will give you a wonderful blessing by severely smashing you." Of course, we should not be in this mood, but it is interesting to consider that when the great devotees curse, their curses bring special benedictions to those who are fortunate enough to receive them. Curses by great devotees result in extraordinary mercy, which will completely alter the lives of those who have offended them. Ultimately, the offenders will be happy, but in the process of undergoing the alteration, they will experience tremendous shock.

Question: How do I transcend my cultural identity in pursuit of Krishna, while at the same time living with loved ones to whom I am linked by birth and *karma*?

Answer: This is a very interesting question. Yes, it is true that our *karma* brings us into a specific body, gender, and culture. Sometimes we think that if our *karma* brought us into a specific culture, then that must be our identity. It is only our temporary identity, however. The whole process of Krishna consciousness is about connecting with our eternal identity. Therefore, as we honor some of our temporary identity, we do not want it to take priority over who we are attempting to become, in an everlasting sense. When cultural traditions and beliefs can be used to aid us in approaching our original identity, then they are to be considered valuable. In general, devotees are not very concerned about ethnic pride, either in antiquity or modernity. We cannot get excited about any culture, because ultimately all material cultures perpetuate lifestyles of incarceration—all cultures, all races, and all nationalities are but temporary designations. Our genuine and eternal culture is a never-ending culture of devotion and pure love.

Basically, what we normally call our culture is simply a set of strategies that people connected with us for some generations have evolved in their struggle to survive in a hostile world. According to various hereditary and environmental factors, we learn to function in various cultures which have evolved different languages, varied ways of gathering food, and diverse methods of social interaction. We must bear in mind, however, that each and every one of these cultures is temporary. Because Srila Prabhupada has given us knowledge about the transmigration of the soul, we know that in this lifetime the soul can be in a European body, while in the next lifetime it may take birth in an African body. In its subsequent lifetime, it may acquire an Indian body. The body is always changing.

We have heard many times that the body is a garment. It is a costume. In the same way that prisoners may compare prison suits, so people on this planet compare their bodies, usually finding their own superior. While one prisoner might be proud of his or her own prison suit, which he just acquired last week, and gloat over a prisoner wearing an old, worn garment, nothing can change the fact that both prisoners are wearing prison uniforms. They are both confined to the jail. In either case, their suits signify restriction imposed because of deviation.

Krishna has a keen sense of humor. Therefore, it is dangerous for us to discriminate on the basis of bodily designations. People who position themselves in opposition to a particular race group in this lifetime stand a high chance of taking birth in that same race in their next lifetime. It is as if Krishna says, "You were so absorbed in hating those people during your past life. Now, I will give you an opportunity to experience the polarity of your hatred, in order for you to feel what it is like on the other side." Some people who were fabulously wealthy in their last lifetime find themselves homeless the next time around. The nature of their *karma* necessitates an extremely opposite experience. If a person in his previous life was a macho body builder who terrorized everyone with his biceps, then Krishna may conclude, "That living entity likes to show off his body. In order to facilitate him, I will allow him to take birth in a nice, pretty, feminine body, which he can also display." Krishna will provide variegated experiences for the living entity to flaunt its material covering until finally it has had enough.

Karma is an interesting science. At times, just by looking at a person's body, we will be able to see much of their past life conditioning. Also in terms of our own *karma*, frequently it will become clear to us why we experience certain things in this lifetime, and why we must develop a greater sense of balance. When we meditate too much in an unhealthy way on material designations, then we begin to create that type of material body for ourselves.

Question: Recently, you gave a very vivid description of how we should become slaves to Krishna's mercy in order get out of prison. Please give some practical advice to householders who usually find themselves enslaved to household life.

Answer: Previously, I used the harsh word 'slavery.' For a *sadhu* it is beneficial to think in terms of being God's slave, even though in a material sense slavery is repugnant. Similarly, the word 'surrender' in most languages is a heavy declaration. It means giving up our identity, being conquered and imposed upon, and having no alternative but to give in to somebody else's power. It does not evoke healthy connotations. However, if we think of surrender in terms of the full protection and care a little child receives as she runs into her mother's arms, then we realize how beautiful surrender can be. When such absolute help and reciprocation is present, then we cannot help but feel inspired to open ourselves to it completely. The idea of being a slave means that we should not hold back, but press ahead without reservation. This is the essence of *Mantra Eighteen—saranagati*, full surrender.

If we are attached to what *we* want to arrange, however, we cannot surrender totally. But, if we use all our property for the pleasure of our loved ones, and if we have an intense level of love for them and they for us, then we feel that we are living for them. As we constantly meditate on how to reciprocate and show our appreciation, we experience a type of blissful slavery. We are happy to be bound by love as it brings us the most satisfying reciprocation. Ultimately, we want to be bound by Krishna's love, exuberantly tied down, and completely protected.

Those in the household *asrama* may feel that life is easier for renunciates, as seemingly we do not have to hold down a job, or interact daily with a husband or wife, and children. In fact, not having a spouse or children produces a different set of complexities and challenges. If one is in a household situation, then one has definite responsibilities that must be faced straight away on a practical level. Our first responsibility is to our immediate environment, and for householders, their immediate environment is their husband or wife and their children. Before we try to save the world, we should first take care of the world right in front of us. As we attempt to be kind to everyone and to share Krishna consciousness, we must keep in mind that our primary responsibility lies with those souls who Krishna has brought into our life space. We should give them the greatest kind of care, addressing all their physical, psychological and, most importantly, spiritual needs.

If we only take care of the physical, we are cheating them. If we are solely concerned about their psychological needs, we are also swindling them. If we cannot address all their needs, then we fail in our task as proper caretakers of Krishna's property. In my book *Spiritual Warrior II: Transforming Lust into Love*, I discuss this subject at some length. If a husband thinks that his wife belongs only to him, then this is problematic. Conversely, if the wife thinks that her husband is exclusively her property, then that is material consciousness. If both the parents consider the children theirs alone, then they cannot love those children completely. Let me explain this statement, which may sound strange initially. If a husband imagines that his wife is his alone, he will not treat her in the proper manner. A husband should treat his wife as if she has been given to him as a gift from Krishna. Therefore, he is to cherish her even more than he would his own property, treasuring her in the spirit of a loving caretaker. The wife should reflect on her husband similarly. If she thinks of her husband as only her property, then she might not think twice if she wants to ignore him, or even to poison him. If he is only hers, then it follows that she can do whatever she wants with him. When we take something or someone to be our property, if we want to deny it, to batter it, or to cheat on it, then we may ask ourselves, "What's the problem? If it's ours, we do what we want, right?" But when we realize that this person is much more than ours alone, then we have to think much more carefully about how we relate to him or her. We should always remind ourselves that this family member is Krishna's gift, and ask, "Am I taking care of this gift in a way that Krishna would be pleased?"

Both husband and wife should visualize their relationship with their children in this light. Instead of thinking of the children as property, we could remind ourselves that these souls have been especially sent to us in order for us to honor them in a way which will fully please Krishna. Will Krishna be pleased if we just tell them to chant Hare Krishna, but we fail to feed them or do not let them get a good education? Will Krishna be pleased if we give them good education and healthy food, but we do not provide them with spiritual nourishment? No, Krishna will not be pleased. The Supreme Lord will be pleased when we value every aspect of what He has made available, and when we take care of all their requirements, while giving priority to their spiritual needs.

Consider how much more loving the world would be if each person were in the mood of not being the proprietor, but of being a genuine, powerful, and compassionate caretaker who is accountable to a higher source. If this consciousness were cultivated, then every devotee would automatically develop greater barriers against deviation as they became more sensitive to one another's authentic needs. As we foster an on-going exchange of selflessness, Maya will have so little chance to get in. Actually, Maya would not want to come anywhere near us because we would be radiating so much love and devotion as we connect with Krishna's mercy and potency.

Mantra Eighteen

Sri Isopanisad is just one of Srila Prabhupada's many volumes of books that offer extremely deep information. Incredible excitement awaits us as we meditate on this final prayer, and as we request Krishna not just to grant us our rights, not just to view us in terms of our responsibilities, not only to give us justice, but to give us mercy. And when Krishna sees that we are being truly merciful, then He will bring more mercy upon us.

Glossary

Abhidheya: The regulated activities of the soul for reviving his relationship with the Lord; devotional service.

Acarya: A spiritual master who teaches by his own example, and who sets the proper religious example for all human beings.

Adhikara: The qualification or ability to understand spiritual matters due to previous spiritual activities.

Adhunika-vada: To apply spiritual precepts practically in consideration of modernity.

Adi-purusa: The Supreme Lord, Krishna, the original person.

Ahankara: False ego, by which the soul misidentifies with the material body.

Ahimsa: Nonviolence.

Aisvarya: Opulence.

Ajnata-sukrti: Pious activities performed unknowingly.

Akarma: Action for which one suffers no reaction because it is performed in Krishna consciousness; free from material desire.

Anartha: Unwanted material desires in the heart that pollute one's consciousness, such as pride, hate, envy, lust, greed, anger, and desires for distinction, adoration, wealth, etc.

Antaranga-sakti: The internal potency of the Supreme Lord.

Aparadha: An offense.

Aprarabdha: Sinful reactions not yet manifest.

Apsara: A heavenly courtesan; the most beautiful women in the heavenly planets who are expert at dancing.

Arca-vigraha: An authorized form of God manifested through material elements, as in a painting or statue of Krishna worshiped in a temple or home; actually present in this form, the Lord accepts worship from His devotees.

Artha-prada: That which gives knowledge of material nature.

Asrama: The four spiritual orders according to the Vedic social system: *brahmacarya* (student life), *grhastha* (householder life), *vanaprastha* (retirement), and *sannyasa* (renunciation).

Astanga-yoga: The eightfold system of mystic *yoga*, propounded by Patanjali, meant for realizing the presence of Paramatma, the Lord in the heart.

Asura: One who does not follow the principles of scripture; atheist; gross materialist.

Atma: The self (refers sometimes to the body, sometimes to the soul, and sometimes to the senses).

Atmarama: One who is self-satisfied, free from external, material desires.

Avatara: Literally means "one who descends." A partially or fully empowered incarnation of the Lord who descends from the spiritual sky to the material universe with a particular mission described in the scriptures.

Avidya: Nescience or ignorance; the illusory energy of the Supreme Lord.

Babaji: A person who dwells alone in one place and leads a life of meditation, penance, and austerity; renounced order beyond *sannyasa* in which one chants and reads.

Bahiranga-sakti: The external potency of the Supreme Lord.

Bhajana: Intimate devotional service; chanting devotional songs in a small group, usually accompanied by musical instruments; solitary chanting.

Bhajana-kutira: A small hut or cottage where a Vaisnava or saintly person performs his or her *bhajana* or personal meditation.

Bhakta: A devotee of the Lord; one who performs devotional service (*bhakti*).

Bhakti: Devotional service to the Supreme Lord.

Bhakti-lata-bija: The seed of the creeper of devotional service.

Bhaya: Fear.

Bhoga: Material sense enjoyment; or food before it has been offered to the Deity.

Bhukti: Material enjoyment.

Brahmacari: Celibate, student life.

Brahmajyoti: The impersonal bodily effulgence emanating from the transcendental body of the Supreme Lord Krishna, which constitutes the brilliant illumination of the spiritual sky.

Brahmana: A member of the most intelligent class of men, according to the four Vedic occupational divisions of society.

Darsana: The act of seeing or being seen by the Deity in the temple or by a spiritually advanced person.

Deva: A demigod or saintly person.

Dhama: A holy place.

Glossary

Dharma: Religious principles; one's natural occupation.

Dhira: One who is undisturbed by the material energy in all circumstances.

Dhoti: A long cotton cloth, traditionally worn by Indian men, that covers the lower half of the body.

Ekadasi: A special day for increased remembrance of Krishna, which comes on the eleventh day after both the full and new moon; abstinence from grains and beans is prescribed.

Gandharvas: The celestial demigod dancers, singers, and musicians of the heavenly planets.

Gopis: The cowherd girls of Vraja, who are generally the counterparts of Sri Krishna's hladini-sakti, Srimati Radharani.

Gosvamis: A person who has his senses under full control; the title of a person in the renounced order of life, *sannyasa*.

Grhamedhi: An envious materialistic householder who lives only for sense gratification.

Grhastha: A married householder in Vedic society.

Guru: Spiritual master.

Guru-aparadha: An offense against the spiritual master.

Gurukula: A school of Vedic learning. Students begin at five years old and live as celibate students, guided by a spiritual master.

Hladini-sakti: The pleasure potency of God.

Isvara: A controller; Krishna is *paramesvara*, the supreme controller.

Japa: Chanting the holy names quietly to oneself, counting the repetitions of the *maha-mantra* on a *japa-mala*.

Jnana: The path of empirical knowledge, culminating in attainment of impersonal liberation (*sayujya-mukti*).

Jnani: A transcendentalist who attempts to obtain impersonal liberation as a result of empirical knowledge.

Kama: Lust.

Kanistha-adhikari: A materialistic devotee in the neophyte stage.

Karma: The law of material cause and effect.

Karma-kandis: Fruitive workers.

Karmi: A fruitive worker who attempts to enjoy heavenly bliss through the process of *karma-yoga*.

Kirtana: Glorification of the Supreme Lord; the devotional process of chanting.

Krishna-prema: Pure love of Krishna, the object of the path of *bhakti*.

Krodha: Anger.

Krpa-siddha: One who has attained perfection by the mercy of superior authorities.

Ksatriya: The martial-spirited, administrative class of Vedic society who protect society from danger.
Laulyam: Greed.
Lila: The transcendental pastimes of the Supreme Lord.
Madhurya-rasa: The spiritual mellow of conjugal love.
Madhyama-adhikari: A devotee in the middle stage of spiritual advancement.
Maha-bhagavata: A pure devotee of the Supreme Lord in the highest stage of devotional life.
Maha-mantra: The great chant for deliverance: Hare Krishna Hare Krishna Krishna Krishna Hare Hare/ Hare Rama Hare Rama Rama Rama Hare Hare.
Maha-tattva: The total material energy.
Mangala-arati: The first Deity worship of the day performed an hour and a half before sunrise.
Mantra: A pure sound vibration that delivers the mind from its material inclinations and illusions when repeated over and over. A transcendental sound or Vedic hymn, prayer, or chant.
Maya: The external energy of the Supreme Lord, which covers the conditioned soul and does not allow him to understand the Supreme Personality of Godhead.
Mrdanga: A two-headed clay drum used for *kirtana* performances and congregational chanting.
Mukti: Liberation from material bondage.
Naistika-brahmacari: One who has been celibate since birth.
Nama: The pure holy name of the Lord.
Nama-aparadha: An offense against the holy name of the Lord.
Nirvana: Freedom from material existence.
Nitya-siddha: An eternal associate of the Lord who was never conditioned.
Pandita: A learned Vedic scholar whose knowledge is based on scripture.
Paramatma: The Supersoul; the localized aspect of the Visnu expansion of the Supreme Lord residing in the heart of each embodied living entity and pervading all of material nature.
Paramartha-prada: That which gives knowledge of spiritual nature.
Paramesvara: The supreme controller, Lord Krishna.
Parampara: The disciplic succession system of spiritual knowledge beginning with the Lord Himself, and continuing down to the present day.
Prabhu: Master.

Glossary

Prajalpa: Idle talk on mundane subjects.

Prana: The life air.

Prarabdha: Reactions of past activities that have already begun to fructify, offering both sinful reactions as well as pious results.

Prayojana: The ultimate goal of life; love of God.

Prema: Love; pure and unbreakable love of God.

Puja: Worship, usually in the form of making offerings to the Deity of the Lord.

Pujari: A priest, specifically one engaged in temple Deity worship.

Rajo-guna: The material mode of passion.

Rasa: The transcendental "taste" of a particular spiritual relationship with the Supreme Lord.

Ruci: Liking, taste; the stage after *nistha*, when a strong taste for devotional service arises in the devotee.

Sabda: Transcendental sound.

Sac-cid-ananda-vigraha: The Lord's transcendental form, which is eternal and full of knowledge and bliss.

Sadacara: Good habits or etiquette.

Sadhana-bhakti: There are nine limbs to the practice of *sadhana-bhakti*: hearing, chanting, remembering, serving, Deity worship, offering everything, friendship, and surrendering everything.

Sadhana-siddha: One who has attained perfection by regular execution of the regulative principles mentioned in the *sastras*.

Sadhu: A saintly person.

Sahajiya: A class of so-called devotees who, considering God cheap, ignore scriptural injunctions and try to imitate the Lord's pastimes.

Sakti: Spiritual energy.

Saktiman: The energetic source, the Supreme Personality of Godhead.

Saktyavesa-avatara: An empowered living entity who serves as an incarnation of the Lord; empowered by the Supreme Lord with one or more of the Lord's opulences.

Samadhi: Total absorption and trance of the mind and senses in consciousness of the Supreme Godhead and service to Him.

Sambandha: The transcendental sentiment of relationship.

Sambhoga: The ecstasy of the meeting and embracing of lovers.

Samsara: The cycle of repeated birth and death in the material world.

Samvit: The knowledge portion of the Lord's spiritual potency.

Sanatana-dharma: Literally, the "eternal activity of the soul", or the eternal religion of the living being.
Sandhini: The existence potency of the Lord.
Sankirtana: The congregational chanting of the holy name, fame, and pastimes of the Lord.
Sannyasa: The renounced order of life in Vedic society.
Saranagati: To approach the Lord for shelter.
Sastra: Revealed scripture; Vedic literature.
Seva-aparadha: Offenses in devotional service.
Siddha-deha: The pure spiritual form of the devotee engaged in pure devotional service; the spiritual identity of the devotee revealed to him by his *maha-bhagavata* spiritual master.
Siddhanta: Conclusion.
Siddhi: Mystic perfections usually acquired by *yoga* practice and natural to residents of Siddhaloka.
Sisya: Disciple.
Sloka: A Sanskrit verse.
Smarta-brahmana: A *brahmana* interested more in the external performance of the rules and rituals of the Vedas than in attaining Lord Krishna, the goal of the Vedas.
Sraddha: Firm faith and confidence.
Sudra: A member of the fourth social order, laborer class, in the traditional Vedic social system.
Sura: Demigods, devotees.
Svarupa: The living entity's original eternal relationship of service to the Lord, the real form of the soul.
Svarupa-laksana: The principal symptom (i.e. surrender to Lord Krishna) of a *sadhu* regardless of *varna* and *asrama*.
Tamo-guna: The mode of ignorance, or darkness of material nature.
Tapasya: Austerity; voluntary acceptance of some material trouble for progress in spiritual life.
Tatastha-sakti: The marginal potency of the Supreme Lord.
Tilaka: Sacred clay markings placed on the forehead and other parts of the body to designate one as a follower of Visnu, Rama, Siva, Vedic culture, etc.
Uttama-adhikari: A first-class devotee who is expert in Vedic literature and has full faith in the Supreme Lord; he can deliver the whole world.
Vaisnava-aparadha: An offense against a devotee of the Lord.
Vanaprastha: Retired family life, in which one quits home to cultivate renunciation and travels from holy place to holy place

Glossary

in preparation for the renounced order of life; the third order of Vedic spiritual life.

Varnasrama: The system of four social and four spiritual orders established in the Vedic scriptures and discussed by Lord Krishna in the *Bhagavad-gita*.

Varna: One of the four Vedic social-occupational divisions of society, distinguished by quality of work and situation with regard to the modes of nature.

Vedas: The system of eternal wisdom compiled by Srila Vyasadeva, the literary incarnation of the Supreme Lord, for the gradual upliftment of all mankind from the state of bondage to the state of liberation.

Vedanta: The conclusion of Vedic philosophy.

Vidya: Knowledge.

Vijnana: The practical realization of spiritual knowledge.

Vikarma: Unauthorized or sinful work, performed against the injunctions of revealed scriptures.

Vipralambha: Ecstasy in separation.

Yajna: Sacrifice.

Yoga: Spiritual discipline to link oneself with the Supreme.

Yogi: A transcendentalist who practices one of the many authorized forms of *yoga*, or processes of spiritual purification.

Yuga: One of the four ages of the universe, which differ in length and which rotate like the seasons.

Reflections on Sacred Teachings, Volume Four

Bibliography

The Bible in Today's English Version. 2d ed. Cape Town: Bible Society of South Africa, 1990.

Krishnapada, Swami. *The Beggar One: Meditations and Prayers on the Supreme Lord.* 2d ed. Washington: Hari-Nama Press, 2001.

———. *Spiritual Warrior II. Transforming Lust into Love.* Washington: Hari-Nama Press, 1998.

Peoples, David A. *Presentation Plus.* 2d ed. New York: John Wiley & Sons, 1992.

Prabhupada, A. C. Bhaktivedanta Swami. *Bhagavad-gita As It Is.* Los Angeles: Bhaktivedanta Book Trust, 1983.

———. *The Nectar of Devotion.* Los Angeles: Bhaktivedanta Book Trust, 1982.

———. *The Nectar of Instruction.* New York: Bhaktivedanta Book Trust, 1975.

———. *Sri Isopanisad.* Los Angeles: Bhaktivedanta Book Trust, 1969.

———. *Srimad-Bhagavatam.* 18 vols. Los Angeles: Bhaktivedanta Book Trust, 1987.

———. *Sri Caitanya-caritamrta.* 9 vols. Los Angeles: Bhaktivedanta Book Trust, 1996.

Reflections on Sacred Teachings, Volume Four

Index

abhava, 9
abhidheya, 143
abhimanyu, 244
acarya, 2, 10, 15, 19, 47, 53, 70, 92, 96, 101, 173, 174, 177, 185, 190, 205, 219, 241, 252, 270, 271, 278, 281, 282, 285
achievements, 136, 242
acintya-bhedabheda-tattva, 27, 83, 101
addiction, 137, 151, 246, 254
adhikari, 69, 71, 88, 89, 90, 93, 94, 201, 253
adhunika-vada, 178
adi-purusa, 27, 229, 250
aesthetics, 2
Africa, 16, 40, 43, 49, 173, 295
aggression, 60, 128
agony, 230, 254
ahankara, 66
ahimsa, 42, 123
aisvarya, 49
aithya, 9
Ajamila, 252, 265, 266, 267, 273
ajnata-sukrti, 14, 125, 235
akarma, 48
alcohol, 116, 133, 204, 225
Allah, 180, 255, 268, 271
amara, 156
ambassadors
  spiritual, 270, 272, 294
ambiguity, 132, 136, 218
America, 2, 3, 9, 117, 146, 154, 159, 161, 168, 232
amnesia, 62, 127, 204, 277, 278, 279, 290
amrta, 187
ananda, 27, 42
anarthas, 164, 243, 246, 258
ancestors, 196, 197
angels, 61, 62
Angira, 263, 264
anguish, 86, 101, 223
animalistic life, 60
antaranga-sakti, 7, 66, 70, 79, 227
anthropology, 176, 177
anticipation, spiritual, 32, 33, 216, 248
antipathy, 31
anxiety, 13, 14, 32, 33, 95, 107, 130, 131, 132, 144, 163, 202, 212, 213, 216, 222, 242, 274, 279
aparadhas, 222, 243
Apocalypse, 64
aprarabdha, 53
apsaras, 62
Arabs, 212
arca-vigraha, 79, 110, 227, 254
archangels, 61, 62, 271
Arci, 28
Arjuna, 5, 14, 20, 26, 30, 38, 59, 78, 85, 96, 99, 107, 125, 172, 197, 203, 204, 207, 208, 224, 225, 233, 234, 268, 292
arsa, 8
artha-prada, 176
arunodaya-kirtana, 181
asa-bandha, 247, 251
asakti, 109

Asoka, 177
asramas, four, 6, 195
assassination, 224
Assisi, St. Francis, 179, 187
astanga-yoga, 2, 8, 174
asuras, 58, 60, 172, 286, 294
Asvatthama, 224, 244
atheists, 54, 58, 59, 61, 68, 81, 104, 116, 179, 200, 219, 221
athletes, 87, 184, 221
atma, 60, 63, 123, 187, 227, 270
atma-hanah, 60, 227
atmarama, 101
attains, 54, 182, 204, 207
attempt, 8, 23, 26, 31, 40, 51, 59, 60, 62, 70, 92, 118, 126, 128, 143, 150, 154, 191, 218, 224, 243, 255, 256, 269, 274, 286, 294, 297
auspiciousness, 50, 127, 137, 140, 141, 156, 263
austerity, 69, 91, 92, 93, 109, 128, 154, 156, 169, 180, 183, 191, 193, 220, 232
  undergoing, 34, 71, 118, 150, 156, 182, 194, 223, 226, 227, 236, 281, 285
Australia, 16
avataras, 28
avidya, 115, 142, 143, 227
Avila, St. Teresa, 180, 187
babaji, 180
Back To Godhead, 123
bahiranga-sakti, 7, 66, 70, 79, 227
Balarama, 232, 279
benedictions, 84, 115, 156, 157, 163, 171, 174, 197, 223, 239, 250, 253, 295
Bernard, St., 180, 187
Bhagavad-gita As It Is, 1
Bhagavan, 83, 215, 250
Bhagavatam, 83, 175
bhajana, 2, 92, 142, 208, 249
bhajana-kutira, 92, 142
bhakti-lata-bija, 5, 126, 142, 143

Bhakti-rasamrta-sindhu, 10, 151, 247
Bhaktisiddhanta, 86, 201, 229, 243, 292
Bhaktivinoda, 143, 161, 175, 176, 178, 181
bhakti-yoga, 8, 11, 18, 148, 218, 247
bhava, 98, 109, 113, 139, 151, 224, 228
Bhima, 224
bhukti, 219, 243
Bible, 50, 64, 116, 173, 180, 262, 268
Bilvamangala, 241, 242
botheration, 174
Brahma, 8, 28, 86, 148, 149, 156, 157, 163, 208, 229, 231, 243, 248, 250
brahmajyoti, 187, 215
Brahmaloka, 86, 180, 208
brahman, 26, 27, 28, 81, 171, 193, 215
Brahma-samhita, 8, 229, 243
brahmastra, 224, 244
breaking spiritual laws, 114
Buddha, 177, 223, 234, 255
Buddhism, 43, 174, 175, 177
building community, 125
Caitanya, 1, 27, 33, 68, 69, 83, 101, 143, 144, 162, 181, 186, 187, 188, 208, 211, 219, 228, 229, 231, 252, 253, 259, 274
Caitanya-caritamrta, 1, 143, 211, 229
Cakravarti, Visvanatha, 53, 88
calamity, 13, 41, 160, 224, 225, 226, 286
cancala, 20
cancer, 148
cannibals, 98, 99
capala-sukha, 114
capitalism, 39, 40
caranamrta, 257
casteism, 116, 173
celibacy, 19, 154
Chandogya Upanisad, 173
chauvinism, 173
Christ, 190, 285, 294

Index

christianity, 43, 176, 179, 182, 190, 230, 294
christians, 63, 129, 167, 175, 176, 180, 182, 190, 264, 270, 294
Cintamani, 241
Citraketu, 262, 263, 264, 265, 267
communism, 39, 40
complacency, 236
Constantine, 176
courage, 183
craziness, 255, 293
cremated, 262
Damodara, 75
death
   dodging, 156
desires
   antimaterial, 272
Devaki, 230, 234
Devil, 160
dhama-aparadha, 257
dharma, 8, 68, 96, 128, 140
Dhrtarastra, 105, 223, 243
Dhruva, 226, 227, 234
dhyana-yoga, 270
diksa, 110
discrimination
   healthy versus unhealthy, 90
diversity, 126
divorce, 16, 147
Draupadi, 224, 234, 243, 244, 245
Dronacarya, 233, 244
Duhsasana, 243
dukhi, 188
duplicity, 131
Durga, 229
Durvasa, 223
Duryodhana, 224
Dvapara-yuga, 50, 71
dvesa, 218
Ekadasi, 257
elements
   anala, 240
   apa, 240

bhumi, 240
buddhi, 240
kha, 240
mana, 139, 240
eliminating distractions, 233
Engels, Friederich, 39
epistemology, 2
espionage, 118, 200
evil, 60, 84, 104, 124, 182, 200, 293, 294
extremes
   avoiding, 159
extremism, 234
faith and trust in God, 245
fanaticism, 61, 129, 176, 178, 182, 200, 234
fatalism, 47
faults, 4
forgiveness, 186, 283, 285, 293
Francis, St., 179, 180, 187
free will versus destiny, 47
fundamentalism, 181
   dangers of, 178
fundamentalists, 158, 178, 179
gandharvas, 62
Gandhi, 144
genitals, 20, 106, 208
ghosts, 196, 205
Gitavali, 181
Glasser, William, 107, 108
Goloka, 67, 84, 177, 188, 193, 194, 203, 206
Gopijana, 247
Gopinatha, 110, 111
gopis, 75, 110, 145, 247, 290
Gosvamis, six, 73
Govinda, 67, 174, 229, 243
gratitude
   and reciprocation, 103
   is essential, 164
grhamedhis, 141
grhasthas, 74, 76, 141, 147
guna, 24, 26, 28, 29, 33, 40, 52, 67,

107, 117, 203, 288
guna-avataras, 28
guru
  all-knowing, 6
guru-aparadha, 257
gurukula, 159, 169
gurus, 2, 7, 18, 61, 68, 79, 86, 91, 129, 133, 156, 167, 172, 173, 175, 176, 181, 185, 186, 190, 211, 213, 214, 225, 240, 241, 253, 254, 256, 259, 270, 285, 286, 289, 292
Hanuman, 249
Hari-bhakti-sudhodaya, 118
hari-katha, 176
harinama, 126, 153, 158
Harinama Cintamani, 287
hatha-yoga, 8
Hildagard, St., 180, 187
Hinduism, 6, 43
hippies, 256
Hiranyakasipu, 63, 156, 157, 163, 245, 294
hladini-sakti, 33, 67, 70
honest with ourselves, 210
hoping against hope, 246
hypertension, 275
hypnotherapy, 46, 167
hypocrites, 60, 293
Indra, 132, 224, 249
intelligence
  applying, 17
Islam, 179, 200, 294
'isms', 39
Isopanisad, 1, 2, 83, 277
Israelites, 271
isvara, 67
Jagannatha, 186, 232
Jaladuta, 219
janma, 49
Janmastami, 19, 88
japa, 208, 222, 279
Jehovah, 271
Jesus, 177, 180, 190, 264, 271, 285

Jews, 175, 180, 190, 212
jihad, 200
jiva-atma, 24
jivas, 25
jnana, 8, 59, 69, 70, 124, 142
jnana-misra-bhaktas, 142
jnana-yoga, 8
jnanis, 57, 59, 92, 117, 119
Judaism, 179
Kabbala, 262
Kali, 1, 50, 68, 71, 82, 108, 134, 139, 141, 142, 179, 200, 218, 219, 249, 251, 256, 282, 283, 287, 294
kama, 13, 84, 210, 216, 231
Kamsa, 182, 230
kanistha-adhikaris, 87, 88
  characteristics, 88
Kapila, 249
karma
  four stages of, 53
karma-kandis, 31, 134, 181
karma-mimamsa, 34, 134
karma-misra-bhakti, 142
karma-yoga, 8
Kauravas, 224
killers of the soul, 60
kirtana, 31, 144, 181, 249, 256, 292
knowledge
  eighteen methods for developing, 127
Koran, 50, 116, 173, 200, 262, 268
Krishna Book, 201, 290
Krishna-prema, 234
kriya-yoga, 174
krodha, 13, 216
krpa-siddha, 71, 75, 76, 134, 287
Krtadyuti, 263, 265
ksatriyas, 226
kuntha, 107
Kunti, 196, 207, 223, 224, 234
Kurma, 28
Kuruksetra, 59, 73, 105, 191
kuta, 53

Index

laulyam, 135, 246, 284
lila-avataras, 28
lilas, 28, 109, 174, 220, 289
lobha, 13, 216
love
  asking for pure, 279
mada, 13, 216
Madhavendra, 252
madhurya-rasa, 180
Madhuvana, 226
Madhvacarya, 8, 177
madhyama-adhikari, 69, 89, 90, 93, 94, 96, 98, 201
  characteristics, 89
Madri, 223
maha-bhagavata, 68, 69
Mahabharata, 80, 197, 233
mahajana, 8
maha-mantra, 55, 126, 220, 222, 227, 231, 279
maha-maya, 101
maha-ratha, 290
mahat-tattva, 23, 38, 62, 121, 188, 217
mala, 279
mangala-arati, 241
Manifesto of the Communist Party, 39
Martyaloka, 204, 208, 211, 217
Marx, Karl, 39
maya, 4, 11, 75, 87, 93, 101, 114, 116, 124, 125, 126, 140, 154, 176, 197, 200, 204, 208, 214, 218, 225, 231, 232, 245, 249, 254, 256, 288
mayavadis, 186
mayayapahrta-jnana, 58, 59, 118, 135
mind
  enemies of, 13, 48, 55, 85, 212, 231
moha, 13, 46, 216
mrdanga, 159
mudhas, 58
mudra, 9
Muhammad, 177, 180, 271
mukti, 219, 243, 281
Mukunda, 110, 111

muslims, 6, 175, 294
Muwatta, 116, 200
Naimisaranya, 164
naiskarmya, 51
naistika-brahmacari, 154
nama-aparadha, 257
namas, 33, 281
narada-pancaratra, 90, 131
naradhamas, 58, 59
Narayana, 265, 266
nava-yauvana, 250
near-death experiences, 266
negativity
  bouncing back from, 141
Nimbarkacarya, 177
nirjana-bhajana, 142
nirvana, 174, 223
nitya-siddhas, 34, 62, 97, 255, 287, 290
nivrtti, 151
niyamagraha, 182
Nrsimhadeva, 28, 157
Pandavas, 223, 224, 233, 243
panditas, 71, 285
Pandu, 223, 224
parama-guru, 286
paramartha-prada, 176, 177, 178
Paramatma, 26, 27, 28, 63, 89, 215, 250, 254
paramesvara, 105
parampara, 59, 172, 202, 225, 253
Pariksit, 84, 201, 224, 225, 226, 234, 245, 249
personalism, 218
phobias, 46
Phuliyagrama, 213
physiognomy, 9
Pitrloka, 193
possessiveness, 11
Prahlada, 63, 249, 253
prajalpa, 211
Prakasananda, 186
pramanas, 8, 10, 28
prana, 86, 226, 270

prarabdha, 53
prasadam, 14, 27, 28, 29, 32, 112, 127, 136, 153, 201, 206, 212
pratyaksa, 9
pravrtti, 151
Prayaga, 228
prayojana, 143
preach by example, 15
prema, 32, 53, 70, 98, 107, 109, 151, 228, 231, 287
promiscuity, 210
propaganda, 118, 275
prostitution, 78, 93, 231, 241, 252, 265, 266
Prtha, 30, 288
Prthu, 28
puja, 12, 110, 286
pujaris, 111
pukka brahmacari, 108
punya-karma, 48, 49, 51
Puranjana, 176
purnam, 23, 24, 27, 34, 42, 82, 101
Putana, 83, 294
Radharani, 33, 40, 70, 109, 145, 159, 188, 228, 279, 289
Raghunatha, 52, 93
rajo-guna, 52
Ramacandra, 28, 220
Ramakrishna, 29
Ramanujacarya, 177, 285, 286
rasa, 42, 67, 81, 189
Ravana, 245, 294
refusing to let go, 254
religious pretenders, 60
renunciation, 11, 24, 43, 70, 82, 124, 138, 150, 151, 154, 155, 163
righteousness, 179
rituals, 15, 63, 69, 71, 97, 134, 226
romance, 82, 162, 279
ruci, 109
rudha, 53
rupas, 28, 33, 34, 119
sabda-pramana, 10, 17, 18, 21
sac-cid-ananda-vigraha, 26, 27, 29, 42

sadacara, 125, 256
sadhana, 11, 18, 19, 109, 143, 151, 152, 183, 209, 229, 247, 287
sadhana-bhakti, 109, 151, 152, 183, 209, 247
sadhana-siddha, 287
sadhu-sanga, 14, 64, 225, 227, 253
sahajiyas, 116, 117
sakti, 12, 26, 28, 29, 66, 78, 172, 185, 208, 219, 253
saktiman, 12, 185, 253
saktyavesa-avatara, 28, 30, 62, 188
samadhi, 270
sambandha, 29, 143, 190
sambhava, 9
sambhoga, 101
samsara, 62, 119, 223
samskaras, 111
samvit, 66, 67, 68, 70, 81
Sanatana, 52, 143
sanatana-dharma, 6, 8, 127, 140
sandhini, 67, 70
Sanjaya, 105
sankalpa, 20, 225
sankirtana, 185, 285
sannyasis, 14, 74, 76, 115, 157, 159, 186, 219, 227
Sanskrit, 1, 156
santana-dharma, 128
saranagati, 6, 277, 283, 297
Sarasvati, 86, 186, 229, 243, 249
sari, 91, 155, 243, 244, 284
Sarvabhauma, 186
sarva-jna, 2
sastris, 71
Satsvarupa Maharaja, 169
sattva-guna, 52
satya-yuga, 50, 71, 82
searching for wholeness, 23
sectarianism, 190
selfishness, 242, 279
selflessness, 15, 279, 291, 298
servitorship
spirit of, 62, 271

Index

seva-aparadha, 257
shame, 201
siddha-deha, 188
siddhanta, 4, 143, 152, 172, 174, 288
sikhas, 43
Skanda Purana, 71
sloka, 2, 159
smarta-brahmanas, 116
socialism, 39
spiritual giving
  principles of, 29
spiritual greed, 242
spiritual warfare
  ammunition, 228
  battlefield, 59, 105
Spiritual Warrior II
  Transforming Lust into Love, 297
spiritualists, 30, 57, 109, 114, 180, 187, 200, 212, 216, 230, 294
spirituality, 38, 39, 40, 42, 50, 60, 63, 82, 133, 162, 167, 169, 175, 176, 177, 180, 181, 194, 195, 205, 207, 236, 250, 251, 256, 265, 275, 278
sraddha, 4, 53, 180, 181
Sri Brahma-samhita, 243, 250
Sri Caitanya-caritamrta, 143, 186, 187
Sri Isopanisad, 1, 2, 5, 6, 58, 61, 65, 82, 103, 107, 108, 115, 118, 119, 138, 149, 162, 172, 182, 203, 215, 239, 243, 261, 277, 281, 289, 299
Sri Upadesamrta, 135
Srila Prabhupada's sacrifice, 232
Srimad-Bhagavatam, 1, 24, 46, 63, 67, 81, 83, 84, 90, 132, 150, 164, 171, 173, 176, 186, 201, 209, 224, 226, 244, 262, 265, 281, 282
sruti, 6
stagnation, 125
Subhadra, 225, 232
suddha-bhaktas, 101, 142, 185, 277
sudra, 71
Sufis, 124, 125, 180
Sukadeva, 84, 226, 249
sukrti, 14, 125

summum bonum, 24, 26, 40, 65, 66, 250, 288
Suniti, 226
suras, 58, 172
Suruci, 226
Suta Gosvami, 164
svarupa, 101, 109, 287, 288
svarupa-jnana, 109
svarupa-laksana, 287, 288
Syamasundara, 65, 66, 245
tamo-guna, 52
tapasvis, 119
tapasya, 69, 149, 171, 278
tatastha-sakti, 7, 66, 70, 79, 227
Tattva Sandarbha, 4, 10, 18
The Beggar One, 244, 247
The Nectar of Devotion, 1, 247, 281
The Nectar of Instruction, 1, 135, 182, 287
tilaka, 91, 188
tolerance, 48, 86, 124, 131
Torah, 50, 173, 262
transmigration, 49, 263, 265, 266, 267, 295
treta-yuga, 50, 71
truth
  essence of, 4
tulasi, 153, 257
  mala, 227
  puja, 145
universal religion, 5
upamana, 8
utsaha, 197
uttama-adhikaris, 69, 81, 88, 90, 96, 97, 98, 121, 201
  characteristics, 90
Vaikuntha, 67, 107, 174, 257
vaisnava-aparadha, 257
Vaisnavism, 235
vanaprasthas, 76
vandanam, 63, 185
varnas, 6
varnasrama, 6, 57

Vasudeva, 185
vayuh, 38, 270
vedanta, 1, 5, 135, 186
Vedas, 1, 4, 5, 6, 8, 10, 17, 20, 64, 65, 116, 118, 193, 207, 244, 262, 271, 273
veda-vada-ratas, 118, 135
vegetarianism, 14, 41, 42, 195, 206
vidya, 115, 117, 142, 164, 172, 227
vidyadharas, 62
vikalpa, 20, 225
vikarma, 48
vilapa-kusumanjali, 52
vinasyati, 135
violence, 41, 55, 115, 117, 125, 144, 212
vipralambha, 100, 101
vipralipsa, 4
Visnu, 69, 226, 266
visnudutas, 266
vrata, 69, 195
Vyasadeva, 1, 18, 107, 108, 239
writing, 116
Yahweh, 271
yajna, 69, 89, 263, 278
Yamadutas, 265, 266, 267
Yamaraja, 201, 227, 257, 265
Yasoda, 75
yoga, 8, 29, 69, 70, 101, 142, 149, 194, 270, 292
yoga-maya, 101
yoga-misra-bhakti, 142
yogis, 28, 29, 57, 92, 105, 109, 119, 180, 182
yugas, 187

About The Author

Bhakti-Tirtha Swami Krishnapada was born John E. Favors in a pious, God-fearing family. As a child evangelist he appeared regularly on television. As a young man he was a leader in Dr. Martin Luther King, Jr.'s civil rights movement. At Princeton University he became president of the student council and also served as chairman of the Third World Coalition. Although his main degree is in psychology, he has received accolades in many other fields, including politics, African studies, and international law.

Bhakti-Tirtha Swami's books are used as reference texts in universities and leadership organizations throughout the world. Many of his books have been printed in English, German, French, Spanish, Portuguese, Macedonian, Croatian, Russian, Hebrew, Slovenian, Balinese and Italian.

His Holiness has served as Assistant Coordinator for penal reform programs in the State of New Jersey, Office of the Public Defender, and as a director of several drug abuse clinics in the United States. In addition, he has been a special consultant for Educational Testing Services in the U.S.A. and has managed campaigns for politicians. Bhakti-Tirtha Swami gained international recognition as a representative of the Bhaktivedanta Book Trust, particularly for his outstanding work with scholars in the former communist countries of Eastern Europe.

Bhakti-Tirtha Swami directly oversees projects in the United States (particularly Washington D.C., Potomac, Maryland, Detroit, Pennsylvania, West Virginia), West Africa, South Africa, Switzerland, France, Croatia and Bosnia. He also serves as the director of the American Federation of Vaisnava Colleges and Schools.

In the United States, Bhakti-Tirtha Swami is the founder and director of the Institute for Applied Spiritual Technology, director of the International Committee for Urban Spiritual Development and one of the international coordinators of the Seventh Pan African Congress. Reflecting his wide range of interests, he is also a member of the Institute for Noetic Sciences, the Center for Defense Information, the United Nations Association for America, the National Peace Institute Foundation, the World Future Society and the Global Forum of Spiritual and Parliamentary Leaders.

A specialist in international relations and conflict resolution, Bhakti-Tirtha Swami constantly travels around the world and has become a spiritual consultant to many high-ranking members of the United Nations, to various celebrities and to several chiefs, kings and high court justices. In 1990 His Holiness was coronated as a high chief in Warri, Nigeria in recognition of his outstanding work in Africa and the world. In recent years, he has met several times with then-President Nelson Mandela of South Africa to share visions and strategies for world peace.

In addition to encouraging self-sufficiency through the development of schools, clinics, farm projects and cottage industries, Bhakti-Tirtha Swami conducts seminars and workshops on principle centered leadership, spiritual development, interpersonal relationships, stress and time management and other pertinent topics. He is also widely acknowledged as a viable participant in the resolution of global conflict.

Made in United States
Troutdale, OR
04/30/2025